D1345831

CUSTOMER SERVICE EXCELLENCE

Edge Hill University
Learning Services

Edge Hill University
LEARNING SERVICES

Renew Online: http://library.edgehill.ac.uk

Help line: 01695 650800

Broadcasting and the NHS in the Thatcherite 1980s

A study of the ways in which changes to the public services and shifts in the concept of 'the public' under Margaret Thatcher's three Conservative governments were mediated by radio and television in the 1980s.

Broadcasting and the NHS in the Thatcherite 1980s

The Challenge to Public Service

Patricia Holland, with Hugh Chignell and Sherryl Wilson

palgrave
macmillan

First published 2013 by
PALGRAVE MACMILLAN

Palgrave Macmillan in the UK is an imprint of Macmillan Publishers Limited, registered in England, company number 785998, of Houndmills, Basingstoke, Hampshire RG21 6XS.

Palgrave Macmillan in the US is a division of St Martin's Press LLC, 175 Fifth Avenue, New York, NY 10010.

Palgrave Macmillan is the global academic imprint of the above companies and has companies and representatives throughout the world.

Palgrave® and Macmillan® are registered trademarks in the United States, the United Kingdom, Europe and other countries.

ISBN 978–0–230–28237–7

This book is printed on paper suitable for recycling and made from fully managed and sustained forest sources. Logging, pulping and manufacturing processes are expected to conform to the environmental regulations of the country of origin.

A catalogue record for this book is available from the British Library.

A catalog record for this book is available from the Library of Congress.

Contents

Acknowledgements

This book has grown out of a project funded by the Arts and Humanities Research Council, carried out at Bournemouth University's Centre for Broadcasting History Research. 'There's no such thing as society?' (AHRC award number AH/E008682/1) looked at broadcasting and the public services under the three Thatcher governments (1979–1990). The original research team comprised Patricia Holland, Hugh Chignell, Sherryl Wilson and Georgia Eglezou. When the book speaks of 'we', this is the group referred to. When it uses 'I', it is the principal author, Patricia Holland, who is speaking. The book also includes contributions from television producers Nick Gray and Peter Lee-Wright, and unpublished research by Heather Sutherland. We are grateful to them for their input. More material from these writers is available on our website at http://www.broadcastingnhsbook.co.uk/.

We also owe a debt of gratitude to the others who contributed to the website and made their considerable expertise and experience available: Ray Fitzwalter, Head of Current Affairs at Granada Television (1987–1993); Steve Iliffe, Professor of Primary Care for Older People, University College London; Kevin Marsh, Editor-in-Chief of the BBC's College of Journalism; Tom O'Malley, Professor of Media Studies, Aberystwyth University; Jonathan Powell, Controller BBC1 (1988–1992); Tony Stoller, Chief Executive of the Radio Authority (1995–2003); and David McQueen and Emma Wray of Bournemouth University. The University's Journalism Research Group gave financial help for creating the Index.

Thanks also to Marcus Prince, of the British Film Institute (BFI), for programming the *The Nation's Health* season at the BFI Southbank, which screened several of the television programmes discussed in this book. It involved a wider audience in discussions around the representation of the National Health Service (NHS) on television, and introduced writers, actors and filmmakers whose work we discuss in this book, including G.F. Newman, Joan Shenton, Paul Unwin and Jeremy Brock. Our thanks go to the London Centre for Arts and Cultural Exchange and Goldsmiths College, University of London, for helping to fund that season. Also, thanks to producer Joan Shenton for lending me copies of her programmes and other materials.

We have had helpful assistance from members of the BFI's National Film and Television Archive, including Becky Vick and Sue Woods, and also from the BBC and some ITV archives in making programmes available for viewing. My own elderly collection of VHS tapes, dating from the mid-1980s, may be scratched and flickering, with strange distorted colours, but has proved invaluable.

Thanks also to Lesley Banks for designing our website, and Ruth Peacock for inputting material into the EndNote database, containing lists of relevant programmes, which is linked to the website. Also, thanks to members of the Southern Broadcasting History Group for their continuing support. The whole project was their idea in the first place.

Some of the research for this book was also drawn on for ' "There is no such thing!": On public service, broadcasting, the National Health Service and "people" in the 1980s' by Patricia Holland and Georgia Eglezou, in *Thatcher and After* edited by Louisa Hadley and Elizabeth Ho (Palgrave Macmillan 2010); for 'Dramatising health care in the age of Thatcher' by Sherryl Wilson in *Critical Studies in Television* (7)1 Spring 2012 13–28; and for Hugh Chignell's *Public Issue Radio: Talks, News and Current Affairs in the Twentieth Century* (Palgrave Macmillan 2011).

Prologue: Echoes of the 1980s

Echoes of the 1980s

This is a book about the 1980s, the decade of the three Conservative governments led by Margaret Thatcher. It is generally accepted that 'Thatcherism' brought a significant shift in the political, economic and ideological climate in the UK. As broadcasting historians, our aim is to trace that shift – in all its conflicts and contradictions – through the radio and television programmes of the decade as they both reflected and mediated the changing climate. Our argument will be that there is a significant, but not straightforward, relationship between the broadcast output and the political climate. To elucidate this, we will seek to map the changes in the important political concepts of 'society' and 'the public', both within the programmes and within the political discourse. Our focus will be on the public services; in particular, on the National Health Service (NHS) and on broadcasting itself.

The book was conceived at an extraordinary moment in political history. Almost 30 years after the election of Margaret Thatcher's radical Conservative government, a devastating 'credit crunch' hit the global markets and, for a moment, it seemed that an era was coming to an end. The market-oriented economic system promoted by the Thatcher governments was in crisis, and the public acceptance that market-centred politics together with their social consequences were necessary, inevitable and, indeed, beneficial, was questioned. As the credit crunch laid waste major financial institutions and threatened the international banking system itself, it seemed that the confidence of the 1980s had been misplaced. Prosperity was built on an illusion; it was nothing but a house of cards. The individualism, personal ambition and get-rich-quick ideology which had pushed out a commitment to social and collective responsibility had simply not worked. In the autumn of 2008, the *Daily Mail* newspaper, a powerful supporter of Thatcherite economics, headlined 'Free-market capitalism lies shredded' (18 September 2008). It was 'Corrupted by the culture of greed' (10 February 2009).

In planning a book about the 1980s, it seemed that we would be illustrating the emergence of a political consensus just as it was coming to an end – or, at least, being radically transformed. Events were forcing a revaluation of Thatcherism's social and cultural assumptions, as well as its economic ones. By mid-2010, however, the election of a right-of-centre coalition government in the UK, dominated by a Conservative Party with a complex relationship to its Thatcherite heritage, made such assertions seem premature. On the one hand, Prime Minister David Cameron espoused what he dubbed a 'big society' as a contrast to Margaret Thatcher's notorious rejection of 'society'; on the other, the aftermath of the banking collapse was used to justify a renewed programme of cuts and privatisation. Many of the changes fought for in the 1980s were reasserted, with a remarkably similar rhetoric.

For the new government, the recession and the credit crunch were to be remedied, not by reshaping a market-based, neo-liberal economic system, but by reinvigorating it. The public sector came under attack, together with the very concept of public service. Within weeks of taking power, the Conservative/Liberal-democrat coalition issued new challenges to the status of the British Broadcasting Corporation (BBC) and the NHS, the two institutions we will be focussing on in this book. 'In his first 100 days Cameron has gone further than Thatcher – and much faster, too', wrote the *New Statesman*'s then political editor Mehdi Hasan (9 August 2010). And Conservative MP Greg Barker claimed, 'we are making cuts that Margaret Thatcher in the 1980s could only have dreamed of' (George Eaton *New Statesman* blog 4 April 2011).

So, it seemed that our book would be tracing the rhetoric of the 1980s at a time when it was being rehabilitated. Yet, as we put the final touches to our work in 2012, several European countries have fallen into crisis, the banking system is once again destabilised by major revelations of fraud, and there is a demand for a change in the 'culture'. The upheavals of the 1980s are still working themselves out.

Programmes of the 1980s

By focussing on programmes concerned with health and the NHS, the research project from which this book has grown sought to explore the complex and shifting relationships between politics, everyday attitudes, lived experience and broadcast programming in the 1980s. It was an era of broadcasting which John Ellis has characterised as 'the age of scarcity', with only four national television channels, but these, together with four BBC radio channels and many more local radio stations, put out hundreds of hours of programming every week (Ellis 2000:39–60). To trace shifting attitudes towards 'the public' and 'public service' across the breadth of this output is a daunting task. It was tempting to pluck out specific examples which appeared to illustrate our argument, but we wanted to give a more secure grounding to our survey, so we compiled lists of programmes across the genres – dramas, documentaries, current affairs programmes, comedies and others – which dealt directly with issues of health, public service and Thatcherite policies.

There were, of course, limitations to this approach – in particular, the very scale of the enterprise. It was impossible within the scope of our study to note every single relevant programme, so we focussed on certain key dates and on specific policy issues, indicating the ways in which programmes related to government initiatives and policy changes. The lists are available on our website. The second problem was the availability of the material. In the case of live broadcasts, such as BBC Radio 4's *Woman's Hour*, very few recordings or transcripts were made. But despite its limitations, our 'listing' exercise meant that we have been able to give an indication of which topics were chosen by the broadcasters, and to map out the competing discourses as they developed across the decade. In this book, we have highlighted a variety of significant programmes for detailed discussion, selected from across the genres because of their particular relevance or their prominence in the schedules. We have also included a chronological selection from our lists, charting the ways in which programme output related to public events. These chronologies, found before Chapter 1 and between Chapters 1 and 2, 3 and 4, 6 and 7, and 9 and 10, are, of necessity, brief and highly selective. Nevertheless, they indicate significant political events in relation to programme output, and they form a background to our review.

Introduction: Thatcherism, the Public and Writing Broadcasting History

I Thatcherism and writing broadcasting history

Mediatised history and the mythology of Margaret Thatcher

The 1980s mark a pivotal decade in British history, heavily laden with cultural as well as political significance, and at the centre is the figure of Margaret Thatcher. Elected in 1979 as the UK's first (and, so far, only) woman Prime Minister, Thatcher's personality dominated the political stage during her years in power, and her shadow has fallen over subsequent decades. Her tone of voice, her style of dress, her mannerisms have become fused in the popular imagination with her political views – declared with such emphasis and conviction. Her image has come to stand as a point of reference, a symbol of the decade, bearing the weight of its significance. It has become a 'cultural marker' threaded through the programmes; condensing within itself meanings, attitudes and ideas about the period; exciting because of its emotive pull. The 'Thatcher' mythology has continued to play a powerful role in facilitating an interplay between culture and politics, intertwining political judgement and cultural expression (Nunn 2002; Campbell 1987).

'History', as an account of the past, can never be innocent. As soon as a moment is gone, it may be told or communicated in some way. It then becomes a 'story' – his or hers, ours or theirs – enshrined in memory or in tangible record. In the totally mediatised society we inhabit today, we negotiate an increasing denseness of such accounts, echoing back and forth across a diversity of media (de Zengotita 2005). Contemporary accounts of the 1980s, like those of any period, come from many, often conflicting, perspectives, whether recorded by commentators, enshrined in official documents or told by participants. As time passes, these are followed by revisions of accounts, retellings,

1

reimaginings, reinterpretations and fictionalisations. Revised readings and rereadings of familiar documents are circulated; new batches of archives become available to scholars and material is published for wider access through online media. (As we write, the archives from Thatcher's first government are being released and studied by historians.) Consequently, any account of a historical moment must also take into account the *histories of* that moment; the accumulation of myth and symbol. It must also pay attention to popular memory and popular forms, in what the historian Raphael Samuel described as *Theatres of Memory* (Samuel 1994; Hobsbawm and Ranger 1983). Possibly the most powerful in creating and circulating such overlapping narratives are the broadcast media.

For broadcasters, revisiting previous decades is partly a way of exploiting the archives, and programmes range from serious historical exploration (BBC4's *Time Shift*; Radio 4's *The Archive Hour*), to various forms of historical tourism built on a fascination with retro fashion, gadgetry, interior furnishings and popular music. (A couple of my 1980s favourites are *Supersizers Eat...the Eighties* in which comedians Sue Perkins and Giles Coren consume piles of expensive dishes and lurid cocktails (BBC 15 June 2009); and the programme in which a 21st-century family is restricted to the technology available in the decade – and struggle with that wonderful new invention, the video-cassette recorder (*Electric Dreams: The 1980s* BBC4 13 March 2011). In this spirit, the visuality of the 1980s has become a familiar part of the television of the 2000s. Its colour, high fashion and general excess are echoed in drama series such as *Ashes to Ashes* in which the glamorous protagonist is mysteriously transported back to the 1980s (BBC1 February 2008). The 'new romantics' glam their way into retrospectives, while anniversaries of major events, such as the Falklands War (1982) and the miners' strike (1984–1985) are reassessed and re-evaluated. The myth of Margaret Thatcher – as a camp icon and a gift to the puppeteers of *Spitting Image*, as well as a political force – finds its place among this output.

The fascination of Thatcher, both reviled and revered, has been reworked and reviewed on numerous occasions in the decades since her resignation. An outpouring of television dramas and documentaries marked the 30th anniversary of her fateful election, and an Oscar-winning film re-evoked her career in big-screen style.[1] Such images carry

---

[1] *The Iron Lady* directed by Phyllida Lloyd with Meryl Streep as Margaret Thatcher (UK 2011).

out cultural *work*. As Graham Murdock put it, 'images do not walk in straight lines. They do not wait to take turns. They work by association, denoting a collision of connotations. This sets up a permanent tension between the pleasures of the image, and the ripples of memory and identity it activates, and the search for explanations that offer a purchase on circumstance and power' (Murdock 1999:14). The effect of the Thatcher image could not be more graphically described.

In this book we are focussing on the imagery, the narratives and the representations produced during the 1980s, both to evoke the cultural aspects of the politics and to illuminate the politics itself. We are concerned with political history, but more importantly we are concerned with the ways in which politics was transmuted into culture and common-sense opinion. As we move back and forth between politics and programmes, the image of Margaret Thatcher will be threaded through them both, and her name will reverberate as a recurring theme. Also, in exploring a mediatised history, we will be identifying some of the *mythologising* practices which characterise the public discourse – and we should make it clear that when we speak of a 'myth', we do not mean that this is a fiction or is untrue, but that an 'image', a story or a cluster of ideas has gained a particular resonance. We will endeavour to unpick the ways in which meanings and emotions can be condensed into such a central symbol – or 'image' – and can be evoked to mark out political opinions, attitudes and allegiances – and can themselves become the centre of a contest over meaning.

The media complex

In the following chapters we will be tracing changing attitudes towards the idea and practice of public service, as we look at those two quintessentially British and frequently compared institutions, the National Health Service (NHS) and public service broadcasting. Although we take later interpretations into account, we are chiefly concerned with the ways in which events and ideas were represented and developed in the 1980s themselves. We want to capture an impression of the 'media complex' in a decade which saw dramatic changes in the technologies and structures of broadcasting, as well as in its politics. By exploring the broadcast output we will demonstrate how certain key ideas were worked on and modified. Factual information and shifting ideologies were embedded in interweaving debates, impressions, opinions, jokes, narratives and emotional attitudes. In ways which were sometimes direct and often oblique, programmes related politics to the experience of everyday life.

This means that our approach is different both from studies of representation and from accounts of broadcasting institutions, although we draw on both. We argue that, by viewing and listening to the programmes of the time, and attempting to understand them as far as possible within the social, political, institutional and cultural contexts in which they originated, we can observe a cultural and ideological shift *as it was happening*. We can endeavour to experience the programmes in real time, close to how they were seen by their original audiences – recognising, but leaving to one side, the accumulation of knowledge which has transformed them for later audiences. By observing the ways in which political and organisational changes were commented on and turned into popular expression and entertainment, we can follow the political project of the 1980s as it entered popular culture and became a new common sense (Hall and Jaques 1983).

In order to get some sense of the changes of the decade, we will look across the broadcast output, and point to the interrelations between different channels and different genres. We take the position that *all* broadcast programmes are potentially of importance, not just those with a high profile or those which have entered an academic cannon. By accumulating examples and making comparisons across the genres, by viewing each programme in the light of the others and when necessary reading between the lines, we will trace how the political ideas of the 1980s circulated, consolidated and took hold. 'Mediated politics goes well beyond the news coverage,' write Kay Richardson and her co-authors (Richardson et al. 2012).[2]

As we highlight case studies from different genres, we will bear in mind that the relations between politics and the media were themselves undergoing a radical change in the 1980s. We will be taking account of the ways in which broadcasting policy impacted on the programme output.

Therefore, we will be giving an account of the challenge to public service in broadcasting and the NHS in several contexts:

- We will consider shifts in *political philosophy*: shifts that were contested as Margaret Thatcher became more influential in the Conservative Party, and developed under the Thatcher governments. In particular, we will look at the concept of '*the public*' and the ways

---

[2] Quoted from the publicity for Kay Richardson, John Corner and Katy Parry, *Political Culture and Media Genre: Beyond the News* (Palgrave Macmillan 2012).

in which it was mobilised in relation to the public domain and to the public services. We will be looking at ways in which the broadcast media themselves responded to and contributed to the renegotiation of the concept, and we will be looking at the debates within academia and other public fora commenting on, contesting and intervening in the changes.

- We will consider the output in the context of *government policy* – particularly in relation to 'public service' in broadcasting and health provision. As the challenge to the concept of 'public service' became stronger and was embedded in official policy, changes in broadcasting legislation influenced the range and content of programmes in important and sometimes unexpected ways.
- Against the background of the broad scope of the broadcast output, we will be making a *close study of selected programmes* and series which illuminate the changing political climate, in particular, programmes related to issues of public health and the National Health Service.

We will be moving back and forth between these three themes in the following chapters.

II 'Public service' in the 1980s

'No such thing?' 'Society' and the public domain

I think we have gone through a period when too many children and people have been given to understand 'I have a problem, it is the government's job to cope with it!' or 'I have a problem, I will go and get a grant to cope with it!' 'I am homeless, the government must house me!' And so they are casting their problems on society and who is society? There is no such thing!

(Margaret Thatcher 1987)[3]

As we think ourselves back into the mood of the decade, this book takes its cue from Margaret Thatcher's notorious declaration that 'there's no such thing as society, only individuals and families' made with emphatic confidence just after she was elected as Prime Minister for a third term. We take up the *political* implications of that statement, but our aim is

---

[3] The quotation comes from an interview with *Woman's Own* magazine (23 September 1987). The texts of Margaret Thatcher's speeches, interviews and statements are available through the Margaret Thatcher Foundation at http://www.margaretthatcher.org/speeches/default.asp.

also to explore its tone and its *cultural* provenance as it came to act as a sort of pivot, a useful shorthand which pulls together aspects of cultural attitudes and social policy in the Thatcherite 1980s. Thatcher's denial of 'society' rapidly entered folk myth. It has been used as the title of programmes, exhibitions, books, articles and photographic projects, and has come to express the uncaring aspects of the free-market policies which Thatcher promoted.

The statement has multiple strands: there is the narrow conceptualisation of 'society' and its responsibilities; the over-simple elision of 'government' with 'society'; and the evocation of mythical 'families' who honour their responsibilities (Nunn 2002:95–133). And it implied a major shift in the grounds of ethical behaviour and practical relationships. In the interview with *Woman's Own*, from which the statement is taken, the Prime Minister moved on to elaborate the place of 'people' within the social structure: 'No government can do anything except through people, and people look to themselves first.' That image of individual men and women who 'look to themselves first' became the ethical centre of Thatcherism.[4] 'No such thing as society' came to encapsulate what David Marquand described, in his reflection on the changes of the 1980s, as a 'hollowing out of citizenship' and a shrinking of the public realm. The public realm, he wrote, is

> the domain of citizenship, equity and service whose integrity is essential to democratic governance and social well-being...In it citizenship rights trump both market power and bonds of clan or kinship. Professional pride in a job well done, or a sense of civic duty, or a mixture of both replaces the hope of gain and the fear of loss...as the spur to action.
>
> (Marquand 2004:1–2)

By contrast in the 1980s, legislation and economic organisation moved away from public provision and public responsibility towards individual choice and individual responsibility; away from public ownership and

---

[4] Unusually, Downing Street issued a clarification of Thatcher's position, published in *The Sunday Times* almost a year later (10 July 1988). It stated that 'society as such does not exist except as a concept. Society is made up of people. It is people who have duties and beliefs and resolve. It is people who get things done...Her approach to society reflects her fundamental belief in personal responsibility and choice. To leave things to "society" is to run away from the real decisions, practical responsibility and effective action.'

the concept of public service, to private ownership and the promotion of finance. The result, according to Colin Leys, in his study of the BBC and the NHS in the 1980s, was that the UK was moved definitively towards

> not just a liberal-market economy, but a liberal-market *society* and *culture*, based not on trust but on the most extreme possible exposure to market forces, with internal markets, profit centres, audits and 'bottom lines' penetrating the whole of life from hospitals to playgroups.
>
> (Leys 2001:34, my italics)

In the following chapters we will consider the ways in which these political and ideological changes were reflected in the broadcast media. Debates about 'the public' and 'public service', both in the political and the academic context, frequently deal in abstractions. This is something broadcasting cannot do. On our screens and through our radios we hear and see actual people, and we encounter stories, images, investigations, conversations, situations and personal accounts. These may be 'real' or 'fictional'; they may reveal important new truths, or may circulate common myths, but all involve embodied individuals. 'Society' and the 'public' appear in these accounts as sets of specific instances. It is through these examples that we will trace the changes in the reality of everyday lives and, at the same time, in the ideas and concepts which influenced those lives. If 'the character of a man depends on his connections to the world' (quoted from Horace by Sennett 1998:10), we can explore possible ways in which those connections may be lived through in dramas, comedies, documentaries, news reports and others. Programmes help to make sense of ways of being in the social world. This is what media theorist John Ellis described as 'working through'. 'Any individual programme has to consider itself part of a larger process,' he wrote (Ellis 2000:72). Moving chronologically through the decade, the book will explore how the concept of 'the public' was worked on, modified and mediated, at a time when the broadcast media themselves were subject to pressures and changes.

We do not begin from a neutral position. We support the view expressed by David Marquand that public service entails an important approach to citizenship and the public domain, and that this was attacked and shrunken during the Thatcherite era (Marquand 2004). We agree with Nick Couldry on the importance of 'voice' in a public space, so that every individual may give meaningful expression to their sense of individuality and selfhood (Couldry 2010); with Colin Leys that a true public service is incompatible with 'market-driven' politics (Leys 2001) and with Richard Sennett that abandoning a live notion of 'the public sphere' has led to a 'corrosion of character' (Sennett 1998).

III The NHS and the medical encounter

'A more onerous citizenship'

> Illness is the night-side of life, a more onerous citizenship. Everyone who is born holds dual citizenship, in the kingdom of the well and in the kingdom of the sick. Although we all prefer to use only the good passport, sooner or later each of us is obliged, at least for a spell, to identify with the citizens of that other place.
>
> (Sontag 1979:1)

Issues of health and sickness demonstrate in a powerful way the manner in which public life is lived out at the very point when the vulnerability and interdependence of individuals becomes unavoidable. This is when the question of whether 'society' exists and what form it takes, matters most. On the personal level, health is a sensitive issue which affects every individual regardless of status. In terms of politics, concern with the nation's health is central to a national public domain, and, in the UK, the publicly funded NHS has been at the heart of political debates. Despite its many imperfections, the NHS has been seen as a reliable and highly respected touchstone of 'public service'. Thus, the challenges which were mounted in the 1980s were particularly significant.

It is notable that Susan Sontag, in her extraordinary book *Illness as a Metaphor*, called on the notion of citizenship rather than the idea of dependency that Margaret Thatcher would evoke. Ill health inevitably creates dependency; dependency on medical knowledge, on expertise, and on the available structures of care, whether from public or commercial health provision, or from family and friends. It is a time when people have no option but to 'cast their problems on society', to use Thatcher's disapproving words. However, Sontag's formulation takes it for granted that a form of citizenship is retained. Citizenship implies a contribution to the social world, as well as a communality of need (Marshall 1950). Yet, as we will see, in the 1980s, the concept of 'citizenship' was disputed and pushed aside. Instead, the users of the service would be invited to see themselves as 'consumers', taking part in a financial transaction.

Attitudes to health care were contested across the 1980s in ways that were not always clear cut, but which had practical effects on the lives of the population at large. We will be tracing changes in the tone and cultural resonance of broadcast programmes about health under the three Thatcher-led governments. We will look at the representation of those citizens who are workers and professionals within the service, as well as those who, of necessity, 'cast their problems' on the NHS. We will observe the language of illness and pain in what we describe as the 'medical encounter': that crucial interaction between medical provision and sick people.

Medical programmes

Doctors and nurses, hospitals and accidents, birth and death have long been attractive as a setting for entertainment media – if only as a source of ghoulish or risqué humour. Some of the most successful comedies of the British cinema have included the staggeringly popular *Doctor* series (1954–1986) and the *Carry Ons – Nurse* (1959); *Doctor* (1967, 1969); *Matron* (1972). The childish naughtiness of these films, with their hints about forbidden body parts, the ever present possibility of nudity and sexual misbehaviour, as well as the comic helplessness of patients at the hands of professionals, is part of a specifically British cultural history. This raucous, disrespectful tradition recurred on television in a somewhat milder form.[5]

Medical dramas have long been a source of fascination on the small screen, from *Emergency Ward Ten* (ATV 1957–1967) and *Doctor Finlay's Casebook* (BBC 1962–1971) to the American *Doctor Kildare* (NBC 1961–1966) and the feistier M.A.S.H (CBS 1972–1983) (Jacobs 2003; Hallam 2000). And medical fantasy, humour and fiction have been paralleled by, and interact with, an equally rich tradition of news, documentaries, current affairs and other factual formats. In the late 1980s, the fictional *Casualty* for adults (BBC1 1986–) and *Children's Ward* for children (Granada 1989–2000) were matched by the life-as-it-is-lived docusoap *Jimmy's* (YTV 1987–1994), and by current affairs reports such as *This Week's* observation of a real casualty department (25 May 1989). Viewers may move easily between these genres. They may watch – and may well compare – both fictional and real medical staff as they cope with daily problems against the background of changing government policies. In the 1980s, as now, viewers will have compared the representations on the screens with their own lives, and will frequently have seen experiences similar to their own reflected, as programme makers

---

[5] Two series of *Doctor in the House*, inspired by the films, ran on London Weekend Television (1969–1970).

sought out 'ordinary people' and everyday examples to incorporate in their programmes (Philo and Henderson 1999).

In the late 1980s, Anne Karpf carried out a detailed analysis of media presentations of health and medical issues, tracing them back to the earliest days in the 1920s (Karpf 1988). Her experience as a researcher on medical programmes gave her an extra insight, and the programmes she describes range from health advice, to news reports and hospital dramas. She observed the possible viewpoints which may be represented in any of the genres: those of doctors, health educators, media critics and the broadcasters themselves; and she charted the delicate relationships between producers and a frequently suspicious medical establishment. As she surveyed the changing styles across the decades, she identified four different approaches:

- a *medical* approach – which stresses medicine's curative powers;
- a *consumer* approach – which challenges the doctor/patient relationship from the patient's point of view;
- a *look after yourself* approach – which encourages changes in personal behaviour;
- an *environmental* approach – which stresses the social origins of illness. This was an approach which, she argued, had significant political consequences and was much more rarely found.

Although this is a schematic classification and there are many hybrids, Karpf argued that these four represent attitudes current in the wider culture. We have found them very helpful in our own analysis.

IV Analysing the programmes: Performance and genre

Populating the programmes

An important function of broadcasting – in both factual and fictional genres – is to represent certain members of 'the public', as they appear in specific, clearly defined roles or situations, to the broad, undifferentiated 'public' at large, the viewers and listeners. In our discussion of the programmes of the 1980s we will be considering who appears and on what terms. We will ask which roles are made possible by a given format, and question how each programme constructs the relationships between those individuals who, for that moment, inhabit those roles.

Bill Cotton, who retired as Managing Director of BBC TV in 1987, notoriously stated that 'television [is] a performers' medium and news and current affairs [are] the side show' (Gray 2008). That may well have been tongue in cheek. Cotton was the first BBC MD to come from the Light Entertainment department and everybody knew that his father was the celebrated cockney band leader. Yet, in a different context, the observer Krishnan Kumar noted that, in the 1970s the BBC was beginning to see itself as 'the "great stage" on which all the actors...parade and say their piece. [As] the 'register' of the many different voices in society' (Kumar 1977:246).

There is a sense in which the idea of *performance* – of the ways in which people or groups adopt particular personae or styles in their interaction with each other – runs through many discussions concerned with the meaning of a *public* presence. Erving Goffman's *The Presentation of Self in Everyday Life* (1959) deals with performance in face-to-face personal interactions, and Richard Sennett's influential *The Fall of Public Man* (1975) is an extraordinary exploration of the shifting ways of performing publicness in Western society. Sennett describes 'performance' as a public display, characteristic of the 18th century, different from the more recent focus on interiority, personality and selfhood. The coming of a mediatised society, he argues (although he does not use that word) led to a move away from the performance of 'publicness'.

However, as we review the programmes of the 1980s, we shall evoke the spirit of Cotton, as well as that of Sennett, and will bear in mind the different ways in which public life is *performed* on the broadcast media. We would argue that communication through broadcasting depends *entirely* on performance. Radio and television are above all stages for public performance. Across the different genres a platform is offered for performances of various types. Professional performers range from stand stand-up comics through to skilled professional actors, journalists, celebrities, television 'personalities', 'experts' and increasingly to media-wise politicians, like Margaret Thatcher herself (Cockerell et al. 1984). Non-professionals, 'ordinary people', are invited on to the airwaves to represent social roles, to illustrate a point, or to take part in an event. In each case they must adopt a suitable persona. Every programme is some form of performance, but each genre poses its own particular demands and has its own generic conventions. This is how the programmes are populated.

'The medical encounter' provides a structured set of roles which we will explore in the following chapters. Programmes open up a space for (at least) three distinct groups of people to appear on the national airwaves, two of them defined by their jobs and status within the service, the third an almost random selection from the public at large. The first group consists of *health professionals and experts*. In factual programmes these tended to carry prestige and respect, and were regularly invited to offer their opinions and share their expert insights. (Although in fiction, and especially in comedy, this established position of power was frequently challenged or mocked.) However, as the 1980s progressed, the authority of doctors, surgeons and consultants was seen to be challenged by a different type of expert; the managers, economists and efficiency specialists who were brought in to restructure the service (Chapter 6).

The second group is made up of others employed by the NHS, such as ambulance staff and *ancillary workers*. Their jobs are crucial to the smooth running of the service, but they are neither authoritative nor of high status. They were frequently presented as militant and appeared most often when they were on strike or taking part in a dispute. Even then, they were rarely invited to offer an opinion, and in fictional programmes they were rarely at the centre of the narrative.[6] *Nurses* held an uneasy position between these two groups. On the one hand they were seen as dedicated to the professional ideal, but they were also low-paid staff, pushed around and taken advantage of (Hallam 2000). Sometimes, they were shown to be as militant as the frequently demonised ancillary workers (Chapter 4).

The third group which populated the programmes is made up of members of the public – random individuals at the point at which they fell sick or became directly affected by health issues – in Susan Sontag's words, at the moments when they take on a 'more onerous citizenship'. These are 'ordinary people', anybody, as they became patients or clients. While the first two groups deliver a public service and carry the weight of that service on their shoulders, this third group has a right to claim the benefits of that service. It was their situation which became the rhetorical focus of the changes of the 1980s as questions were asked about the nature of that right (Chapter 5).

In the real world, there were changes to the limits within which these roles could be performed, as each of the groups came under pressure. The upheavals were reflected on the screen: workers, who had established an assertive militancy in the 1970s, were pressured to become compliant and their jobs became less secure; professionals were challenged by a managerial culture; users of the health service moved from being conceptualised as 'patients' to becoming 'consumers' or even 'customers'. The changes were reflected – and acted out – across the genres.

---

[6] One exception was *The Cause* (BBC *Play for Today* 3 February 1981), in which an elderly union official is called in to deal with a 1980 hospital dispute.

Political pressures affected the ways in which each group was defined, and those changes in definition themselves had a deep effect on actual relationships within the health service and beyond. We will observe ways in which those assigned to a given role – whether as nurse, or surgeon, ambulance worker or patient – increasingly needed to balance their understanding of that role with the expression of a personal 'voice'. In all three roles we will observe attempts to hang on to one definition while being pressed to adopt a different persona.

Among those who populate the programmes there are two groups of shadowy figures who are present, but not necessarily visible. These are the writers, producers and others who create the programmes, and also the invisible audience – those who watch and listen. We will be discussing the roles of writers, directors, journalists and others, and we will also be aware that each genre builds up its own expectations of its audience. It has a view about who they are; an awareness of their presence. A genre-based relationship between programme creators and their audience is of great importance and itself came under stress with the changing policies of the 1980s. We will observe how changes to the structure of broadcasting, as well as ideas about public service in broadcasting, were led by a changing conceptualisation of who the audiences were; what they had a right to expect from the broadcast media; and how they were expected to respond (Chapters 5, 7 and 12).

Genres: Centripetal and centrifugal

To use John Corner's formulation, broadcast genres are both centripetal and centrifugal, they 'ingest' ideas, attitudes and events current in society, then 'project' them out towards the audience. And each genre does this in its own particular way (Corner 1995:5).

Jeremy Tunstall, who carried out a survey of the working lives and professional ethos of television producers in the early 1990s, observed that 'each genre has its own specific goal or goals: it has a characteristic style of production... its own internal system of status and prestige, its own values and its own world view' (Tunstall 1993:3). Of course, over the half-century of broadcasting which preceded the 1980s, there had been boundary disputes, reorganisations and forms of hybridisation (and these have continued apace). Nevertheless, in the 1980s, the major genres inhabited relatively separate worlds and, in the intertwining narratives of illness, health and public service, each broadcast genre offered a platform of a specific type. However, as restrictions on broadcasting hours were lifted and more spaces became available, there was increased opportunity for new genres to develop. Many of these new formats designed for off-peak viewing times, tended to be seen as lower status, attracting smaller audiences than the prestigious, peak-time staples. Judgements about the status of genres, and their role within the broadcasting output would play an increasingly important part in debates around 'public service' in broadcasting (Chapters 7 and 8). In our review of programmes on health and the NHS, we have argued that the range of genres offered a fruitful variety of platforms for the staging of both public performance and personal voice. The interaction between genres, and cross influences from one to another will be central to our observations and to their political significance.

We offer here some of the ways in which genres could be assessed as contributing to broadcasting as a public service. Each genre has its own specific qualities and purposes, but many of the characteristics listed below can be traced across the output, from high to low status, from 'serious' to 'popular'. We will be unpicking these 'generic possibilities', in our study of the significance and social place of health care provision in the 1980s.

Generic possibilities

- Narrate stories and experiences – factual and fictional: probable or hypothetical.
- Make visible, or imagine, a multitude of differing social contexts and relationships.
- Pass on information.
- Analyse and explain.
- Circulate and debate ideas, opinions and worldviews.
- Pose hypotheses.
- Reflect moods, trends, the spirit of the age.
- Create a public space for citizens from all sections of society to be represented in various different ways.
- Allow participants to 'give an account of themselves': (to have a 'voice' in Nick Couldry's sense).
- Make space for the representation of specific social roles, such as doctors, and for formal and informal organisations, such as trade unions, political parties and campaigning groups.
- Create well-known 'personalities': entertainers, commentators.
- Provide emotional outlets – laughter, provocation, relaxation – sometimes shock and horror.
- Mock and question established ideas and attitudes.

In the broadcasting schedules, real worlds were juxtaposed with possible worlds, laughter with shock, information with distraction. We shall be moving between these different modes in the following chapters, asking, for example, what possible worlds are posed by the radical threats to life itself of pain and disability, and the ways in which society could or does deal with these challenges.

By observing the presentation of roles in the medical encounter, we will suggest that, during the 1980s, a wide range of genres was contributing to the totality of broadcasting *as* a public service.

Analysing the programmes

In analysing programmes across the genres, and exploring their relationship with the politics of public service, we will be noting three major aspects which interweave with and influence each other. As we will demonstrate, none of these aspects fully makes sense without the others, since they interrelate in the ways in which they are presented to viewers and listeners:

- We will consider the *flow of information*, provided by the broadcast output. In particular we will look at the news and current affairs strands which reported and reflected on politics and the policies which affected the public services. Bill Cotton may joke that they are a 'sideshow', but, of course, these are the programmes that set the agenda, circulate the language and influence the limits of the debate. They provide a showcase for politicians and other public actors. They are taken very seriously by governments and are intensely scrutinised by those in political life.

- Then there is the *cultural creativity* of the rest of broadcasting, ranging from serious drama through to lifestyle, comedy, chat shows and numerous other lightweight formats. We will argue that this outflow of narrative, entertainment, rumour, attitudes, provocation and spectacle across a range of genres has its own purchase on politics. In their differing ways the various generic possibilities map public changes of mood, reflect shifts in vocabulary and adjust conceptual frameworks. We will explore the ways in which the different emotional and intellectual appeals characteristic of these diverse genres interleaved personal experience with argumentation, attitudes and political commentary. Of course, the range of programming is so great that it is impossible to pin it down precisely. We do our best to indicate the penumbra of hints, suggestions, images, considered ideas and instant reactions, all jostling for space across the airwaves.

- While studying the cultural and informational output, it is essential to take on board the ways in which institutional changes affected that expression. This brings us back to the context of broadcasting policy and the ideologies which drive it. Hence, we will be considering the very *conditions of possibility* for the production of broadcast output: the changes in the finances and structures of television and radio, driven by the political, economic and ideological commitment of governments. It is of crucial importance to view the broadcast output within the context of a broadcasting structure which was, in the 1980s, under considerable pressure as its public service foundations were challenged, contested and transformed.

We will be keeping a rough chronology through the chapters as we give an account of the developments of the 1980s, moving back and forth between these three aspects as, taking our cue from the programmes, we observe the changing discourse around broadcasting, the NHS and the concept of 'public service'.

The first three chapters set the stage for the Thatcherite 1980s by exploring the opposing ideologies of the 1970s as the ideas of 'Thatcherism' were first evolving. Chapters 4, 5 and 6 look at moves towards restructuring the three main roles in the medical encounter, workers, patients and professionals, in the early 1980s. Chapters 7 and 8 look at the middle years of the decade, when major government reports were produced on both broadcasting and health. Chapter 9 considers the dramatic challenge to public health with the arrival of the AIDS epidemic, Chapter 10 takes up the development of popular programming towards the end of the decade, and Chapters 11 and 12 discuss 'third-term politics' and the two major Acts of Parliament of 1990.

V   Changing values: 'What is true, possible and desirable'

More important than the immediate practical effects of Thatcherism...has been its effect on how people think...it has fundamentally changed political attitudes in Britain. It has changed the conception of what is true, what is possible and what is desirable.

wrote Margaret Thatcher's supporter, Shirley Robin Letwin, reflecting on 'Thatcherism' in 1992. (Letwin 1992:v)

The project of the Conservative 1980s, it emerges, was not so much an abolition of society but a restructuring. This involved restructuring the ways in which individuals relate to one another, and restructuring the ways in which individuals inhabit specific social roles – both in their daily lives and as they are represented in the media.

In the 1960s, the marxist historian of culture and politics, Raymond Williams, described a process of creating 'meanings and values as they are actively lived and felt' (Williams 1965:64–88). This was what he called the 'structures of feeling', which underpin a society at a point in time: not just an ideology, a mere set of ideas, but a way of *living through* particular values and cultural experiences. The Thatcher years brought a change in the 'structure of feeling'. Changes to what was *possible* had the effect of changing what was *desirable*, and ultimately what was *true*. Thatcher herself stated 'economics are the method; the object is to change the heart and soul' (*The Sunday Times* 3 May 1981).

We will be tracing these shifts in the coming chapters. But first, we will need to look at the background of public service in broadcasting and the NHS, and the arguments, debates and campaigns which surrounded them before Margaret Thatcher came to power in 1979.

Chronology and Programmes: 1927–1970

1927   **BBC** becomes a public organisation incorporated by Royal Charter. John Reith is Director General.

1936   2 November: World's first public launch of television. Re-launched in 1946 after the Second World War.

1942   **Beveridge Report.**
Report of the Committee on Social Insurance and Allied Services outlines a 'welfare state'.

1945   Friedrich von Hayek's *The Road to Serfdom* published.

1948   **National Health Service** launched by the Labour government.

1953   BBC television's *Panorama* begins.

1954   **Television Act.**
Establishes Independent Television (ITV) regulated by an Independent Television Authority (ITA).

1955   22 September: **ITV** launched.
By 1962, 16 regional companies were broadcasting.
Institute of Economic Affairs founded.

1956   Associated-Rediffusion launches *This Week*.

1958   *Your Life in Their Hands*. BBC medical series featuring operations.

1961   Granada launches *World in Action*.

1964   Launch of **BBC2**.

1964–1970   *The Wednesday Play* anthology of single plays on BBC1, succeeded by *Play for Today* (1970–1984).

1968   ITV contracts reallocated. Thames replaces Associated-Rediffusion.
Carry On Doctor comedy film. Director Gerald Thomas with actors Frankie Howerd, Kenneth Williams and Sidney James.

1970   *Analysis* begins on BBC Radio 4.

1
Myths of Origin: Public Service or the Road to Serfdom?

I 'A truer citizenship': Public service in broadcasting and health

Myths of origin: Intellectual and moral happiness

'We realised the stewardship vested in us, and the responsibility of contributing consistently and cumulatively to the intellectual and moral happiness of the community... We have tried to found a tradition of public service, and dedicate the service of broadcasting to the service of humanity in its fullest sense... Down the years [this] brings the compound interest of happier homes, broader culture and truer citizenship,' wrote John Reith on the foundation of the BBC.

(1927 quoted by Pratten 1998:401)

But for Margaret Thatcher, 'Broadcasting was one of a number of areas – the professions such as teaching, medicine and the law were others... – in which special pleading by powerful interest groups was disguised as high-minded commitment to some greater good.'

(quoted from Thatcher's memoirs by O'Malley 1994:67)

Although very different in their activities and outcomes, both broadcasting and the National Health Service (NHS) were created within a rhetoric of public service and a dedication 'to the service of humanity in its fullest sense' so eloquently expressed by John Reith. Both were set up at significant moments in UK history: BBC radio began when the memory of the First World War was still painful; the NHS immediately after the Second. These were moments when the idea of a unified national 'public' had a particular potency, when there was a desire to overcome social divisions and inequities. Both services addressed a broad and inclusive 'public' with a scope way beyond those who were 'casting their problems on society'. Both were funded by 'the public' at large through a universal payment and were free at the point of use; both reached out to a population seen as sharing certain needs. For John Reith, founder and spiritual father of the BBC, this broad public needed education, information and entertainment, too, even though this was rather reluctantly tagged on (Scannell and Cardiff 1991). For William Beveridge, whose 1942 Report gave birth to the UK's post-war welfare state, the public needed physical care and medical attention 'from the cradle to the grave' (Thane 1982:246–254; Fraser 1984:214–221).[1] Although the historical realities which surrounded the foundation of the two services were complex, both continued to carry with them these powerful myths of origin, and these contributed to the embedded expectations and attitudes of practitioners and users of the services.

To make sense of the shifts which occurred across the 1980s, it will be important to look at the ways in which this notion of 'public service' had evolved over the previous decades. We will be arguing that, rather than seeking hard and fast definitions of 'public service', we will need to consider *clusters* of notions, which can be traced as they developed and fluctuated over the years, modulating with the changing social and political environment. We will observe the ways in which the concept evolved in the *practices* of the two services, against the background of contested popular understanding. What Margaret Thatcher dismissed as the 'high-minded commitment' to provide for body and spirit/mind had been challenged throughout the history of both, and in both cases the institutional structure was forged out of compromise and pragmatism (Curran and Seaton 2010; Griffith et al. 1987). Both were forced to adjust to changing circumstances and by the end of the 1970s the concept of public service was strongly challenged. Margaret Thatcher was not alone in viewing the professionalism of the institutionalised public services as arrogant, patronising and centrist, denying a voice to users and opportunities for providers. On the left, libertarian movements demanded responsiveness and inclusion, while on the right, neo-liberal think tanks were campaigning for privatisation and competition. Both attacked elitism and claims to leadership. In 1977, media sociologist

---

[1] Report of the Committee on Social Insurance and Allied Services, chaired by Lord William Beveridge. Cmd 6404 1942.

Philip Elliott argued that 'cracks have appeared in the moral-political consensus in society'. There was a growing division between claims to 'cultural and moral leadership' and ideas of 'brokerage and mirroring society'. 'It has become less clear in which direction society wishes to be led, or indeed whether, as a whole, it will stand for being led in any one direction' (Elliott 1977:152).

Despite criticisms, the BBC and the NHS remained deeply rooted in the life of the country. Both had created a live popular memory, and both commanded a great deal of public respect and affection. Their powerful myths of origin helped make sense of the ways in which they were experienced, and ensured a coherent point of reference for practitioners, users and society in general. This commitment would continue to find many forms of expression in the broadcast programmes of the 1980s.

However, in 1979 the situations of the two services were very different. The NHS was in crisis, and had been subject to cuts, reorganisations and industrial disputes. Broadcasting was also going through a turbulent but somewhat contradictory phase. In important respects, the practice of public service in broadcasting was expanding, and would enrich its scope when Channel Four (C4) was launched in the early 1980s. But before we can discuss the output of the 1980s, it will be important to take a closer look at the evolution of the two services and the challenges of the 1970s.

'The service of humanity in its fullest sense': The practice of public service in broadcasting

Broadcasting in the UK had been established in the 1920s, and it was the powerful influence of the BBC's first Director General, John Reith, which ensured that it would be seen *as* a service for the public (Briggs 1961; Scannell and Cardiff 1991). The new 'wireless' service was among those institutions established in the late 19th and early 20th centuries in the spirit of Victorian philanthropy, which aimed to broaden the scope of public culture and public education. As well as magnificent town halls, which celebrated municipal pride, educational institutions included libraries, schools and adult education institutes as well as public facilities, such as swimming baths, parks and open spaces. Most were endowed by wealthy benefactors: created out of that Victorian sense of 'service' – a sense of moral purpose and a social duty on behalf of the community – which Raymond Williams described as one of the defining achievements of the Victorian middle class. But, middle-class 'service' was balanced by working-class 'solidarity'. A significant number of institutions were set up by energetic working-class self-education groups, such as the Workers' Education Association and the Co-operative Movement (Williams 1961:313–317; Simon 1965:327–342; Scannell 1990:22). Together they demonstrated a spectrum of approaches to the practice of public service and its links to civic life, ranging from paternalism and charity, to municipal localism and grass-roots self-help. This is an important and often neglected background to the origins of broadcasting as a public service. It existed alongside the elitism rooted in the intense class divisions of the time, and posed several possible relationships between a service and its 'public'. We will be observing some of the ways in which adjustments between paternalist provision and forms of public participation have been threaded through the history, not just of the BBC, but of broadcasting as a whole.

The commercial British Broadcasting Company gained a Royal Charter and became a Corporation in 1927. Broadcasting was a 'public utility'. Like the post office, electricity and water, 'the wavebands available in any country must be regarded as a valuable form of public property' wrote the government's Sykes Report in 1923 (Scannell 1990:13). These utilities were considered to be natural monopolies and were centrally controlled at a time when, particularly during the First World War, competition was seen as inefficient (Curran and Seaton 2010:105–108). Broadcasting, too, was a universal service, in which a signal was sent over the airwaves to be picked up by anyone with the appropriate equipment. In the spirit of the Victorian and Edwardian philanthropists, Reith extended the routine meaning of a public utility. The *content* of broadcasting would entail a moral and cultural commitment. Central control is desirable for practical reasons, but it is also 'essential ethically, in order that one general policy may be maintained throughout the country and definite standards promulgated' (Memorandum to Crawford Committee 1925). For Reith, broadcasting had a 'spiritual' dimension: 'to apply it unworthily to the dissemination of the shoddy, the vulgar and the sensational would be a blasphemy against human nature' (quoted by Coase 1950:48, 53).[2]

The BBC's status was underpinned by its funding by 'the public' themselves. Rather than government-controlled general taxation, its funds came directly from its users in the form of a licence fee, which would sustain not only the Corporation's radio and later television output,

---

[2] The quotation is from a *Times Literary Supplement* review of Reith's book, *Broadcast Over Britain* 15 January 1925.

but also its transmission facilities and commitments in technology, engineering, training, research and development and many other related fields which supported the programming. Listeners paid the basic fee, regardless of their tastes and preferences, their social status or income. The 'public' addressed was undifferentiated – and *broad*. Historian Paddy Scannell argued that broadcasting 'brought into being a radically new kind of public – one commensurate with the whole of society' who 'now had access to a wide range of events previously only for privileged publics ... it equalised public life through the common access it established for all members of society'. It was a form of 'social cement' (Scannell 1990:16, 23).

But from the earliest days, this public service structure was contested. John Reith's conceptualisation of broadcasting as a public service needed, in practice, to find expression in specific programmes, specific schedules and specific managerial decisions on funding and structure, and that, many argued, was elitist and non-democratic.

An early modification to Reith's puritanical, educational vision was a recognition of the validity of entertainment and popular taste. Despite his reservations, entertainment programmes from dance music to irreverent comedy found their way on to the airwaves, and the coming of the Second World War put pressure on the Corporation to broaden its appeal (Scannell and Cardiff 1991:Part III). After the war, the BBC began to expand its television service. By this time, Reith had left the Corporation, but he continued to distrust the visual medium, as did most of the radio establishment (it 'was generally considered to be a light-weight service' wrote producer Grace Wyndham Goldie (1977:40)). Reith remained firmly committed to the patrician, educational interpretation of public service, and was of the view that the 'brute force of monopoly' was necessary to maintain the BBC's commitment to a suitable range of programming. This was definitely not accepted by many who wanted a stake in broadcasting, and a post-war campaign to break the monopoly was many pronged. Campaigners included entrepreneurs and advertisers who stood to profit from the commercialisation of broadcasting, but there were others who argued from a democratic perspective that monopoly allowed the BBC to be insufficiently responsive to its audiences (Wilson 1961). Conservative politician Selwyn Lloyd had reiterated the dangers of the 'four scandals of monopoly, "bureaucracy, complacency, favouritism and inefficiency"' (Curran and Seaton 2010:153).

However, when Independent Television (ITV) was launched in 1955 as a network of regionally based, advertising-funded commercial companies, the regulation set in place to bind it to public service principles was rigorous. 'Tonight, 7.15 September 22nd 1955, a new public service is about to be launched over the rooftops of old London,' declared its announcer (*How TV Changed Britain* C4 June 2008). An Independent Television Authority (ITA) was established to act as a broadcaster and to supervise content and quality of the output, as well as the viability of the new companies. Its powers were strengthened in 1963 when the first ITV schedules were thought to be too commercial. The ITA ensured that the network's programmes were diverse and did not neglect the less profitable areas. The Corporation retained its status as a national institution, and gained a second television channel in 1964. Nevertheless, with the coming of ITV and then of commercial radio in 1972, 'public service' in broadcasting had evolved into a much more flexible commitment. The structure ensured that there was 'a rivalry for audiences but not for finance' wrote Jeremy Potter, ITV's official historian who had himself been a director of London Weekend Television (LWT) (Potter 1989:2). The commitment of ITV to more than money-making and audience maximisation was embraced by energetic executives like Jeremy Isaacs at Thames and Sidney Bernstein at Granada (Holland 2006; Goddard et al. 2007). Potter argued that it had 'evolved into the best of all systems' based on 'regulated competition'. 'The BBC and ITV were different faces of a similar reconciliation between the opposing desiderata of freedom and control.' ITV was 'embraced as a fellow public-service broadcaster' (Potter 1989:2–3). Meanwhile, 'competition detached BBC from apron strings of the state' (Scannell 1990:24).

The balance established between the BBC and ITV produced schedules on both channels which intermixed politics, high culture and social purposes, with a multitude of lighter genres: game shows, soap operas, consumer advice. Programmes were interspersed with advertising on ITV, but all were freely available in exchange for a modest licence fee. The regionally based commercial franchises which contributed to the ITV network were regularly reviewed, and the ITA and its successor – the Independent Broadcasting Authority (covering commercial radio, as well as television) – did not hesitate to terminate the contracts of companies whose programmes it judged to be of insufficient quality. The Annan Committee on Broadcasting, which reported in 1977, recommended that this diversity of funding should remain a basic principle for any new broadcasting organisation. But the mood would change. A decade later, the Peacock Report (1986) condemned what it described as a 'comfortable duopoly' (see Chapter 8). The space between the two reports, both in time and in ideological positioning, demonstrates the gulf which was opening up in relation to broadcasting as a public service. A long-running debate between producing what the public 'needs' and setting out to broaden horizons, and giving it what it 'wants', by producing programmes guaranteed to be popular, would intensify, as would the difference between approaching the 'public' as a whole, and seeing it as fragmented, with many different tastes (Pratten 1998).

However, when the Conservative government was elected in 1979, the broadcasting structure seemed secure. The two BBC television channels were in competition with the ITV network. Radio was now offering 19 independent, local commercial stations (ILR) in addition to the BBC's four national radio services, its regional services and 20 local radio stations. Listeners could also access a number of short-wave and long-wave overseas-based radio stations (Stoller 2010). Together, these broadcast outlets created a varied range of spaces to reflect (among many other issues) issues of health and the NHS, as we will see.

The history of the NHS, and the ways in which it exemplified the meanings of 'public service', had been rather different from that of broadcasting, and during the 1970s the service had been going through a particularly turbulent period.

'Full preventive and curative treatment': Public service and the NHS

> The NHS has shown the world the way to healthcare, not as a privilege to be paid for, but as a fundamental human right. The values of the NHS – universal, tax funded and free at the point of need – remain as fundamental today to the NHS as they were when it was launched in 1948.
>
> (From the official website on the 60th anniversary of the NHS July 2008)[3]

> The NHS functions as a metaphor...a social imaginary that works as the collective protection from painful realisations of death and decay, ensuring symbolic survival.
>
> (Gorsky 2008:439)

Public broadcasting had started (more or less) from scratch early in the 20th century (Street 2002, Chapter 1). By contrast, health provision

---

[3] http://www.direct.gov.uk/en/Nl1/Newsroom/DG_078760 (last accessed July 2012).

had a long history. When the National Health Service was founded, long-established and respected institutions were already in place, involving voluntary, professional and contributory funding schemes, as well as commercial interests. There were traditions, hierarchies, established ways of going about things and a great number of entrenched practices. However, from the point of view of the patient, because of the uneven patchwork of services there was great inequality of provision. Even so, the new public service structure, set up in 1948, needed to be carved out of existing institutions, as well as establishing new ones. As a result there was, from the beginning, a balance between the NHS, funded from taxation, and the elements of paid-for, private provision which continued to supplement it. Rather than creating a structure which could, as in the case of broadcasting, provide a productive interaction between public and private funding, from the beginning there were political and commercial pressures, disputes and compromises (Griffith et al. 1987).

The Beveridge Report, published in 1942, at the height of the Second World War, had envisaged

> a health service providing full preventive and curative treatment of every kind to every citizen, without exceptions, without remuneration limit, and without an economic barrier at any point to delay recourse to it.

For William Beveridge, long-term campaigner for planning and centralisation, and author of the report, disease was one of the 'five giants' which had disfigured pre-war society and must be vanquished. The others, all of which arguably contributed to ill health, were ignorance, want, squalor and idleness (Hopkins 1991). Like the BBC, the NHS was set up to offer universal provision, and like the BBC it would be free at the point of delivery. Its public was made up of equal citizens, and whereas the BBC had set out to contribute to a 'broader culture and truer citizenship', the National Health Service aimed to ensure good health and general well-being among those citizens.

Aneurin Bevan, the Labour minister who doggedly guided the NHS legislation through the minefields of politics and vested interests, stated that he drew his inspiration from grass-roots and municipal forms of public service earlier in the century. He was brought up in Tredegar, in industrial South Wales, where the Tredegar Medical Aid and Sick Relief had been set up by the mining community, backed by local philanthropists and politicians. At a time when working men's institutes and miners' libraries were catering for the cultural and intellectual needs of working communities, the Tredegar Medical Aid provided health services free when needed, its cost covered by a small contribution from its members. 'We are going to "Tredegarise" you,' Bevan told the nation. In many ways, the NHS can be seen as an achievement of working-class activism.[4]

Funded from taxation, the NHS was established in 1948, just as the BBC's television service, relaunched after its wartime absence, was tentatively getting into its stride. Despite the hardships brought by the destruction of homes and infrastructure during the war years, despite the continued rationing of food and other goods and the legacy of disability and ill health, this was a moment of great national optimism. In cinemas across the country, public advertisements and excited news flashes announced the arrival of a universal service to replace the patchy and inadequate health care of the pre-war years ('It's coming! Are you ready!' 'Have you chosen your doctor yet?' 'No-one will be left out').[5] Their anticipation and optimism are tangible. But the NHS had 'a difficult beginning' as the title of a 60th-anniversary television programme made clear. In particular, it encountered opposition from many of those professionals already engaged in health care who were afraid of loosing their independence (*NHS: A Difficult Beginning* BBC2 5 July 2008). The British Medical Association (BMA), which represented most family doctors, was deeply opposed. 'Let's make sure your doctor does not become the state's doctor; your servant not the Government's servant,' declared the BMA secretary, Dr Charles Hill. Ironically, Dr Hill was working for the BBC at the time. He was the well-known and trusted 'radio doctor' who gave health tips and advice, as well as putting over public service messages. Despite his mistrust of public service, he would later become Chair of the ITA (1963–1967) and then Chair of the BBC Governors (1967–1972). 'It was like inviting Rommel to command the Eighth army on the eve of Alamein,' said Sir Robin Lusty, the Acting Chair who handed over to him.[6]

---

[4] http://en.wikipedia.org/wiki/Tredegar_Medical_Aid_Society (last accessed July 2012).

[5] British Film Institute (BFI) online resource *InView British History Through the Lens* includes a number of films related to health, including the 1948 government information films (http://www.bfi.org.uk/inview/).

[6] Quoted on the Wikipedia website for Charles Hill, Baron Hill of Luton (http://en.wikipedia.org/wiki/Charles_Hill,_Baron_Hill_of_Luton).

Back in 1948, Bevan guaranteed independence to the general practitioners (GPs) and made concessions to the surgeons, who had considerable political clout. They were allowed to continue with private as well as NHS work. NHS historian Steve Iliffe describes its structure as 'a mixed economy: it was both nationalised (the hospital network) and franchised (general practice, dentistry, optics and pharmacy), with a loose, decentralised management structure' (2010).[7] The service continued to face problems with funding, and subsequent governments needed to continue horse trading with the various interest groups and commercial interests (Webster 1998:13). By the 1970s, problems of inequality of provision had not been solved. The radical GP Julian Tudor Hart proclaimed an 'inverse care law': 'The services available to an area are inversely proportional to the needs of the area. This is most true where market forces operate,' he wrote in *The Lancet* in 1971 (quoted by Iliffe 1982:6). Iliffe commented that consultants with the greatest stake in the private sector continued to have the greatest influence on services and facilities.

The international oil crisis of 1973 was followed by severe spending cuts and complex reorganisations which affected every part of the service (Gorsky 2008:441). There was considerable discontent among those working within it, and the changes were opposed with unprecedented vigour, leading to a number of strikes. The reorganisations created a complex three-tier arrangement, and there were moves to 'professionalise' nursing, creating different categories of qualification without addressing their low pay and poor conditions. And the position of matron, one of the few roles in which women could automatically claim positions of authority, was reduced (it was a role affectionately caricatured by Hattie Jaques in at least four *Carry On* films, the last being *Carry On Matron* 1972). For the first time, the Royal College of Nursing, which had prided itself on its 'no strike' position, engaged in a public campaign, which went down in nursing history as the 'raise the roof' campaign (Hallam 2000:79, 81). The 1975 doctors' dispute proved another watershed. From the point of view of an NHS manager, 'It was not until the end of the decade that management attitudes again stiffened' (Edwards 1993:45, 48).

There was also pressure from the commercial sector, which saw the opportunity to cash in on potentially profitable parts of the service. In 1973, the Conservative government legitimised pay beds in NHS

---

[7] On the website of the 'No such thing as society' research project (http://www.broadcastingnhsbook.co.uk/

hospitals and made access to them more flexible (Iliffe 1982:24). This led to more industrial action by the public employees union NUPE, then, in 1976, the Labour government established a Health Services Board to control private hospitals and nursing homes. The Board reduced the number of private homes, but a separate private sector remained 'dominated by insurance schemes and American companies' (Iliffe 1982:27). The productive relationship between public and private funding which characterised broadcasting was not reflected here. In fact, when Margaret Thatcher's government took over, for many working in the service the new programme of cuts, privatisations, reorganisations and hospital closures seemed like a continuation of policies from the previous administrations.

Nevertheless, the public service ethos reflected in the myth of origin remained live in the consciousness of those working within the NHS and those who used it. And its centrality was constantly reaffirmed by politicians of all parties. By the end of the 1970s, the service accounted for 11% of government expenditure, and was the largest single employer in the country. Colin Leys notes that it was 'spectacularly economical' compared with the USA and elsewhere (Leys 2001:167–168). But the 1979 election brought a government with a radically different approach to public service, and one which had its own, rather different, myths of origin. The 1979 Conservative Party manifesto promised to end what it described as 'Labour's vendetta against the private health sector' and stated its intention to 'decentralise the service and cut back bureaucracy' (p. 17). NHS historian Charles Webster notes that voices 'representing the political left, the health professions or local government were very much relegated to the sidelines' (Webster 1998:22).

II It all comes down to money: Thatcherism and neo-liberalism[8]

Getting our fundamental intellectual message across

Thatcherism had a long pre-history and its own mythology. It drew on a coherent economic philosophy in which monetarism was a key component, and 'was flanked and supported by new pressure groups, think tanks, an ideological reorientation of the mass media and the passage of some key social democratic intellectuals to the new right', wrote Bob

---

[8] This section draws on research conducted by Hugh Chignell for *BBC Radio 4's Analysis, 1970–1983: A Selective History and Case Study of BBC Current Affairs Radio*. PhD thesis: Bournemouth University 2004.

Jessop in 1988, in one of the many attempts by those on the left to analyse and account for the shift in mood (Jessop et al. 1988:19).

According to her biographer, Hugo Young, Margaret Thatcher had been deeply influenced by Friedrich von Hayek's *The Road to Serfdom* published in 1945, as the Second World War was drawing to a close. In it, he argued that economic planning would inevitably end in tyranny. At the time, Hayek was Professor of Economic Science at the London School of Economics, but this was more than a dry academic text. It appeared in an accessible condensed version in the popular *Reader's Digest* series, illustrated by some terrifying cartoons which reflected Nazi Germany as well as the Stalinist Soviet Union. The dire results of planning would be whips, soldiers on the streets and burning books. 'If you're fired from your job, it's apt to be by firing squad... Thus ends the road to serfdom!' The jacket notes for the first edition read like a rousing exhortation: 'Is there a greater tragedy imaginable than that in our endeavour consciously to shape our future in accordance with high ideals, we should in fact unwittingly produce the very opposite of what we have been striving for?' (Hayek 1945/1999).

Hayek's ideas were promoted by campaigning think tanks, especially the Institute for Economic Affairs (IEA) (which republished the *Reader's Digest* edition of *The Road to Serfdom* in 1999). Founded in 1955, the IEA set out to convert intellectuals and opinion formers. To this end, it published numerous pamphlets promoting monetarism, economic liberalism and the 'free market'. These argued that a government should not aim to achieve full employment, but should ensure that the only money circulating in the economy was generated by the economy itself. Government spending would lead to state control which was akin to 'socialism': the road to serfdom! Although these ideas were considered eccentric at a time when the political consensus was to generate employment within nationalised industries and to build a welfare state, the Institute made converts among influential journalists and academics. In his book on the right-wing think tanks, Richard Cockett discusses how the IEA was used by the leaders of the 'counter-revolution' in the Conservative Party as a source of arguments and education:

> it was the attention that Mrs Thatcher, Sir Keith Joseph and Sir Geoffrey Howe paid to the IEA that gave the Institute its critical political influence, as they became, of course, the three leaders of the 'counter-revolution' in the economic management of Britain that the IEA had been urging on all who would listen since 1955.
>
> (Cockett 1994:176)

The IEA held meetings and lunches at its headquarters in Lord North St, close to the Houses of Parliament in Westminster. Margaret Thatcher began visiting from the early 1960s (Beckett 2009:276). In 1974, together with Keith Joseph, she set up a new think tank, the Centre for Policy Studies, which aimed, according to its website, to 'convert the Tory Party' to economic liberalism. Joseph was praised by Thatcher for appealing to intellectuals at a time when much theorising was of the left:

> If Keith hadn't been doing all that work with the intellectuals, all the rest of our work would probably never have resulted in success... It was Keith who really began to turn the tide back against socialism. He got our fundamental intellectual message across, to students, professors, journalists, the 'intelligentsia' generally.
>
> (quoted by Chignell 2004:8)

It came from nowhere: 'An ideological reorientation of the mass media'[9]

'Thatcherism came as an astonishing surprise to the BBC, it came from nowhere,' Michael Green told Hugh Chignell (27 October 2000). Green, who went on to become Controller of Radio 4 (1986–1996), had previously been an influential radio current affairs producer. Yet, the ideas which Margaret Thatcher's governments would seek to put into practice, were, by the mid-1970s, exerting a significant influence on prominent journalists in all branches of the media. By 1979, there were many who contributed to the broadcast output who were certainly neither astonished nor surprised.

The Institute of Economic Affairs had worked hard to make converts among influential journalists who were linked to politicians of both main parties. They included William Rees-Mogg, editor of *The Times* from 1967, and a committed Conservative. He had been an 'unofficially sanctioned' speech writer for Prime Minister Anthony Eden, for whom he wrote the words, 'Socialism is about equality but... Conservatism is about opportunity,' a sentiment that would be frequently echoed by Margaret Thatcher. Rees-Mogg employed Peter Jay as *The Times* Economics Editor, although he was part of the Labour establishment, the son of a Labour minister and married to Prime Minister James Callaghan's daughter. However, he, too, had become a convert to

---

[9] The quotations from participants in this section come from interviews conducted by Hugh Chignell. Dates of interviews are given in brackets.

monetarist economics, and *The Times* became a leading advocate of monetarism (Cockett 1994:183–187). The Labour government itself proposed monetarist solutions when it faced a major financial crisis in 1976 and applied for a bail out from the International Monetary Fund. Peter Jay became a speech-writer for James Callaghan, at that time. He later claimed to have been the first to explain monetarism to Margaret Thatcher: 'I felt like the geography teacher who first showed the map of the world to Genghis Khan' (*Tory, Tory, Tory* Programme 1 BBC4 June 2006).

In one of the complex ironies and cross-influences which characterise the movement of influential figures in this story, when Rees-Mogg left *The Times* in 1981 he was invited by the then Director General of the BBC, Ian Trethowan, an ex-*Times* columnist, to become Deputy Chair of the Corporation – hardly a neo-liberal stronghold. Meanwhile, Peter Jay had been working for the ITV company, London Weekend Television, where he was presenter on the high-brow political series *Weekend World*. The series was later presented by Brian Walden, a former Labour MP who, according to IEA director Ralph Harris, 'became a scalp we treasured. Later he would often have our chaps on his TV programmes' (Beckett 2009:275). Walden presented *Weekend World* between 1976 and 1986, then fronted his own series *The Walden Interview* (1988–1989) and *Walden* (1990). He was said to be Margaret Thatcher's favourite interviewer, and, according to the political journalist, Michael Cockerell, they formed 'a mutual admiration society' (1988:258).

Despite Michael Green's surprise, neo-liberal ideas were influential in parts of the BBC, too. Hugh Chignell has made a detailed study of radio current affairs and below he describes how the ideas promoted by the right-wing think tanks and pressure groups influenced journalists working on the Radio Four series *Analysis*, launched in 1970.

Hugh Chignell writes:

Analysis began to establish itself as a 'right-leaning' programme just as the group of ideas which would become known as 'Thatcherism' was developing as a coherent approach with intellectual appeal. It was an extraordinarily ambitious series. Presenter Ian McIntyre and George Fischer, Head of Radio Talks and Documentaries, were driven by their commitment to getting the most distinguished contributors and basing their programmes on the most rigorous research.

'The distinction that *Analysis* had', said Fischer '– and people sometimes don't seem to get this – we worked only with primary sources.

In other words: we didn't work from news cuttings. If there was a House of Lords report we did actually read the...thing from beginning to end (or Ian did if I didn't). I can't recall many occasions when we had journalists in the programme. It was always "from the horse's mouth" ' (22 September 2000).

The audience was felt to be small and knowledgeable, and this facilitated the intimacy and informality which can be detected in existing recordings. Producer Greville Havenhand explained:

'You were aiming at an elite audience...you were actually aiming at opinion formers...When you got someone for the programme you actually explained what the audience was and said this is not a mass audience, this is an opinion former's audience...they had their guard down and they also didn't talk down' (30 October 1998).

Analysis chose themes that would reflect the Thatcherite agenda. During the 1970s, editions addressed the power of trade unions, the importance of profits and the problems of nationalised industries, reflecting the concerns of the 'counter-revolution' in Conservative thinking. At a more speculative level, the 'mood' of Thatcherism was also important. Intolerance of vested interests and patriotism combined with a frustration at Britain's decline, admiration for the simple virtues of hard work and family life, and dislike of the 'nanny state' interfering in the lives of individuals.

As well as contributors and topics, the 'counter-revolution' influenced the series through its choice of presenters. Central to the success of *Analysis* was the performance of Ian McIntyre, followed by one of the finest broadcasters of her generation, Mary Goldring. Both were influenced by free-market ideas. 'It was a challenge to the BBC to seek out the intellectual underpinning of the Right,' said Michael Green. '*Analysis* was probably the one recognisable place where [right-wing thought] started to get airspace and I think the programme was really quite prescient in that domain.' He recognised the role of the presenters: 'it was clearly partly driven by the kind of people...I mean Ian and George particularly, who I think would both describe themselves as of right of centre persuasion but who spotted something different' (27 October 2000). Green is suggesting that not only can a single programme adopt a political position, but also that a current affairs series broadcast over a period of years can 'lean' (to use his word) in a particular direction because it is balanced by other programme output. As much of the other output embraced what he calls 'the liberal/progressive ticket' there would be balance in the overall schedule.

The series seems to have become a well-protected territory where the usual rules of impartiality did not apply. Its intellectualism gave a licence to the presenters, together with the valued qualities of 'professionalism' and 'calibre'. 'It had always been understood that, because presenters were chosen for their quality of intellect he or she was allowed a degree of involvement not permitted elsewhere,' stated a programme review board in 1976 (28 July 1976). This meant that the green light shone brilliantly for *Analysis* presenters of sufficient 'calibre' who wanted to use the series as a platform. Two presenters were of particular interest: the academic economist, John Vaizey, who helped present the programme in 1975 and 1976, and Mary Goldring.

Although a Labour Party member at the time, Vaizey had argued, 'Monetarism is a doctrine that a large number of people think is correct.' Like Thatcher herself, he dramatised politics into a battle over the very survival of capitalism. He concluded a programme transmitted on 14 November 1974 by quoting the then Shadow Secretary of State for the Environment Margaret Thatcher, on the need to defend profit, and added, 'there's no doubt that many people would agree with her... " Profits, he concluded, 'should be renamed the blood transfusion that the economy needs' and he asked how viable the mixed economy of private and state owned businesses really was.

From 1975, as a journalist with a reputation for plain speaking, Mary Goldring took the long *Analysis* interview into much more confrontational territory. From her first edition as presenter (1 May 1975) she quickly revealed her priorities and concerns: the failures of nationalised industries, the inadequacies of state education, the abuse of the social security system and the dangers of the trade unions.[10] Over the following years she returned repeatedly to the problems of the British economy and the public services. *Analysis* became a sounding board for concerns about the state of the Britain and its economy, and tough solutions to those problems. In fact, Goldring used *Analysis* to voice the very concerns which defined Thatcherism. And not only did she speak for Thatcher, she spoke *like* Thatcher. A didactic, impatient and morally certain woman, she spoke her mind and challenged the orthodoxies of the consensus politics of

---

[10] 27 November 1975: 4 July 1979: 20 January 1977: 25 October 1978.

the post-war period. For the small, elite audience of *Analysis* perhaps Mary Goldring was a surrogate Margaret Thatcher, hectoring her listeners about the awesome power of trade unions, the failure of state institutions and the fecklessness of the unemployed.

Journalists and 'the intelligentsia' from both political parties would play an important role in the history of broadcasting and the media, but, at the end of the 1970s, with a general election approaching, the NHS was a particular focus of attention for the right-wing think tanks. They were mounting what historian Charles Webster described as 'the most spirited pamphlet and press campaign to be witnessed since the idea of a National Health Service was first debated' (Webster 1998:22). Colin Leys would praise the service for its 'strong spirit of public service and equality', but words such as 'collectivity' and 'equality' – just like Margaret Thatcher's 'society' – were used by neo-liberal campaigners as terms of abuse. In 1980, the Centre for Policy Studies published a pamphlet entitled *A National Health Dis-service* in which Dr Ivor Jones of the BMA fulminated, 'NHS medicine is infected by *egalitarian* politics' (my italics – and note the medical metaphor of 'infection'). He condemned 'the cynical subordination of the health of the people to political dogma' (in Seldon (ed.) 1980:90). Arthur Seldon, President of the Centre and editor of the pamphlet, stated that 'improvement [to the NHS] will only come by motivating *individuals* – doctors, nurses, administrators etc – by varying the resources at their disposal according to the effectiveness with which they use them'. There should be 'additional payment...for good work and diminished payment for bad work'. In other words, 'the real engine of improvement is *the flow of money*' (p. 146).

Faced with questioning from within, as well as such attacks from right-wing campaigners, by the end of the 1970s the secure status of the two public services could no longer be taken for granted. While the myths of origin remained powerful, the practice of broadcasting and the NHS was coming under fierce attack. The next chapter will explore campaigns of both the left and right, as they challenged the concept of 'the public' and put pressure on the very idea of 'public service' in health and in broadcasting. It begins with a discussion of 'freedom' as advocated by the neo-liberal economist Milton Friedman, and goes on to discuss the counterculture and the energetic 'new social movements', which flourished in the decade.

Chronology and Programmes: 1970–1980

1972   **Sound Broadcasting Act** allows for the setting up of commercial radio stations.
June Independent Local Radio (ILR) begins.
London Weekend Television (LWT) launches *Weekend World* (1972–1988).
General Hospital ATV/ITV (1972–1979). Drama series set in a large, modern hospital.
BBC establishes the Community Programme Unit.
Salmon Report on Senior Nursing Staff (1966) implemented.

1975   Margaret Thatcher elected leader of the Conservative Party.
2 December *Through the Night* in the *Play for Today* series BBC1.
The Good Life BBC1 (1975–1978). Comedy series: a couple try to be self-sufficient in a suburban home.
Angels BBC1 (1975–1983). Drama series: 'For the first time focussed on the detail of day-to-day nursing practice.'
This Week: four programmes on smoking and health, Thames/ITV (1975–1976).

1977   **Annan Report on the Future of Broadcasting** recommends an Open Broadcasting Authority.
October–December *Hospital: The Bolton Hospital Story* BBC2. Documentary series filmed in hospitals in the Bolton Area Health Authority.
File on Four current affairs series launched on BBC Radio 4.

1978   September *This Week* replaced by *TVEye*.

1978–1979   **Winter of discontent**: strikes among public sector workers including hospital porters, ambulance workers, hospital cleaners and nurses.
30 November 'What are we here for, brothers?' *Analysis* BBC Radio 4.

1979   15 February 'Hospital in Crisis' *TVEye* Thames/ITV. The strike at St Andrew's Hospital, Bow, London.
January–March *Telford's Change* BBC2. Drama serial on an 'international banking hotshot' who downsizes.
Party Election Broadcasts. Advertising agency Saatchi and Saatchi promotes the Conservative Party campaign with the slogan 'Labour isn't working'.
May **General Election**. Margaret Thatcher becomes Prime Minister.
5 June 'Staff relations at Liverpool hospital' *File on Four* BBC Radio 4.
25 September *Question Time* launches on BBC1.
17 November *Health: Who Cares?* Community Programme Unit/BBC2. How ordinary people can influence decisions about the health service.

1980   February *Yes Minister* comedy series. A wily civil servant manipulates a government minister BBC1 (1980–1984).
February–March *Free to Choose: A Personal Statement by Milton Friedman* BBC2. 'If everyone is left to work for their own self-interest it is inevitable that society as a whole will benefit.'

2
Freedom and the Public: Campaigner, Participant, Consumer

I Freedom

'Freedom' versus class politics

The theme of the 1979 election would be 'freedom'. In the neo-liberal view, personal freedom was linked to economic freedom and both rejected the fusty ties of a class society. The election campaign set the tone. *The Sun* newspaper, owned by one of Margaret Thatcher's favourite entrepreneurs, Rupert Murdoch, printed a three-page article urging its huge popular readership to 'Vote Tory This Time' with some impressive capitalisation: 'FREEDOM to run your life as YOU want to run it, or to be shackled by the bureaucrats and the political bully boys. FREEDOM to work with or without a Union card – or be shackled to a dole queue in a declining economy' (Lamb 1989:154). The Conservatives' election broadcast claimed: 'Those who want to work are left feeling guilty.' Aspirant parents and hard-working businessmen plead 'guilty' to the sin of ambition. 'Do you want better schooling?' 'Guilty.' 'Did you make a profit?' 'Guilty: I'll try not to do it again.' 'You're sentenced to *nationalisation!*' The interests of workers were presented as being in opposition to the interests of trade unions, and the interests of trade unions were characterised as 'socialism'. 'It's a free society versus "socialism",' the right-wing Conservative politician and intellectual Enoch Powell had written back in 1965. For him, 'everyone who goes into a shop and chooses one item instead of another is casting a vote in the economic ballot box' (quoted by Letwin 1992:74). A debate between planning and competition, which dated back to the 19th century, was being revived (O'Malley 2009).

But this was still 1979. The Conservatives were not yet in power. While news and current affairs journalists were obsessed by strikes and the coming election, an independent production company was working on a series of films which publicised the views of the most outspoken exponent of the free-market neo-liberal approach, Nobel Prize-winning American economist, Milton Friedman.

Milton Friedman: Free to choose

In 1980, scarcely nine months into the new government, six of the films were broadcast on BBC2 (16 February–22 March1980). Friedman was introduced as 'the chief contemporary prophet' of monetarism, and he staked out his ground: 'If everyone is left to work for their own self-interest it is inevitable that society as a whole will benefit.' The title of the series was *Free to Choose*; the programmes ranged from an hour to 90 minutes in length, and the films were followed by debates chaired by Peter Jay. Jay noted that Friedman's views were 'personal and controversial', but pointed out that 'the Conservative Government [had] based its economic philosophy' on them.

The evocation of 'freedom' echoed across the programmes, and was associated with 'health' as well as with 'vigour' and self-reliance. 'Free market forces are the best regulator of economic activity in a healthy society,' stated Friedman (programme 1). As the relations between the economics of 'freedom' and the daily experience of living in the social world were spelt out, it became clear that this included freedom from traditional social obligations. Sometimes directly, sometimes through implication, Friedman evoked a world in which it was possible for an individual to shake off social ties and responsibilities, to step beyond familial networks and emotional commitments, and to engage only in financial relationships. From the sweatshops of New York to the slums of Hong Kong, what counted, he argued, was the freedom to buy and sell. The principles of monetarism and their links to personal self-interest were laid out with a confidence and starkness which clearly shocked some of the eminent economists, trade unionists and politicians who acted as respondents.

The films made the most of their global locations, as Friedman bounced back and forth between Japan and India, New York, Hong Kong and London. However, it soon became clear that this was largely an American story. The series began by recalling the early 20th century when the immigrant boats arrived in New York, crammed with desperate people who had left everything behind, including traditional ties and social obligations ('For the first time in their lives they were free to pursue their own objectives') and it ended with the punters who risked all in Las Vegas. In New York, Friedman visited a garment workshop, similar to the one where his mother had worked. It was poorly ventilated and the workers were paid below Union rates. 'It breaks every rule in the book... but if it were closed down, who would benefit?' Here was a telling myth of origin, to be laid against those myths which, as we have seen, characterised broadcasting and the NHS in the UK: 'Our parents and grandparents went through this for us.' But unlike the UK, these new Americans were not held back by the weight of history. 'These workers won't stay here long,' Friedman reassured his viewers, 'they will better themselves'. However – and here followed his recurring theme of the limits on freedom – 'we've been squandering that inheritance by allowing government to control more of our lives instead of relying on ourselves'. Strikingly, the films did not feature those bankers, multinational corporations or wealthy entrepreneurs who stood to make most from a market society. Instead, viewers met shopkeepers, traders running small businesses, consumers and welfare recipients. This was an argument on behalf of the working classes. These, Friedman argued, are the potential beneficiaries. They should claim their 'freedom'.

He had little to say about health-care issues, but, observing a practitioner of Chinese medicine in Hong Kong, he commented, 'This does not come from official certification. The patient's trust comes from experience – his own or his friends. The doctor treats him not because he's ordered to, but because he gets paid. The transaction is voluntary. If both parties don't benefit it doesn't take place' (programme 2). Issues of sickness, vulnerability, expertise, reliability of treatment – the special qualities of the medical encounter – were overlooked, as well as the ability to pay and the glaring possibility of exploitation. There was no such thing as society or social obligation in the world Friedman was presenting. 'The doctor treats him... because he gets paid.' Any motivation such as pride in one's work, expertise or compassion was simply not considered. 'Consumers' were simply 'free to choose'.

Throughout the series, Friedman relished the apparent paradoxes he posed. 'We're less well protected than before' *because of* regulation which aims to protect (programme 5). 'Egalitarian policies *take from* the poor. They create a permanent class of poor' (programme 4). And 'human greed and self interest *promote* the welfare of consumers' (programme 6). When Michael Douglas in the Hollywood film *Wall Street* (1987) declared that 'Greed is good', the phrase became notorious. For Milton Friedman it was a self-evident part of a coherent world view.

At a time when very few independent companies were producing for television, *Free to Choose* was made by Video Arts, a training company which had expanded into production. It was led by a number of influential television figures and chaired by producer Anthony Jay, who had been Head of BBC Talks and Features (1963–1964) and was at the time co-writing the knowing political sitcom *Yes Minister* (1980–1984). Jay was explicit about his own aim to promote free-market ideas. He wrote in 2008, 'I am a Friedmanite. My company produced Milton Friedman's 10-part documentary series *Free to Choose* back in 1979, but I was a convert to market economics long before that. In fact, that was why my company got the gig.'[1] Friedman, together with his American supporters, had been looking for television outlets. He later wrote that it was 'interesting that Britain, the fatherland of the welfare state and the home of a major avowedly socialist party, should be where we would find producers sympathetic to free markets'. It was certainly ironic that in the USA this hymn to commerce was backed by WQLN (We Question and LearN), a struggling, non-commercial, educational station, while in the UK it was the publicly funded BBC which screened six of the ten original films.

All but the first were followed by discussions in which Friedman engaged with economists, trade unionists and politicians. The seriousness with which these presentations were taken was reflected in the grandeur of the setting and the status of the respondents. With some irony they were set in a wood-panelled City of London hall, heavy with tradition, with glittering chandeliers and distinguished portraits. Respondents included the current and previous Chancellors of the Exchequer, Geoffrey Howe and Denis Healey (Friedman mischievously welcomed the Labour ex-Chancellor as 'the first to introduce monetary targets. I have two monetarists here'). Peter Jay was a suitably weighty presenter and known as an avowed monetarist. As well as his work as a journalist on *The Times* and *Weekend World,* and as a speech-writer for Labour Prime Minister James Callaghan, he had, until the previous year, been Britain's Ambassador to the USA (1977–1979).

In the six programmes, Friedman summarised his economics in apparently simple slogans, which revolved around an evocation of 'freedom'. It is worth recording them here, as they underpin the Thatcherite monetarist approach which would put such pressure on the public services, including broadcasting and the NHS:

---

[1] This quotation and the next are from the Power Base website's page on Anthony Jay at http://www.powerbase.info/index.php/Antony_Jay#cite_note-8 (last accessed July 2012).

1. 'The power of the market' meant that if markets were left unregulated, as in the chaos of Hong Kong, prosperity would follow.
   Friedman approved of 1970s Hong Kong. In the slums, people were
   desperately poor 'but the people are free'. Hong Kong was a place
   where the free market really worked. No duties, no tariffs . . . the free-
   est market in the world. 'If they fail they bear the cost, if they succeed
   they get the benefit' (programme 1).
2. There should be no government regulation of the market. 'Self-
   interest will produce public welfare' through the market's 'invisible
   hand'. The phrase was coined by the economic philosopher of the
   Scottish enlightenment, Adam Smith, who had been adopted as a
   founding father by the neo-liberals. (At this point in the programme,
   viewers saw a few mountains and heard a swirl of bagpipes.) Government interference would *cause* recessions, Friedman argued, and
   it did so in the 1930s (programmes 2 and 3).
3. Similarly, consumer protection was unnecessary. Friedman met an
   American woman with asthma, who travelled to Canada to buy a
   drug prohibited in the USA because of its side effects. 'Therapeutic
   decisions which used to be the preserve of doctor and patient are
   now taken at national level.' 'Let the government give us information
   but let us decide what chances we want to take with our own lives'
   (programme 5).
4. Welfare did more harm than good. 'Government money *always* cor-
   rupts.' Friedman visited public housing projects in the USA and the
   UK. These tenants 'lose independence and dignity. They are treated
   like children.' Many welfare recipients were afraid to take a job.
   'I couldn't risk it . . . jobs are low paid,' says a man from Hulme in
   Manchester. Friedman responds, 'It's the fault of the system. If the
   welfare is taken away he would find a job.' Alternatively, he may
   have to rely on private charity. 'Trying to do good with other people's
   money simply has not worked' (programme 3).

At this point, MP David Ennals, Social Services Secretary in the previous
Labour government, responded that the film was irrelevant to British
society. This was not *other* people's money, it was *our* money. 'People
should be allowed to live in dignity and that's the state's responsibility.' 'The state has no responsibility,' responded Friedman briskly. '*People
do* . . . your approach is *collectivist*.' Any form of collectivity and collective
action was unacceptable. Here he took a sideswipe at a hospital workers'
strike. 'There were cancer patients turned out of their beds,' he claimed.

'The attendants acted as a group as they would never have acted as individuals.' And he swept aside trade unionist Jack Jones's description of the North of England, where unemployment was a result of changing technology. For Friedman, it was the trade unions that created unemployment by forcing up wages.

5. Attempts to create equality were counterproductive. 'It goes against the most basic instinct of all human beings.' At this point, he was standing beside the Thames. 'The growth of criminality in Britain owes much to the drive for equality.' 'The society that puts equality before freedom will end up with neither. The society that puts freedom before equality will end up with a great measure of both' (programme 4). He went on to argue that differences were valuable and equality was boring. 'Life would be no fun without winners and losers.' Just like Las Vegas, life involved gambles.

As the language and ideas of monetarism became more familiar during the 1980s, they were accompanied by attitudes towards social relations and morality. Freedom, in Milton Friedman's presentations, had no truck with traditional or emotional ties. It did not recognise the 'professional pride in a job well done, or a sense of civic duty' described by David Marquand (2004:1). It flourished best when people, as individuals, left all commitments behind them and moved to a new and (apparently) empty land, an unregulated space. This new individual was exposed, unprotected, at risk; not rooted within any supportive social network. It was a staggeringly simple but extreme expression of 'no such thing as society'.

II Counterculture and new social movements

Counterculture

Most assessments of the 1970s have tended to be gloomy, focussing on the repeated financial crises and the strikes which raged across the country (Marr 2007; Beckett 2009). Already in 1979, *Daily Telegraph* columnist Christopher Booker predicted that the decade would be remembered as 'a long and rather dispiriting interlude ... the prevailing mood was one of a somewhat weary, increasingly conservative, increasingly apprehensive disenchantment' (Booker 1980:5). But others have seen it very differently. 'The 1960s was a decade of dreams ... the 1970s was the decade ... which tried to harness those dreams into reality' (Forster and Harper 2010:4). Rejecting tradition, there were experiments with new forms of solidarity, new ways of constructing identities, different concepts of 'society' and 'the public'. The 1970s saw many 'cracks in the moral-political consensus' in society (Elliott 1977:152), and the discourse of social class was revised and renewed.

In this atmosphere of radicalism, Margaret Thatcher and her advisers were not the only ones to argue for 'freedom' and to condemn the idea of 'public service' as a disguise for the exercise of power. This was the age of the counterculture: as sceptical, anti-authoritarian and impatient of traditional deference as Friedman himself, but with a completely different analysis and set of solutions. While the radical right had been building think tanks, publishing pamphlets and setting out to influence politicians and journalists, an equally radical and highly energetic set of mainly left-wing campaigners addressed a grass-roots constituency. In a coming together of culture and politics, the political became personal as campaigns challenged gender, sexuality, ethnicity and tradition as well as social class, and explored new ways of inhabiting everyday life. Alongside the surge in trade union activism, the decade saw a flowering of feminism, gay rights, children's rights, antiracism and the beginnings of campaigns from black and Asian groups. It saw social experiments, alternative lifestyles, street demonstrations, festivals, community-based activism and single-issue campaigns. Some were linked to left-wing political groupings; many identified themselves as socialist, others as anarchist or libertarian. There was a renewal of left-wing politics, a growth in far-left political parties, and a valorisation of working-class perspectives and working-class experience. In a decade of ideological turbulence, many options seemed wide open.

The outlets were fringe magazines, radical publishers and alternative bookshops. And there was backing from a radical academia which had embraced the critical agenda developed during the student campaigns of the late 1960s. Jeremy Potter, historian of the IBA, called his chapter on the 1970s 'The heyday of the marxist sociologist' (1989:8), and marxism, in several different guises, did indeed, provide an influential critique. New, disrespectful disciplines flourished – cultural studies; media studies; radical sociology – which challenged established institutions, including those of broadcasting and health.

Critiques of health

'We have a right to know and decide about procedures … that affect our bodies and our lives,' wrote feminist historian Barbara Erenreich (quoted by Karpf 1988:59). The medical profession had become arrogant and disdainful; insitutionalised medicine was impersonal and reduced patients to a state of helplessness; patients were not treated as individuals; many treatments were, in any case, inappropriate, and the wider context of ill health was not recognised. These were the views of many who were campaigning for a radicalisation of contemporary approaches to health care. Some distrusted those very advances in technology and treatment which created the sophisticated medical practices of the 20th century. For others, the recognition of inequalities in health provision meant that issues of social class were still firmly on the agenda, while feminists identified a 'sexual politics of sickness' in which medicine had become dominated by a largely masculine hierarchy. Historians traced the 'medicalisation' of women's bodies, which removed their agency even from such natural processes as childbirth (Oakley 1984). The professionalisation and technologisation of health care, they argued, had devalued the practical skills which had been the province of women, in their capacity as mothers and carers (Erenrich and English 1979). As with many of the activist movements of the 1970s, detailed critiques of established structures were balanced with the development of alternative and collaborative practices. This meant the creation of spaces where the rigid distinction between experts and clients could be broken down; professionals could share their skills, and the users of a service gain expertise and control. In 1970, a women's health collective of this sort, set up in Boston, USA, published advice and information based on their experiences. *Our Bodies Ourselves*, still regularly updated, became a key feminist text, supporting workshops and self-help groups, which drew together women health workers, community activists and 'health care consumers' (Boston 1971/2011).

A more radical view argued that conventional medicine was itself a sham, and should be rejected. 'The medical establishment has become a major threat to health,' wrote Ivan Illich in his introduction to *Medical Nemesis*. 'The disabling impact of professional control over medicine has reached the proportions of an epidemic.' The only solution was a total rejection of institutionalised health care, since 'medicine only does harm' (1976:3). Professionalised medicine 'tends to mystify and to expropriate the power of the individual to heal himself and to shape his or her environment' (p. 9). It changes 'pain, impairment and death from a personal challenge into a technical problem' (p. 10). It was a message that was shared by many, and would be expressed in a series of angry plays by G.F. Newman transmitted on Channel 4 in 1983 (see Chapter 6). Alternative forms of healing, such as acupuncture and homeopathy, had a long history, and the 1970s would see a renewed interest.

Although many critiques of medical care were politically neutral – or at least disinterested – others questioned institutionalised medicine from an explicitly left-wing perspective. The alternative medicine movement wanted nothing to do with the professionalism and expertise of modern medicine, but the socialist approaches recognised the importance of the NHS and those who worked within it. Jeanette Mitchell, a member of the Politics of Health Group, wrote: 'although to outsiders the National Health Service may seem like a monolith, there are arguments and discussions going on within it all the time about how health care could be better' (1984:11). Campaigning organisations such as Politics of Health made common cause between those who worked in the NHS and those who used its services. They argued for patient participation as part of a democratisation of the service; for a 'convivial' (Illich's term) collaboration between those with specialised knowledge and skills, and those who must take on Susan Sontag's 'more onerous citizenship'. Those who are sick should remain autonomous citizens, neither 'patients', submissive to the control of professionals and science, nor 'consumers' in the market place, whose 'freedom' depends on their financial clout. 'Our problems are less a matter of biology than politics,' wrote Mitchell (p. 41). Within the NHS, campaigning organisations included the long-standing Socialist Health Association (founded as the Socialist Medical Association in 1930) and the Radical Nurses Group (founded 1980). Ultimately, 'the struggle for health can only be part of a wider struggle to effect basic changes in economic and social relationships', a group of British feminists wrote in 1973 (Doyal et al. 1973:16).

The ideologies, campaigns and alternative practices of the 1970s were mounting a significant challenge to the patrician view of public service embedded in the myths of origin and well-established traditional approaches. They were paralleled by a wider sense of dissatisfaction and willingness to challenge medical authority. In the best-selling *Health Rights Handbook* (1980), Gerry and Carol Stimson insisted, 'Your body belongs to you and only you should decide what to do with it and what to have done to it.' Their message was that 'health service consumers should attempt to improve the system', and the book outlined how to complain and how to claim your rights, as well as recommending the setting up of health pressure groups and patient participation groups. 'I doubt if the authors of this book will be surprised if it irritates the doctors who read it,' wrote a reviewer (Selley 1980). Anne Karpf described how television and radio programmes took up the challenges. She wrote: 'Consumerism was the new ideology. In the 1960s we were all re-constituted as consumers...class seemed old hat.' By the 1970s, 'consumer discontent about medical practices became...a significant strand in medical and consumer programming' (1988:57).

III   Publics

Consumer, campaigner or participant?

The single-issue campaigns and new social movements which thrived in the 1970s challenged established views of 'the public'. As the decade drew to a close and debates around the 'public services' intensified, it is possible to derive a typology of possible 'publics' which were being evoked. They include:

Two traditional positions, embedded in social structures and in social class differences:

- 'The public' as passive *clients*: a paternalist, professional approach.
- 'The public' in their capacity as *workers*: finding a distinctive voice through trade unions and workplace activism.

Two contemporary pluralist positions:

- 'The public' as participating *citizens*.
- *Diverse publics*: demanding space for many different groupings.

Two opposing libertarian views:

- Left libertarians: 'the public' made up of self-determining, *de-institutionalised individuals*: the 'Ivan Illich' option.
- Right libertarians: individual *consumers*, competing with each other and exercising choice in the market place: the 'Milton Friedman' option.

Traditional positions: Older definitions of public service

1. The paternalist, professional approach: the public as clients
Within both the BBC and the NHS, there was a continuing stress on professionalism and commitment to 'service' to a broad and unified 'public'. But critics argued that 'professionalism' characterised an entrenched establishment. Members of the professional classes were part of a network with an easy access to decision-making and power, and many opportunities to put their view in the media.

2. *Workers' rights within the public service structure: the public as workers*
   At the other end of the social spectrum there was a challenge from working-class organisations, especially the trade unions, campaigning for rights and equality for members of the public in their capacity as workers. The heavy industries were disappearing but still dominated the UK economy and sustained the communities in which they were based. In the 1970s, trade unionism was more than a political structure – it was a culture and a set of relationships. It could evoke a history of self-reliance and of self-education, and could draw on the image of the 'self-improved, politicised working man'. There was a vivid sense of class awareness and solidarity, which went way beyond the sterile condemnation which filled the newspapers. It was 'not only a cause ... it was ... something approaching a workers' faith ...', wrote historian Raphael Samuel (quoted by Beckett 2009:56).

Pluralist positions

3. *Campaigning for participation: The 'public' as participating citizens*
   The radical movements of the 1970s put class politics on the agenda in a different way, by posing a view of the public which focussed on *citizenship and participation*. This view rejected a clear distinction between professionals and 'publics'. For many, 'participation' went beyond mere 'access' and implied a role in controlling and managing the monolithic public services.

4. *Broadening public service: Diverse publics; multiple participation*
   From the 1960s, a *pluralist* view of the public had extended to specific campaigns for participation by many who argued that they were disadvantaged, *as a group*, and that their voices were not heard. The 'new social movements' of the 1970s posed forms of solidarity and identity which cut across traditional social strata. They posed smaller 'publics' whose members shared a particular understanding. Individuals insisted on speaking from their social position, as women, as people with disabilities or as people from specific communities – the regions or nations, black or Asian. These were not representative of 'the public' as a whole, but they drew attention to the diversity of that wider 'public' beyond the broad strokes of class differentials.

Libertarian positions: There's no such thing as 'the public'

5. *'Left' libertarian: Suspicious of public service, rejecting all structures*
   In this view the 'public', are seen as self-determining, deinstitutionalised individuals. An opposition to all institutions and to the claims

of professionals was expressed most strongly by the anarchist and alternative lifestyle movements of the 1970s which threw off stifling traditions in the name of personal autonomy and set up their own non-hierarchical ways of living and working, including producing alternative media (see Chapter 3). And a deep suspicion of claims to authority and established structures was more widely spread, with an insistence on individual differences and preferences, and increasing dissatisfaction with public services seen as condescending and paternalist.

6. *Abandoning public service: Deregulation and 'freedom'*
   Here the 'public' become individual consumers, exercising choice in the market place. The libertarian thrust of the countercultural movements had much in common with the language of neo-liberal economists, who equally opposed the entrenched power of professionals and the inflexibility of institutions. Their attitude was also characterised by a passionate opposition to interference from 'the state' and from government as it sought to plan the economy and regulate enterprises. For a thinker like economist Milton Friedman, the key was *consumer* choice, which would be achieved by economic competition among providers. In this view the 'public' does not exist as a single entity – there is no such thing as 'society'. It is not made up of social classes, nor of social or interest networks, nor of communalities defined by ethnicity or gender. What the sociologist Richard Sennett described as 'connections to the world' are here organised through individuals alone and, sometimes, in family groups (1998:10). Unlike the left libertarians, self-interest is prioritised. Individuals compete in the market place and assert their rights through commercial transactions, buying and selling. Private enterprise is free from the paternalism and coercion of public service.

This was the approach taken by the right-wing think tanks which influenced Margaret Thatcher as she became leader of the Conservative Party in 1975. It was echoed by the Party's 1979 appeal to a specifically working-class public. This was the public envisaged by *Sun* editor Larry Lamb when he gave over three pages of his newspaper to urge his readers to vote for 'freedom'.

The great moving right show

First published in 1964, *The Sun* newspaper had grown out of the trade union-backed *Daily Herald*. But when Rupert Murdoch bought the paper in 1969, his project was to address its working-class readers in terms of fun, pleasure and a bit of a laugh – anything but 'work' ('Life's more fun in your number one *Sun*' the newspaper trumpeted) (Holland 1983). This was a new working class, with disposable income and time for leisure. In his 1979 election leader column, editor Larry Lamb wrote: 'The roots of *The Sun* are planted deep among the working class. We are proud to have a working-class readership' but 'the Labour party no longer carries any torches. It does not excite...with Margaret Thatcher there is a chance for us to look again to the skies' (1989:154–155).

It was the left-wing cultural theorist, Stuart Hall, who detailed this 'Great Moving Right Show' in the journal *Marxism Today* (January 1979). *Marxism Today* had been moving from its orthodox Communist Party origins to become an influential source of contemporary ideas. Its writers, inspired by the work of Italian theorist Antonio Gramsci, had been carrying out a penetrating analysis of the political, economic and cultural forces which together characterised this moment in UK history. By 1979, at a time when some were arguing that it came as a complete surprise, for Hall and his co-writers, Thatcherism had already pushed 'popular ideologies sharply to the right' as various strands in 1970s restlessness were coming together. The Conservative Party's election broadcast claimed that trade union leaders were among those who pushed you about and told you what to do, and in an further article Hall considered the 'two ways of taking democracy seriously': 'Traditional working class "us/them" has been displaced, as social democracy is aligned with the power bloc, and Mrs Thatcher is out there "with the people"' (1980:177).

'Thatcherism', he argued, provided 'a particularly rich mix', not just because of its economics, but also because of the resonant traditional themes – nation, family, duty, authority, standards, self-reliance, which had 'been effectively condensed into it' (Hall 1979:170). This was the new 'common sense' which was echoed by *The Sun* and appealed to by the Conservative Party broadcast. By the end of the 1970s, there were many different perspectives from which the discourse of 'public service' could be criticised. It was part of an old-fashioned us/them division which the new common sense would reject as outdated and oppressive. The next chapter will explore these critiques in relation to broadcasting.

3
Broadcasting into the 1980s

I Radical, popular, challenging, informal

Broadcasting in the 1970s

In 1973, Nicholas Garnham wrote a polemic about television for the British Film Institute:

> What in fact we have is a system in which two powerful institutions, responsible not to the public, but to the real, though hidden, pressures of the power elite, government, big business and the cultural establishment, manipulate that public in the interests of that power elite and socialise the individual broadcaster [i.e. programme maker] so that he (sic) collaborates in this process almost unconsciously.
>
> (Garnham 1973:12)

How does this passionate critique of the *structure* of broadcasting, with its parallels with the radical criticisms of the health service, and its denunciation of traditional definitions of public service as a sham, square with the broadcast output of the time? This chapter will be looking at the *practice* of broadcasting in the 1970s, and the radical campaigns which challenged and sought to reform it.

Many working in the BBC and the ITV companies at the time shared in the new critical mood and certainly did not accept that they were, even unconsciously, collaborating with a power elite. In certain ways, the programme *output* of the 1970s echoed both the disrespectful mood of the counterculture and the new assertiveness of the consumer movements. So, before looking more closely at the challenges to the broadcasting establishment, I will first consider some of the programming of the time. Focussing on output that dealt with health and the

NHS, I will highlight four significant trends – four approaches which would, in different ways, become central to discussions of 'public service' in broadcasting and the changing ideas of who 'the public' were. They can be roughly categorised as *radical, popular, challenging* and *informal*. Although they were loosely mapped on to particular genres, they were not confined to them. More importantly, they created different platforms – different conditions of possibility – through which medical themes, among others, could be addressed, and through which we will be able to trace the shifting, contradictory and often overlapping concepts of the public and public service as they developed across the 1980s.

Radical: 'Dissipating the ivory tower stuffiness'

At the BBC, Director General Hugh Carlton Greene (1960–1969) had already set out to transform the Corporation's stuffy 'Auntie' image, and had encouraged a distinctly anti-establishment approach across the board, from late-night satire, to searing dramas, especially *The Wednesday Play* (1964–1970). Both the BBC and the major independent companies set out to nurture new writers from a much wider range of backgrounds, and commissioned plays which reflected working lives and made powerful attacks on established interests. In 1969, the BBC set up Pebble Mill in Birmingham to specialise in regional drama, and by the 1970s, in the words of broadcasting historian Jeremy Potter, 'in dramas and documentaries she ['Auntie' BBC] sunk her teeth into every sacred cow in sight: the British Empire, the Church of England, the medical profession' (Potter 1989:8). It was, according to Lez Cooke, historian of television drama, a time of 'realism and ideology' (Cooke 2003:90–127). Its radicalism prioritised deep-rooted working-class themes, but also reflected the newer, more individualist mood. Trevor Griffiths's *Through the Night* (*Play for Today* BBC 1975) took on the medical establishment from the point of view of the vulnerable patient. The team made a conscious decision not to use the documentary-style filming which had become associated with 'gritty' working-class topics. Instead, they it filmed in a studio, using costumes, make-up and camera styles familiar from popular soap operas. The aim was to lull the audience into expecting a cosy, reassuring plot, 'but they got something very different', said Griffiths. The heroine, played by Alison Steadman, wakes from an operation to find her breast removed after signing a consent form that was not properly explained to her. The play follows her struggle to cope with the aftermath. Based on Griffiths's wife's experience with breast cancer, it clearly struck a chord with the viewers. He received hundreds of letters and referred to it as 'without question...my best known piece'.[1] However, the BBC felt it necessary to consult a number of medical experts before the programme was made, and, as a consequence the text was revised considerably (Karpf 1988:197–198). Producer Tony Garnett said, 'I made sure we finished after the *Radio Times* deadline, so if they were going to ban it would cost them dearly in publicity.'[2]

Despite the critical acclaim won by *The Wednesday Play* and *Play for Today*, the dramatists and producers who worked on them saw themselves as an embattled enclave standing up against a highly conservative Corporation.

Popular: 'Not to preach but to entertain'

Some prestigious single plays like *Through the Night* were certainly popular in that they attracted a substantial audience, but their serious intent did not fit the criteria for a 'popular' format, which set out to please rather than provoke. 'This programme is not to preach but to entertain,' stated the 1977 publicity for ATV's *General Hospital*. ATV, based in Birmingham, was known for its comforting early evening soaps. It had had a great success with the long-running *Emergency Ward 10* (1957–1967), whose writers, far from challenging the medical establishment, had declared that they wanted to 'overcome the pre-war attitude of the British public to hospitals as institutions, places to be avoided' (Karpf 1988:183). After all, this was less than a decade after the creation of the NHS. Chief Executive Lew Grade reflected that cancelling the series had been one of the biggest mistakes he had ever made, so, when restrictions on broadcasting hours were lifted in 1972, ATV launched a (slightly) tougher hospital soap in a twice-weekly afternoon slot. In 1975, *General Hospital* (1972–1979) was promoted to Friday evenings, 'with a new, more gritty dramatic theme tune'.[3] The BBC responded with *Angels* (1975–1983) which followed the lives and loves of student nurses at St Angela's hospital.

In classic soap-opera style, both series focussed on the personal relationships of doctors and nurses rather than the pressures of hospital life,

---

[1] Quoted in the British Film Institute's *Screenonline* website. http://www.screenonline.org.uk/tv/id/1086102/index.html.

[2] Quotations from Tony Garnett and other dramatists and producers come from *Left of Frame: The Rise and Fall of Radical TV Drama* BBC2 31 July 2006.

[3] Episodes from *Emergency Ward 10, General Hospital, Angels* and *No Angels* were shown in the National Film Theatre season 'The Nation's Health'. BFI Southbank May 2011. Quotations are from the programme notes.

but even so, the critical attitudes of the 1970s came through. An episode of *General Hospital* from 9 January 1975 included plenty of pretty nurses with frilly caps, strained relationships and a nurse who was pregnant by a doctor. However, when a consultant used his contacts to land a high-paid private job, a woman colleague was scornful. 'What sort of person will you be treating?' she demanded. 'Rich oil sheiks... the neuroses of film stars. You'll be a surgical pimp for wealthy hypochondriacs.' Concerns about the power of drug companies were hinted at: 'You've been reading too many medical advertisements,' his superior told a know-all young doctor who recommended a branded medication. And racial prejudice was challenged. A black sister gave instructions to a white trainee, and an African doctor succeeded in a job interview ('there's nothing wrong with my skin, man').

Angels began with a more radical brief. It was written and produced by women in the context of the outspoken feminist movement, and aimed to reflect the sharp end of health-care delivery at a time when nurses' organisations were under stress (Karpf 1988:212; Hallam 2000:80). The main actors, together with script editor Paula Milne, prepared themselves by working as auxiliaries in hospitals. Even so, when the actors discussed the show with their real-life equivalents, the nurses were emphatic that it did not capture the real experience of life on a ward. It was good on the petty restrictions and the frictions between nurses and difficult patients, but did not convey the speed and pressures of hospital life. Nor did it show the contempt with which nurses were treated by many doctors ('they just throw their needles on to the bed for the nurses to pick up: "you're a nurse, you're there to do the dirty work". You're *under* them'). And, they added, *Angels* never addresses the important issue of pay. 'Nurses don't expect to be well paid, but they never stop wondering about being so badly paid' (*Radio Times* 3–9 April 1976).

Even so, the series was criticised for its realism. Sexual promiscuity and nurses drinking heavily came under fire (although compared with more recent series like *No Angels* (C4 2004–2006) these were mild), and 'we get people complaining about small touches of realism – like nurses who have untidy hair', producer Ron Craddock told Sherryl Wilson. Clearly many viewers expected all nurses to live up to what Julia Hallam described as a 'particular professional idea of nursing' (2000:80).

And the hospital context provided a fascinating setting for factual programmes which were able to balance entertainment with insight. When *Hospital: the Bolton Hospital Story* (BBC2 1977) became the first fly-on-the-wall documentary to follow hospital life, it attracted viewing audiences of more than 5 million. As the *Daily Mail* put it: 'Birth, death, humour, pathos, even union action – this is the everyday face of the Health Service TV has never dared to show before.' Although it was a documentary format, it followed the popular conventions. 'Heroes are inevitably the doctors and its heroines, or "angels", the nurses, and its villains invariably heartless bureaucrats and striking ancillary workers,' commented NHS manager Brian Edwards (1993:42).

While seeking a broad audience who wanted relaxation and entertainment, the popular output could also provide a light-hearted commentary on the age. Home-grown revolutionaries were mocked by the accident-prone *Citizen Smith* (BBC1 1977–1980); the self-help movement found its limits in *The Good Life* (BBC 1975–1978), and in the ten-episode BBC serial, *Telford's Change*, 'an international banking hot-shot downsizes to a local branch against the wishes of his wife'. The popular dramas of the late 1980s which celebrated ambition and luxury (*Howard's Way* BBC1 1985–1990; *Capital City* Thames/ITV 1989) would reflect a completely different world.

Challenging: Journalists with dust on their boots

While the popular formats set out to provide entertainment which would not be too demanding, what I have described as the *challenging* formats treated their audiences as engaged citizens with a right to be informed. These were mostly investigative programmes in the classic current affairs mode, and many journalists and others with a long-term commitment to the genre have looked back on the 1970s as a 'golden age' (Goddard et al. 2007:59–70; Barnett 2011:67–76; Holland 2006:60–86). On television, a number of 'fixed common elements' from the ITV companies were protected in peak-time viewing by the regulator, the IBA. They included Granada's *World in Action* and Thames Television's *This Week*, both challenging the BBC's prestigious *Panorama* (Sendall 1983:232). On BBC radio, producer Michael Green chose to launch *File on Four* (1977–) from Manchester, the home of radical left-wing broadcasters in the pre-war days. He wanted it to be a programme where journalists 'actually got dust on their boots...they went out in the field; they spoke to real, in quotes, people as well as people in authority' (interview with Hugh Chignell 29 July 2008).[4]

---

[4] Hugh Chignell conducted research on *File on Four* for the AHRC-funded project ' "There's No Such Thing as Society": A Study of Broadcasting and the Public Services under the Three Thatcher Governments, 1979–1990' at Bournemouth University. This research is also included in his book *Public Issue Radio: Talks, News and Current Affairs in the Twentieth Century* (Basingstoke: Palgrave Macmillan).

During the 1970s, two distinct approaches to current affairs had developed. One was committed to investigation and on-the-ground reporting, getting close to the individuals who may be feeling the effects of a political decision – whether doctors, nurses, managers, patients or ancillary workers in a hospital. The other argued that it was the job of such programmes to stand back, to analyse policy initiatives, to question politicians and experts, to inform the public and to generalise. On BBC radio, this position was taken by the Radio 4 series *Analysis* (see Chapter 1). On television, perhaps surprisingly, it was an ITV company, London Weekend Television, which adopted this more cerebral approach with its series *Weekend World*. As it happened, both of these series were more sympathetic to the sorts of views which were being expressed by Margaret Thatcher and her advisors. The investigative approach was more contentious, and by the end of the decade, was running into trouble. *This Week* would be a test case. When it came to health issues, *This Week* managed to annoy the regulator, the advertisers, the IBA and the government.

Instead of the softer medical topics, reporter Peter Taylor took on the tobacco companies. His four dramatic films on smoking and health began with a notorious sequence of cancerous lungs kept in buckets in a hospital laboratory: 'This is the work of a hospital,' says a surgeon prodding yet another pallid lumpy growth. 'Buckets and buckets of lungs…If this man had not smoked he would be alive and this lung would be in his chest now' (*Dying for a Fag* 3 May 1975). The programme followed the final months of a 42-year-old smoker dying of lung cancer. *Licence to Kill* came a week later, and a third programme followed a group of volunteers who had decided to give up. *Ashes to Ashes* (11 September 1975) included an interview with the head of an advertising agency, who later complained that his arguments had been presented unfairly compared with those of his critics (Holland 2006:107–108). Even though the company depended on advertisements for its income, there had, initially, been no opposition from Thames's management. However, the IBA upheld the complaint (Elstein 1979).

Here was an example of what Anne Karpf described as an 'environmental' approach to health. As Peter Taylor explains in his book *Smoke Ring*, his original concern, caused by his wife's smoking, led him beyond issues of personal health to challenge big business and the global interests which controlled the industry (Taylor 1984:xiii–xxi). His fourth film took its cue from advertisements for Marlboro cigarettes, featuring stirring music, galloping cowboys and wide open spaces. *Death in the West* showed real cowboys crippled by lung disease (9 September

1976). The film became the subject of an injunction by tobacco company Phillip Morris, and an out-of-court settlement meant that to this day it cannot be shown publicly. However, it was pirated almost immediately by anti-smoking campaigners in the USA and circulated informally on VHS tape (Holland 2006:107–108). The reaction of Thames's management to this unwelcome controversy and other sensitive critiques – notably of government policy in Northern Ireland – was to take *This Week* off the air and replace it with something less challenging.

The renamed series *TVEye* (1978–1986) had a brief to make something more palatable for 8.30 on Thursday evenings. Its editor, Mike Townson, thought that programmes should concentrate on 'stories' rather than 'issues' and avoid the politicised context which caused so much trouble. It was a sign of the times. The conditions of possibility for challenging programmes were changing. Many on the *This Week* team were outraged and accused Townson of being 'unable to distinguish between the significant and the sensational' (Holland 2006:171). And medical topics could well be sensational. The very first *TVEye* gained a scoop with a programme on the birth of Louise Brown, the first 'test tube baby', surrounded by much hype and PR (*To Mrs Brown a Daughter* 7 September 1978). As it sought out 'soft' medical topics with a definite audience appeal, *TVEye* was described as indulging in 'medical alarmism', and became known in the trade as 'TV Eye, Ear, Nose and Throat' (Phillips 1995:24–25). However, for the moment, the series remained protected in its mid-evening slot, and retained much of its journalistic clout. One of its first programmes was *Hospital in Crisis* (see Chapter 4), which followed a strike in a London hospital.

Informal: Consumerism, social action and committed programming

Our fourth significant context for 1970s broadcasting was the development of a much more casual and intimate style across the genres, together with an increase in informal, low-key programmes and series. The loosening of restrictions on broadcasting hours in 1972 opened a space to experiment with casual, less structured formats in the new, off-peak slots. Chat shows, audience-participation programmes, consumer advice, lifestyle, news magazines, game shows and youth programming contributed to a flow of action on the screen which was light and entertaining, mildly informative and involved lots of chatter, lots of personalities, some music and plenty of laughs. This was a type of output which was television's own, in which the small small-scale domestic medium, with its incessant words and images, seemed more like another group of people in the corner of the room than any sort of demanding political or cultural experience.

Despite its low prestige, it has been in the flow of this routine television that many innovations that are characteristically televisual have evolved: the low-key, continuous format, with weak boundaries between programmes; the development of the presenter as a friend, with a relaxed and easy address directly to the audience; the phone-in exchange between presenter and viewers; the presence of 'ordinary people' on the screen (Holland 2000:131). Since these were the days before domestic videotape recorders made time-shift possible, this output of 'ordinary television' was viewed at off-peak times, mornings, afternoons or late at night and was directed at the audiences thought to be available at those times, in particular, women (Stossel 1987).

The regional base of the ITV network meant that programme makers were seeking out a more localised public. Especially in local news magazines and similar formats, the companies set out to get closer to their immediate audience with relaxed and chatty presenters, local people on screen and regional accents, ignoring the cultural norms laid down by the metropolitan centre (see Chapter 5).

From 1973, a number of local radio stations became a significant part of the broadcasting landscape. Pirate broadcasters like Radio Caroline had been banned and a network of advertising-funded Independent Local Radio (ILR) stations set up. These were licensed by the IBA, which required them to produce a full range of speech content, including hour-long documentaries, regular features, extended news programmes and phone-ins. Like ITV, ILR became a 'fusion of private enterprise and public service'.[5] Through their numerous talk shows and informal phone-ins, the stations built up a sense of easy familiarity with their audience. Listeners could engage in banter and relaxed conversation with presenters and their guests. In the view of Tony Stoller, Chief Executive of the Radio Authority in the 1990s, the obligations placed on ILR by the ITC 'underpinned the success. It caught the mood of the times, socially, politically, economically.' By the beginning of the 1980s, there were 26 stations with an audience of more than 14 million (Stoller 2010; Lewis and Booth 1989).

Across the broadcast media, the more conversational style of address brought broadcasters closer to everyday life, and questions of health

---

[5] Discussions of ILR by Tony Stoller and Emma Wray can be found on the research website at http://www.broadcastingnhsbook.co.uk/ Quotations are taken from their papers.

and well-being came to play an important role. 'Social action' programming, such as Thames Television's *Help* (1979–1991), responded to
viewers' questions and offered advice on everyday problems. Series of
this sort could create a space for self-help, for sharing experiences, for
consumer concerns and also for educational material. They also created
a space for oppositional and radical ideas in what Peter Lee-Wright, who
worked as a producer and director in the BBC's Community Programme
Unit, called an 'efflorescence of committed television'.[6] The Unit had
'emerged from a happy accident', writes Lee-Wright:

> when a team from the legendary BBC2 show *Late Night Line-Up* was
> dispatched to the Guinness brewery in Park Royal to canvass views
> on the 1972 BBC Autumn schedules. Invited in out of the rain to the
> works canteen, they were subjected to a cogent critique of the BBC's
> bourgeois preoccupations. This led the show's then Editor, Rowan
> Ayers, to argue successfully for the setting up of a unit to make pro-
> grammes with and about people who were largely excluded from
> the media. For nearly 30 years, until 2000, the CPU made what was
> called 'access' television with members of the public in the *Open Door*
> series, *Take the Mike*, and with self-help groups in *Grapevine*, disaf-
> fected youth in *Something Else*, the deaf *See Hear* and many other
> groupings, including the innovative *Video Diaries*.

'Access' programmes which dealt with issues of health and the NHS,
and which allowed campaigning groups to challenge NHS practices
from the patient's point of view, were part of the move to what Anne
Karpf categorised as 'consumer' programmes. But this was a 'humanist'
consumerism, concerned with participation and activism rather than
competition and financial values.

Into the 1980s

The broadcast output of the 1970s reflected the 'war of position'
between the conflicting and overlapping ideologies of the decade.
In some ways, broadcasting was itself part of the radical mood, prepared
to challenge entrenched attitudes, inequalities and traditional structures
of power. At the same time, both the BBC and the independent companies were responding to a new, assertive consumerism by building up
their popular output, and creating a more equal relationship with their
publics through the development of informal styles. Radical series like

---

[6] Peter Lee-Wright's comments are quoted from the research website http://
www.broadcastingnhsbook.co.uk/

Play for Today had only been a small part of the output, and gradually, on all channels, the confidence to make space for material that challenged rather than pleased would be undermined. As the 1980s progressed, 'the sort of radicalism found in *The Wednesday Play* became almost impossible' according to producer Tony Garnett, while director Ken Loach spoke of 'an implied instruction to broadcasters' to 'respect the spirit of the times' in what he described as 'the Thatcherite onslaught'.[7] Pressures to be popular would intensify, and the terms in which 'the popular' was understood would themselves be subject to pressure. But, although the conditions of possibility were changing, forms of radicalism did not disappear. Instead, they gained a major new outlet with the arrival of Channel Four in 1982.

II Critiques of broadcasting

Critiques of broadcasting

Despite the spaces for radical programming on both the BBC and ITV, and in some cases *because* of them, broadcasting would become a prime target for the critical mood of the 1970s. The BBC, in particular, was subject to bitter criticism: on the one hand for narrowness, elitism and 'biased' reporting, and on the other for immorality, vulgarity and what critics such as Mary Whitehouse, and her 'clean up television' campaigners, saw as a drive downmarket (Whitehouse 1994). Both groups saw the Corporation as run by arrogant professionals and not responsive to its audiences (Heller 1978), and many of the strongest critiques came from those working within the industry itself. Nicholas Garnham (who was working at the BBC at the time) had concluded that the concept of 'public service' simply 'softened' 'any guilt that broadcasters might feel about the apparent elitism of this stress on "professionalism"' (1973:33).

Critical commentary on the media was spirited as it echoed across the decade. Beyond established academia, teachers and researchers in polytechnics, at the newly established Open University (whose first students enrolled in 1971), and at educational institutes – in particular the British Film Institute (BFI) – saw themselves as critical outsiders. They produced work driven by an enthusiasm for popular media and a recognition of their democratic force, as well as by arguments for a participating public. Inspired by innovators like Raymond Williams and Richard Hoggart,

---

[7] Quotations from *Left of Frame The Rise and Fall of Radical TV Drama* BBC2 31 July 2006.

writers insisted that popular culture and the mass media should be taken seriously. Television and radio were firmly at the centre of social and cultural life, and their economic and political aspects should be explored as well as their literary and cultural ones (Hall and Whannel 1965; Williams 1974). 'A knowledge and understanding of television in the public at large is a prerequisite for public control over the medium,' wrote Ed Buscombe, laying out a programme for the study of television in schools (1974). There was a real sense that this work was new and urgent. Pamphlets, monographs and dossiers, some of them circulated as duplicated typescripts, looked at the structure of broadcast media; reported on European and American television; analysed 'low status' genres such as soap opera and sitcom, and conducted research among audiences.

News, in particular, was exposed to scrutiny and stringent criticism. The Glasgow University Media Group meticulously documented ways in which broadcast news neglected dissident voices and misrepresented trade unions and working-class organisations, particularly in reporting the strikes which raged across the decade. 'What underpins media coverage is scrutiny of working people, rather than an analysis of "normal" operations of the economy and its ability to generate crisis,' they wrote (1982:43). There were studies into absences, stereotyping and (mis)representation. It was pointed out that many of the interest groups identified by the new social movements – ethnic minorities, workers' interests, regional interests, women – were not only misrepresented (and often mocked) on screen, and inadequately catered for as audiences, but were largely excluded from employment within the media.[8]

There were investigations into the broadcasters' accountability to these diverse publics and how it could be ensured. For the BFI, Caroline Heller carried out a rare study of the BBC Governors and their views (Heller 1978). There were questions about who the broadcasters were, and how the structures of broadcasting could be democratised. It was

---

[8] Examples include: BFI Television monographs; stencilled occasional papers from the Centre for Contemporary Cultural Studies at the University of Birmingham; statements from campaigning filmmakers, documented in Margaret Dickinson (ed.) (1999) *Rogue Reels: Oppositional Film in Britain 1945–1990* (London: BFI). Influential academic studies included Stanley Cohen and Jock Young (eds.) (1973) *The Manufacture of News: Deviance, Social Problems and the Media* (London: Constable); Charles Husband (ed.) (1975) *White Media and Black Britain* (London: Arrow); Annette Kuhn (1982) *Women's Pictures* (London: RKP).

argued that 'the public' should not be conceptualised merely as con-sumers of media output. They should have some *control* over that output, too. The Free Communications Group, set up in 1969 by some well-connected journalists and media insiders, stated in their samiz-dat publication, *The Open Secret,* 'the Free Communications Group believes in the social ownership of the means of communication. This will not happen without a radical change in the present struc-ture of society' (FCG 1969:1). In 1974, the Labour Party, advised by some of the campaigners, published a discussion paper titled *The People and the Media* which promoted a new, decentralised broadcasting sys-tem, with democratic control over policy (Freedman 2003:85–95). The technicians union, the Association of Cinematograph and Television Technicians (ACTT), was campaigning for workers' control and workers' participation.

An energetic set of theoretical studies underpinned the critiques. Pro-moted by the journal *Screen,* contemporary versions of marxism were brought together with feminism, semiotics and psychoanalysis to create a heady mix which has continued to influence media studies (Hall 1977; Fiske and Hartley 1978). Its reflexes were oppositional, with a strong campaigning spirit. Despite the apparent abstraction of theorising, the influential work of feminist writers, in particular, was deeply embed-ded in political activism; part of a broader attempt to link a theoretical challenge to a changing practice.

Media activism: A participating public

Media activists included many who were working within the established structures and campaigning to open them to a broader range of voices. But, as with the health service, there were also those who rejected the broadcast mainstream and set out to create an alternative media. They saw themselves as part of the counterculture and posed different forms of solidarity and community. Feminists, in particular, argued that that new meanings could not be conveyed in the old, well-worn formats. The media language must itself be radicalised. A woman's cinema must be a counter-cinema, wrote Claire Johnston. It must stand outside the mainstream and explore new, often avant-garde, forms (Johnson 1973; Mulvey 1975). The women's film collectives of the 1970s, including the London Women's Film group to which Johnston belonged, were part of a thriving independent movement, which had begun in the 1960s. Individual filmmakers, co-operatives, workshops and collectives set out to explore topics beyond the range of the broadcast media. Some followed the progress of strikes and demonstrations; others set out to represent local communities in a number of towns and cities; others to explore topics of particular relevance to women and other excluded groups. Some were concerned to experiment with visual and aural styles, and to expand the possibilities of film and the new video technologies. There was a move to develop forms of collaborative work which rejected the hierarchical structures and craft-based skills of the established industry, and aimed to break down the rigid distinction between those who created programmes, those who appeared in them and those who watched them. A new group of distribution circuits was established, including small businesses with expanding catalogues, such as The Other Cinema (established 1970) and the women-only Circles (established 1979). There were numerous informal screenings and discussions, where a film may be part of an exchange on health issues, or be screened to cheer on the participants in a strike (Dickinson 1999; Nigg and Wade 1980).[9]

As the 1970s progressed, critiques of a centralised media became stronger, and many independent filmmakers were less satisfied to remain on the margins. They too wanted to see their work broadcast to a wider public, and argued that that 'public', in all its diversity, should be envisaged not just as consumers but as participants. To the regional activists, women's groups, video artists, black and Asian film workshops and many others, the 'public service' commitment of the BBC and ITV implied a highly restricted access to the airwaves as well as a narrow and a limited range of programming styles. The unoccupied fourth channel offered a new opportunity and, in 1974, many of these diverse groups came together to form the Independent Filmmakers' Association (IFA).[10]

---

[9] Margaret Dickinson's *Rogue Reels: Oppositional Film in Britain 1945–1990* includes an account of these projects as well as interviews with participants and copies of the numerous documents and manifestos produced. Heinz Nigg and Graham Wade give a contemporary account of 'community media' in the UK.

[10] The campaigns which led up to the establishment of Channel Four have been documented, among others, by: Michael Darlow (2004) *The Independents Struggle: The Programme Makers Who Took on the TV Establishment* (London: Quartet); Simon Blanchard, Chapter 1 in Blanchard, S. and Morley, D. (eds.) (1982) *What's This Channel Fo(u)r? An Alternative Report* (London: Comedia); Sylvia Harvey in Stuart Hood (ed.) (1994) *Behind the Screens: The Structure of British Television in the Nineties* (London: Lawrence and Wishart); Stephen Lambert (1982) *Channel Four: TV with a Difference* (London: BFI).

A democratic fourth channel?

> Our broadcasting structures should be as inventive as our pro-
> grammes and as varied ... tidiness is tyranny.
>
> (Smith 1977:35)

> Pluralism has been the leitmotif of all of us in this report.
>
> (Annan Committee 1977, para. 9.31, p. 108)

> The public must not be seen as a statistical aggregate of abstract
> individuals, but as a complex body of diverse and distinctive
> people.
>
> (Blanchard 1982:17)

Before the arrival of digital media, there was limited space on the
'airwaves' – the electromagnetic spectrum which carries the broadcast
signals – hence a limited number of broadcast channels. However, the
technology did allow for at least one more television channel, and competition for access to this bandwidth had been intensifying since the
launch of BBC2 in 1964. From the early 1970s, the fourth channel
became the focus of some energetic campaigning from a number of different interest groups. The biggest difference of opinion was between
the ITV companies, which began planning for an ITV2 to balance the
BBC's second channel, and those who argued that a new channel offered
an opportunity for something completely different. 'The heart of the
debate on TV4 is the desire to make television more democratic,' stated
the Free Communications Group (Darlow 2004:115).

A 'TV4' campaign, set up in 1971, was emphatic that the fourth channel should not go to the ITV contractors. There was a multitude of
possible uses, they argued; it could be educational, community-based
or experimental. Theirs was a loose alliance of television producers,
politicians, trade unionists and advertising executives, as well as media
pressure groups. More radical was the Independent Filmmakers' Association (IFA), which included established freelance filmmakers as well
as the activist workshops and collectives who wanted to see their
community-based and campaigning work on-air. The argument was that
space should be made for a wider range of professionals, but also for
many different *kinds* of voice, for the publics which had hitherto been
excluded by the overwhelmingly white, male, middle-class and largely
metropolitan broadcasters. There was lobbying of ministers, numerous
public meetings and the debate spilled over into the pages of the press
and the trade journal, *Broadcast*. Proposals for the new channel were put

forward, notably a contribution from Anthony Smith, who had been a BBC producer, and, in 1979, would become Director of the BFI. He argued for a National Television Foundation, which would act as a publisher of programmes and would 'make room for the sort of experiment which broadcasting authorities shun' (Darlow 2004:148). There should be a commitment to 'openness rather than to balance, to expression rather than to neutralisation' (Smith 1974).

In response to the increasingly vocal campaigns, a the Government Committee on the Future of Broadcasting, which had been set up in 1970 then cancelled, was reinstated by the incoming Labour government of 1974. Under the chairmanship of Lord Noel Annan, it sat for nearly three years and took evidence from all interested parties: the BBC, the IBA, advertisers, ITV companies, the broadcasting unions, business entrepreneurs, grass-roots campaigners and many others. In the words of Michael Darlow, evidence to Annan represented

> a decade of cross-fertilisation of ideas, aesthetic and political values, between those in the relaxed, open and democratic world of independent filmmaking...and those who worked in the much more hierarchical and layered world of the broadcasting institutions.
>
> (Darlow 2004:160)

And the critics set the agenda (Freedman 2001:203).

'It has been put to us that broadcasting should be "opened up",' wrote Lord Annan when his Report was published in 1977 (p. 20). In a fat book which quoted from the numerous submissions made over the years of the enquiry, the report recognised that the nation 'is now multi-racial and pluralist...the structure of broadcasting must reflect this variety' (p. 30). It echoed the view that 'broadcasting in Britain today is controlled by closed and almost autocratic institutions' (p. 32), and that broadcasters 'must accept the principle of industrial democracy' (p. 428). ITV's pitch for a fully commercial ITV2 was rejected in favour of a radical new experiment on the lines suggested by Anthony Smith. But instead of a Foundation, Annan proposed an 'Open Broadcast Authority' which would act 'as a force for plurality in a deeper sense...a new kind of broadcasting publishing'. It would not make programmes itself, but commission independent producers (p. 235). It would be able to broadcast committed programmes and only need to achieve balance across the schedule. This would allow for the expression of opinions not normally sanctioned by other channels. Annan also praised the idea that channels should not compete for funds, but should be funded from different sources. Although the report was not specific about sources of funding, it was certainly a victory for the 'years of campaigning by small shifting groups of committed programme makers' (Darlow 2004:170). Campaigners looked forward to the new channel with great anticipation – but they recognised the need to keep up the pressure, especially when Labour lost the 1979 election.

In a presentation to the 1979 Edinburgh Television Festival, the IFA reasserted its democratic view of a participating public:

> One of the main goals of TV4 must be to lessen the gulf between professional communicators (including ourselves) and the public we observe, question and on whose behalf we speak… The public must not be seen as a statistical aggregate of abstract individuals, but as a complex body of diverse and distinctive people, with a whole hitherto unexplored range of potentialities, desires and concerns… the audience, or rather audiences, should be enfranchised.
>
> (Blanchard 1982:17)

The Annan Report would become the basis of Channel Four, which eventually launched under the Conservatives in November 1982.

III   General Election 1979

Although the Labour government produced a White Paper, largely supporting Annan's proposals, Labour Prime Minister James Callaghan had other things on his mind, including a major financial crisis, an IMF bailout and industrial unrest following the imposition of a 5% ceiling on pay rises. His government was not popular. In the autumn of 1978, the Conservatives' dynamic new advertising agency, Saatchi and Saatchi, created a poster that became notorious. 'Labour isn't working' it shouted, under the image of an apparently endless dole queue. It was said that the impact of this campaign caused Callaghan to delay the planned election, with disastrous consequences for Labour (Scammel 2008). The winter of 1978–1979 became the 'winter of discontent' which was to gain mythical status in UK political history. Between November 1978 and March 1979 there were strikes among rubbish collectors, dinner ladies, traffic wardens, printers, pilots, school caretakers, train drivers and civil servants, as well as ambulance workers, hospital cleaners and nurses.

Backed by some virulent reporting from right-wing newspapers and a whipping up of anti-union sentiment, the Conservatives maximised their advantage. Andy Beckett notes that 'union power in general began to stop being a dilemma for the Tories and started to become their key to office'. Thatcher's advisor, John Hoskyns, headed the relevant chapter in his memoirs, 'Saved by the Unions' (Beckett 2009:469). 'Strikes backlash brings big swing to Tories' reported the *Daily Express*. 'MAGGIE LEAPS AHEAD!' (TUC 1979:11).

The Conservatives under Margaret Thatcher won the election and the long Thatcherite decade began at a moment of old-fashioned class confrontation. The theme of class realignment would continue across the 1980s, and would be central to the development of Thatcherism, involving new forms of social identity and shifts in the concepts of the public and 'public service'. Arguments for democracy and participation would be reconfigured. Despite the famous slogan 'there's no such thing as society', rather than being abolished, 'society' would be restructured.

In order to trace these political changes though the broadcast output, the next chapters will look at moves towards restructuring the three main roles we have identified as being part of the 'medical encounter': workers, patients and professionals. As we have seen, when Margaret Thatcher came to power, both broadcasting and the National Health Service were in an unstable state. In the following chapters, we will observe how the politics of broadcasting shifted the conditions of possibility of broadcast programming, and affected the ways in which television and radio reflected the turbulence which was affecting the NHS.

Chronology and Programmes: 1979–1983

1979	15 February 'Hospital in Crisis' *TVEye* Thames/ITV. Peter Williams reports on a strike at St Andrew's Hospital, Bow, London.
	May **General Election**. Margaret Thatcher becomes Prime Minister.
	July Report of **Royal Commission on NHS** published.
	December **Patients First**. Government consultative document published. Proposes streamlining the NHS administration.
1979–1982	*Only When I Laugh* Yorkshire/ITV. Hospital comedy. Three hypochondriacs avoid leaving the security of their ward.
1979–1984	*Medical Express: Your Weekly Health Report* BBC1. News programmes on the latest developments in medicine and health.
1980	**Broadcasting Act** widens Independent Broadcasting Authority's remit to include a fourth channel.
	30 January *Newsnight* launches on BBC2.
	25 February *Yes Minister* begins on BBC1 (1980–1981). Comedy in which civil servant, Sir Humphrey, manipulates naïve government minister, Jim Hacker.
	22 May *Your Life in Their Hands* BBC2 (1980–1986). New series. In programme 1 a cancer sufferer faces a major operation.
	A National Health Dis-service edited by Arthur Seldon, published by the Centre for Policy Studies.
	August **The Black Report** *Inequalities in Health*, originally commissioned by the Labour government, is released on a bank holiday.
	5 November–10 December 'Unmasking medicine' *Reith Lectures* BBC Radio 4, delivered by Dr Ian Kennedy.
1981	New ITV franchises begin.
	5 February 'Going Private' *TVEye* Thames/ITV.
	5 June *Going Gently*. Directed by Stephen Frears in BBC2's *Playhouse* series. Norman Wisdom and Fulton Mackay play terminal cancer patients.
	29 July Wedding of Prince Charles and Lady Diana. The global television audience was estimated at 750 million.
	Rupert Murdoch (News International) buys *The Times* and *The Sunday Times*.
	8 September *Only Fools and Horses* begins a 15-year run on BBC1. Comedy in which Del Boy and Rodney devise get-rich-quick schemes in a Peckham council block.
	12 October–22 December *Brideshead Revisited* Granada/ITV. Prestigious drama series based on an Evelyn Waugh novel set in upper-class Britain.
	Inner-city riots.

1982   In January, unemployment in the UK tops three million for the first time since the 1930s.

8 February *Sick in Sheffield, Broke in Beverley Hills* Yorkshire/ITV. 20 family doctors from Beverley Hills visit Sheffield to find out how the NHS works. In California, doctors and patients discuss the US system of medical insurance.

29 July–5 September *The Best of Health* Central/ITV. Documentary series filmed in a Birmingham health centre over a period of a month.

September: **Report of Hunt Enquiry into Cable Television**. 'Opportunities for new forms of entrepreneurial activity'.

Long-running strike by NHS workers.

16 September 'Hospitals: an Unhealthy Dispute' *TVEye* Thames/ITV.

10 October–7 November *Boys from the Blackstuff* BBC1. Unemployed tarmac workers cope with life on the dole.

2 November **Channel Four** launches with a remit to be innovative and to appeal to diverse tastes and interests.

S4C (Sianel Pedwar Cymru) launches in Wales.

Walter Channel Four's first-night drama about an institutionalised mental patient. Director Stephen Frears criticises 'heritage dramas' 'about an England that no longer exists'.

12 November *Well Being*: C4 series on healthy living in association with the Royal College of General Practitioners begins (12 November 1982–11 February 1983).

1983   April–June Falklands War.

April–June *Kill or Cure*: Meditel for C4. Series on damage from prescribed drugs.

Terence Higgins, one of the first British victims of AIDS, dies. A group of his friends set up the Terence Higgins Trust to increase awareness and support.

NHS restructuring: Area Health Authorities abolished. Cuts in local health services; doctors and nurses given independent pay-review bodies.

Brass Granada for C4 (1983–1984). Comedy series about the wealthy Hardacres and their employees, the Fairchilds.

Questions of Leadership Central for C4. Series of documentaries directed by Ken Loach. Not transmitted.

6–27 October *The Nation's Health* C4 drama series. Each episode was followed by a discussion programme: *Follow the Nation's Health*. The IBA commissioned research to investigate whether the public's trust in the health service was diminished after watching the drama.

4
Restructuring Social Class

I Restructuring social class: Restructuring workers

'The children of Margaret Thatcher': New forms of social identity

'She defined the country we still live in today' wrote journalist and historian Andrew Marr, looking back from 2007, 'we are all of us, like it or not, the children of Margaret Thatcher.'

(Marr 12 June 2007)

Reviewing her memoirs in 1993, *The Times* columnist, Janet Daley had argued that Thatcher's greatest achievement had been the transformation of the class structure. Her personal toughness had helped to legitimise the 'right of working-class people to be self determining'. On BBC2's *The Late Show* (27 October 1993), Daley pointed out that it was ambitious working-class voters who had kept Thatcher in power.

For Margaret Thatcher herself, a restructuring of class relations had been central to a very personal project, and she made this clear in the television version of *The Downing Street Years* (BBC1 1993).[1] The six documentaries were built around one of the most revealing of her television interviews. In it she asserted her unwavering political convictions and justified her every decision with a withering glare. She emphatically linked her conviction politics with her views on the structure of society and her determination to change what was 'true, possible and desirable' across the whole social spectrum. On the one hand this involved

---

[1] The *Late Show* discussion and the series *Thatcher: The Downing Street Years* (a Fine Art production, Series Producer Denys Blakeway) were part of the BBC's *After Margaret* season, which marked the publication of Volume 1 of Thatcher's memoirs, *The Downing Street Years* (London: HarperCollins).

a rejection of older Tory values and attitudes. 'I spoke with a direct-ness to which they were not used,' she declared of her dealings with upper-class Foreign Office diplomats (programme 1). 'I'm very proud I don't belong to *your* class', she told the aristocratic Sir Anthony Par-sons. 'You see everyone else's point of view.' Members of the privileged class could afford to be patronising and condescending without conced-ing an iota of their status. But Margaret Thatcher's driven personality had no energy to waste on 'everyone else's point of view'. The 'grandees' embodied a set of Victorian values of which she did not approve. Theirs was a commitment to the long tradition of 'service'-based patronage and deference. It was a tradition which John Reith had inherited, but which she passionately rejected. 'It was important to have a sense of duty and responsibility,' said Lord Carrington, her first Foreign Secre-tary and a wealthy peer. 'I would counter that very toughly,' responded Thatcher. 'They had a *guilt* complex. If you feel guilty don't take it out on the policies which create the wealth!' The exchange demonstrated one way in which the economic reorientation of the 1980s not only entailed changes to the established structures of society but also *demanded* them. This meant a change in upper-class attitudes on the one hand, but an even more dramatic change in working-class values on the other. The validation of an identity *as a worker* would be progressively undermined.

1979: Hospital in crisis: The ancillary workers

It is early morning and cold. A group of men in duffle coats is standing around a brazier warming their hands and stamping their feet. They are surrounded by placards and banners declaiming 'End low pay' and 'Toot if you support us'. Together with images of rubbish piled in the streets, empty ambulances and locked graveyards, such pictures of picketing strikers became the iconic images of the winter of 1978–1979. Hospi-tals came under particular media scrutiny as the strikes took hold, and, in tune with much of the reporting across the 1970s, the focus of the news coverage was on the inconvenience to the public rather than the grievances of the strikers (Glasgow 1976). And who could be subject to greater inconvenience than hospital patients.

'Is more money worth a *life*?' 'Are you seriously saying that dedi-cated men are going to leave other people to *die*?' television interviewers demanded of union officials (*Thames at 6* ITV 19 January). The tone of the questioning was apocalyptic. 'One understands the basis of your claim, but isn't the strike by ambulance men potentially one of the most disastrous things that could happen to society?' demanded John Stapleton on BBC *Nationwide* (BBC1 16 January) (TUC 1979:30). On

31 January Margaret Thatcher herself appeared on Radio 2's *Jimmy Young Show*, described as 'one of her favourite soapboxes'. She declared, 'Some of the Unions... are confronting the sick. If someone is inflicting injury, harm and damage on the sick... my god, I will confront them!' (Beckett 2009:473).

The following day a team from *TVEye* went to St. Andrew's Hospital in the East End of London as a strike was called by the National Union of Public Employees (NUPE). They returned every day to document the progress of the action, 14 days in all. *Hospital in Crisis* was transmitted at peak viewing time on the day the strike ended (8.30 p.m. 15 February 1979). In the half-hour report, viewers met representatives of the main groups who populated programmes on the NHS: patients, doctors, nurses, members of the local community – here acting as volunteers to keep the hospital going – as well as the striking ancillary workers. The patients complained about delayed operations, paper sheets and a lack of blankets; the doctors helped out on the wards and worried that it was impossible to do operations without support from the porters. The views of the volunteers, who ranged from the local pastor shifting rubbish to an inept young man pushing a dinner trolley, were expressed by a group of middle-aged women: 'It's for the patients and for our local hospital... I've got a lot to thank St Andrew's for.' Then there were the porters and other ancillary workers who were taking part in the strike. Although this group of health service employees was rarely represented in current affairs broadcasting, now, together with other low-paid workers, they had effectively forced their way on to the screen and into the public debate. As the pickets gathered around the brazier, they argued that there was no other way to publicise their situation. 'We want a living wage, and we are prepared to fight for it.' This was a local hospital, embedded in its community – a not very well-off part of London[2] – and a division of opinion between patients, professionals and manual workers was by no means clear-cut. The strikers were supported by many of the patients, and the pickets explained that they were doing their best to liaise with management. After seven days the cameras were present as the ancillary workers voted overwhelmingly to stay out for another week. After 14 days they voted to go back. *Hospital in Crisis* was transmitted at peak viewing time on the day the strike ended (8.30 p.m. 15 February 1979).

---

[2] By 2011, the abandoned building featured on a website called 'Derelict places' (accessed 16 March 2011) at http://www.derelictplaces.co.uk/main/showthread .php?t=3344.

Most journalists missed the point that the growing unionisation was partly in response to the increase of managerialism in the NHS and the devaluing of the less skilled jobs (Karpf 1988:29). These changes were also resented by many nurses.

The nurses' dilemma

Nurses were possibly the most significant group in *Hospital in Crisis*. Of all the participants in the developing narratives of the NHS, it was nurses who found their public image most difficult to negotiate, especially, as they were overwhelmingly female. In fact 'the cultural ideal of nursing was a sort of professionalised femaleness', wrote Anne Karpf (1988:208). Jane Salvage, a vigorous campaigner on nurses' behalf, commented on the well-known stereotypes of nurses as angels, battle-axes or sex symbols, and observed that the 'angels' accepted 'with grace and composure everything thrown at her (or him) and self sacrifice is seen as a virtue', while the sex symbols tended to age into embittered battle-axes (Salvage 1987).

In British popular culture the screen comedies of the *Carry On* and the *Doctor* films had projected these masculine fantasies of the female nurse – both desired and feared – into the repertoire of national humour. Both Barbara Windsor, as the pert little sex-symbol nurse who stopped men in their tracks with her improbably aggressive breasts, wriggling high-heeled walk, and cap perched on a huge bush of hair, and Hattie Jaques, as the battle-axe Matron with a stately presence, upholstered figure and underlying kittenishness, had become national treasures. Although the BBC drama series *Angels* was, at the time, creating a much more down-to-earth world in which the daily routine of nursing practice was interweaved with the lives of recognisable young women, the triple image continued to lurk in the popular consciousness. It inevitably affected how nurses were represented, and also, as Julia Hallam demonstrated, how nurses saw themselves and how they performed their real-life roles (Hallam 2000:130–175). Their situation is interesting, because, despite the popular tongue-in-cheek image, nurses commanded a great deal of public respect and affection. Despite their low pay they were seen as highly trained and dedicated professionals. At the same time, their position as women remained significant, their femininity enhanced by their traditional uniforms, with swirling capes, starched white aprons and frilly caps. The TUC's study of the 1979 media coverage noted that

> Some groups of workers are more sympathetic than others ... When nurses came to the fore there was a large number of news items

examining in detail their pay, their work and living conditions. The BBC TV *Nationwide* programme did one such item, the *Daily Express* and *Daily Star* both gave sympathetic coverage to the nurses and the *Daily Record* in Scotland on March 9th devoted two pages to an examination of nurses' conditions.

(TUC 1979:19)

Nurses could be placed in contrast to the more 'militant' NUPE strikers, who were mostly men. In many ways they escaped the easy class categorisation which marked ancillary workers on the one hand and doctors and surgeons on the other.

However, nurses' self-image was changing dramatically as the 1970s came to an end.

As those interviewed by the *Radio Times* had pointed out, they must deal with 'the professional predicament' in nursing (see Chapter 3). They were 'highly valued as individuals, but nursing, as women's work, is devalued and given a low status in society' (Davies 1995 quoted by Hallam 2000:7). Also, the nursing profession was internally divided. The reorganisations of the mid-1970s introduced a two-track training which was reflected in a conflict between the Royal College of Nursing (RCN), committed to 'professionalism' and opposed to strikes, and those nurses who belonged to the Confederation of Health Service Employees (COHSE) and the National Union of Public Employees (NUPE), which both took a more militant stance. The 'raise the roof' campaign of the early 1970s had marked the first time the RCN had sought positive media coverage in its efforts to increase nurses' wages (Hallam 2000:79).

The reporter on *Hospital in Crisis*, Peter Williams, specialised in social issues and had covered the problems of the nursing profession in 1974. In *You Can't Put Dedication in the Bank* he had visited King's College Hospital, London (*This Week* 9 May 1974), where it became clear that nurses were indeed 'underpaid and overworked'. Consequently, they were leaving the NHS for agencies where they could earn twice as much (£1 per hour). This had led to the paradoxical situation in which the hospital was seriously short of full-time nurses and was forced to supplement its staff from the agencies – at a higher cost. According to one busy nurse, if NHS nurses don't get better pay, 'the standard of nursing is going to carry on dropping'. Nurses no longer saw it as 'a vocation in the old sense', claimed another. Motivation for work was a major issue. A doctor commented that for 'someone who's a professional, that is, who's in it for the *job* – the enjoyment eventually goes when you press them too hard'.

Across the documentary representations of hospital life, similar references to job satisfaction and to the ethos of the health service recur. They are linked to a sense of identity through work at all levels, and to debates over the nature of work in a public service. A well as workplace camaraderie and bonds formed through common experience, 'professional pride in a job well done' was a recurring theme, as was the tension between pride in the job, and the need for a living wage.

This was the hinterland of the strike at St Andrews in 1979. As the action took hold, the nurses came under extra pressure. Those who were NUPE members held a meeting to debate whether to join. It was conducted with compassion, good humour and concern. 'We are trained to care for patients,' said one. 'How can you watch them suffer – or allow the ward to get dirty?' And another warned against the inevitable headlines: 'you'll get "a baby dies due to the strike" . . . they always think of something to blame you for'. The filmmakers recorded the arguments and the vote, and they followed the nurses who decided to join the pickets. This was a blow-by-blow, non-judgemental observation of the daily experience of a strike, bringing an understanding far more nuanced than the crude headlines and glib condemnation. As the 1980s progressed, current affairs series, such as *TVEye*, Granada's *World in Action* and Yorkshire's *First Tuesday* would continue to engage with the dramatic changes brought by the Thatcher government and the increasing pressures on nurses and others working within the NHS.

Trade unions

'Hospitals have become a political and social battleground in recent years,' announced Peter Oppenheimer, presenter of BBC Radio 4's *File on Four*. 'One of the main factors behind this has been increasing trade union membership. There are 46 different trade unions operating in the health service [...] 10 years ago twenty per cent of hospital staff were unionised, today the figure is close to seventy per cent' (5 June 1979). This was June 1979 and Margaret Thatcher was one month into her premiership. Rather than following a single event, as *TVEye* had done, *File on Four's* reporter, David Henshaw, gave an overview of the general situation in the Royal Liverpool Hospital. Hugh Chignell writes:

> Henshaw described the hospital saying that it had become, 'synonymous with unrest'. There were 'demarcation disputes' in which workers from different unions were in conflict over who did what, and the hospital was 'filthy'. One trade union leader described social class problems in the hospital, claiming that workers were looked

down on by other staff. This point of view was expressed by a chef who claimed that, 'We're the pawns on the chessboard getting used to make someone feel good higher up. The doctors don't want to associate, you know, they look down on us – we're just cooks in the basement.' There was conflict over the consistently late meals, and nurses were critical of ancillary staff who they felt did not take responsibility. Meanwhile of the two hundred laboratory technicians one hundred and twenty were members of a union and in dispute with management over their status compared to doctors. The programme painted a picture of class-related tensions between doctors, nurses and the ancillary staff.

Despite these conflicts between the different unions and differences of opinion between union members, the judgement of many reports was that 'the unions' were a unitary and far-too-powerful force. In *Analysis*'s 'What are we here for Brothers?' Mary Goldring remarked, '...we have become conditioned to think of unions as bodies corporate so powerful they can pull down governments with the twitch of a muscle...' (25 October 1978). And Margaret Thatcher herself was unwavering in her position. Her dislike of traditional class solidarities applied to working-class organisations even more strongly than the despised 'grandees'. In January 1979, she rejected an invitation to appear on *Panorama*, and turned instead to a more sympathetic Brian Walden on *Weekend World* for her first major interview as Prime Minister (7 January 1979).[3] 'Someone's got to grasp this nettle,' she declared, and went on to outline what historian Andy Beckett describes as 'jaw-dropping' proposals, which went well beyond Conservative policy at the time: strikes in essential services should be outlawed, strikers' benefits should be taxed, strikers should have their benefits taken away if they acted without a secret ballot. The long-established structures of working-class solidarity and self-organisation needed to be broken. 'I had broken ranks,' Thatcher wrote in her memoirs. 'People could see that I was going to fight' (Beckett 2009:468).

The Employment Act of 1980 was one of the first from the new government. 'The Trade Union movement certainly has cause to worry about [its] effects,' wrote the *British Journal of Law and Society*. 'Many

---

[3] Thatcher's preference for Walden as an interviewer was made clear in her papers released in 2011. Reported in *The Guardian* 19 March 2011 at http://www.guardian.co.uk/politics/2011/mar/19/margaret-thatcher-papers-bbc-itv?INTCMP=ILCNETTXT3487.

supposedly fundamental freedoms of trade unions are coming under severe attack from the present administration' (Vol. 7, No. 2 quoted by Edwards 1993:45). In particular, there were restrictions on picketing and secondary action, in which a union from one industry would support another. Even so, the first half of the 1980s would be riven with confrontations which linked different industries, including the NHS. In 1982, a long-running health workers' strike over low pay and job losses was supported by miners, steelworkers and dockers. In August, the secretary of the London Press branch of the Electrician's Union, Sean Geraghty, was fined for holding up the Fleet Street presses in support of a health service day of action. NHS workers marched to the High Court in London to support him.[4]

Although cooks and other ancillary workers had their say in *File on Four* and *TVEye*, reporting rarely came from the perspective of strikers. Journalists were more interested in the consequences than the causes of a strike, 'returning repeatedly to the possibility of fatalities and pressing a consultant to confirm them', wrote Anne Karpf, describing BBC2's *Newsnight* (12 July 1982). 'Hospital workers complain that journalists wait like vultures for patients to die'. Behind much of the coverage was journalistic indignation that porters and ancillary workers were interfering in areas considered medical or clinical (Karpf 1988:29–30). However, off-peak and local programmes made space for a less stark dichotomy. LWT's *The London Programme* reported the crisis by focussing on the ways in which unions were trying to prevent government cuts to the service (21 March 1980).

Discrediting workers' organisations played a role in the project of restructuring working-class identity, and the interests of 'the unions' were consistently presented as separate from those of their members. Leaders were identified and frequently vilified in the popular press. Perhaps surprisingly a somewhat similar judgement came out of an utterly different politics. This argued that it was the rank-and-file union members, the local shop stewards and activists, who were the real campaigners, while trade union leaders were power-hungry compromisers who sold out on the interests of their members. This had been the theme of several radical dramas of the 1960s and 1970s, including *The Big Flame* (1969), *The Rank and File* (1971) and *Days of Hope* (1975), all made for the BBC by the celebrated left-wing director Ken Loach. Under the new Thatcherite regime, Loach felt he was not able to

---

[4] http://cohse-union.blogspot.com/search/label/1982 (last accessed July 2012).

make the dramas he wanted so turned to documentaries. In *Questions of Leadership* (1983), he bitterly attacked a number of Union leaders as he followed the disputes of the early 1980s from the point of view of the rank and file, including those in the NHS. 'The people in these films have rarely, if ever, been seen on national television, putting views that are never acknowledged,' he asserted, following accusations of bias (*Guardian* 31 October 1983). The films were commissioned by Channel Four, but following complaints from the Union leaders represented, threats of litigation, and extended negotiations between Channel Four, the IBA and the producing company, Central TV, they were not transmitted, despite recutting and the preparation of 'balancing' programmes. 'Effective censorship is best achieved not by an outright ban, but by delay and inaction,' responded Loach. And he attacked the new channel. 'The Reithian tradition of discreet but rabid support for the existing social order is in safe hands' (*Guardian* 31 October 1983; Petley 1997).

Nevertheless, the radical dramatists of the early 1980s reflected the crisis in working-class traditions. Alan Bleasdale's *Boys from the Blackstuff* (BBC2 10 October–7 November 1982), was mostly written before Thatcher came to power, but it was widely interpreted as a comment on the mood of Thatcherite Britain. The tragicomedy of the five plays perfectly reflected a balance of anger, despair and bleak humour. Yosser Hughes's desperate 'Gissa job' became a catchphrase which resonated across the decade. Hospital workers never gained the mythical status that Bleasdale gave to his unemployed tarmac workers, but the characters in *Boys from the Blackstuff* were faced with illness and death as well as degradation and unemployment. In the opening sequence of episode 5 'George's Last Ride', George, the ex-shop steward who was deeply respected across the dockside community, was in hospital with a terminal illness. He was cared for by a sympathetic doctor who was part of the community and treated George with respect and affection. It was a scene which would become unthinkable as the 1980s wore on.

Porters and others in ancillary jobs would occasionally appear on the screens in sympathetic roles, where their contribution to the life of a hospital was recognised, but more often the comic figure of a union militant would be mocked in both drama and comedy. In the highly popular BBC satire, *Yes Minister* (1980–1982), the only aim of the smooth-talking Sir Humphrey was to protect the civil service (precisely the charge that Margaret Thatcher levelled at professionals of all kinds) even if that meant colluding with union activists. *Yes Minister* kicked off its second season with 'The Compassionate Society' (23 February 1981), in which a new hospital was kept empty because of the prohibitive cost of employing medical staff. When the Minister insisted on opening it, Humphrey made sure a 'firebrand agitator' was recruited and set about provoking a strike. The hospital was rapidly closed again and, of course, the civil servants did not lose their jobs.[5]

As the 1980s progressed, structural changes to conditions of employment would further undermine the position of ancillary workers (see Chapter 8).

Participation and a voice that matters

'The offer of effective voice is crucial to the legitimacy of modern democracies' argues Nick Couldry, adding, 'having a voice is never enough. I need to know that my voice matters' (2010:1). As we study the broadcast output of the 1980s we can note the differences in access to a voice that matters. Those who inhabited the role of ancillary workers had far less opportunity to express themselves fully on the airwaves. Not only did the available spaces in factual programmes continue to diminish, but the comic stereotypes regularly called up in fiction made effective personal presentation more difficult. Nurses, too, needed to negotiate the ambivalent position in which they found themselves (see above), but there remained a rich and varied range of possibilities available for doctors and surgeons, including the right to dissent and to express less orthodox opinions.

Within the NHS itself, activists had been pressing for participation, and the representation of those who worked within the service and those who made use of it. The service had some lay representation in its structures: Community Health Councils, set up in 1974, were made up of lay members from local authorities and other local bodies, and from 1976 trade union representatives joined the Area Health Authorities. A system called 'consensus management' had broadened the input of nurses and others, and managers were 'required to involve staff more closely as industrial democracy became more fashionable', wrote manager Brian Edwards (1993:56–57). But despite these tentative moves, the distinction between workers – especially low-paid, manual workers – and the managers and professionals was rigidly maintained. If workers were to be restructured in the Thatcherite world, it would not be as participants in management.

---

[5] Andy Beckett suggests that the militant was based on Jamie Morris, leader of the 1979 NUPE strike at Westminster Hospital (Beckett 2009:477).

However, they may be restructured as entrepreneurs. 'Inside every unemployed person there's a self-employed one', declared an advertisement for a 're-start' enterprise allowance scheme. New types of jobs defied the old categories of blue and white collar, and certainly did not involve trade unionism or worker participation. 'Work wasn't some great, shared experience any more. We were on our own,' was the conclusion of presenter Kirsty Young in a 2011 television review of work in the 1980s (*The British at Work*: programme 3 BBC2 24 March 2011).

II The vigorous virtues

The vigorous virtues and class politics

After Margaret Thatcher's resignation, Shirley Robin Letwin, a member of the Centre for Policy Studies, set out to define 'Thatcherism' as a way of thinking. She argued that it was not based on a coherent ideology, but that its apparent inconsistencies were held together by a pragmatic approach to specific social situations, backed up by firm moral convictions. Most important was a belief that people should be given the opportunity to be successful and self-reliant. This approach held together the drive for privatisation and enterprise with support for family structures and traditional morality (Letwin 1992:18). It also informed Thatcher's attitude to class politics. Letwin sums it up as a commitment to what she described, in a rather Nietzschean formulation, as the 'vigorous virtues'.

She described the 'individual preferred by Thatcherism' as 'upright, self-sufficient, energetic, adventurous, independent-minded, loyal to friends, and robust against enemies'. These attributes are '*virtues*', which could belong to anyone, regardless of class or position in society. They are the *vigorous virtues*, which Thatcherites assume have been neglected in recent British history. And significantly she mobilised the metaphor of sickness as she continued, '[Thatcherites] have drawn attention to the healthy and vibrant rather than the *sick, the halt and blind*' (pp. 32–34 my italics). As healthy and vibrant workers, individuals would be on their own. Work would be redefined. But the sick must equally call on their own resources. Recognising the uncaring impression given by her approach, Letwin added that Thatcherites were

> willing to sound harsh in order to avoid the rhetoric of socialism...which – by emphasising the need for public support of those who cannot look after themselves, may all too easily... suggest that

everybody is in some way sick or incapacitated, and thus discourage or enervate people who could well stand on their own two feet.

(Page 34)

People should look to government 'not for "care" as a child looks to a parent or *a patient to a doctor* but for something quite different… a set of arrangements that will allow each person to pursue his (sic) projects, whether alone or in co-operation with others, in security and without conflict' (p. 34 my italics). Sickness, together with dependence, had gained a powerful, metaphorical significance within class politics.

III   Casting their problems?

'Does it hurt? Only when I laugh'

One of the best-loved comedies of the early 1980s explored the experience of being in hospital in terms of social class. *Only When I Laugh* (1979–1982), from the thriving and energetic Yorkshire Television, featured three ill-assorted patients sharing a hospital ward where the claustrophobic environment provided a classic set-up for a situation comedy – the desperate humour of a setting where incompatible individuals are tangled together in a situation they cannot escape. In *Only When I Laugh* a perverse dynamic keeps three men together in the security of their ward. The basic joke is a reversal of the usual fears. These hypochondriacs *want* to be in hospital. None of them can cope with leaving. So, stroppy lorry driver, upper-class snob and naïve bookworm continue to annoy each other and the doctors. There are endless forms of malingering, and they became known as the longest-staying-ever hospital patients.

The theme of class runs through the series. The posh Archie Glover (Peter Bowles) (although referred to as 'middle class', he goes shooting, wears tweeds and has all the accoutrements of the English upper classes) was at a public school. He can pull strings, and claims solidarity with the surgeon. 'The middle classes stick together,' complains Figgis (James Bolam). '*They* don't get rusty scalpels. It's different for us – it's all cut and thrust' (Episode 2 5 November 1979). Playing up his own class allegiance, Figgis demands workers' solidarity with the cleaners and catering workers. Neither man succeeds. Glover gets the best bed, but that leads to confusion and the wrong operation. Figgis stirs up a strike among ancillary workers, but that goes disastrously wrong when the kitchen staff block all meals.

Questions of dependency become an issue since these patients depend on the skill, good will and human fallibility of the professionals. Richard Wilson, as the bumbling surgeon, turns up for an operation with a hangover and quivering hands ('Everything's going wrong today,' he complains to his hapless victim (episode 2)). The role of the patient had long been explored in comedy. The clueless doctor and his mishaps – a specialism of the *Doctor* series – is the funnier because of the genuine helplessness of patients who depend on him and because it derived from very real fears. The joke of *Only When I Laugh* was that Glover, Binns and Figgis were fantasists who refused to face the outside world, whereas in real life, sickness and dependency were unwelcome and usually unavoidable.

Across the 1980s, the question was repeatedly posed: what did it mean to be a patient in a regime which despised dependency and preferred to draw attention to 'the healthy and vibrant'? Just like the other significant roles in the medical encounter, 'patients' would be subject to redefinition and restructuring. What was 'true, possible and desirable' would change for the three groups – workers, patients and professionals – and the changes would be reflected in the style and approach of the programming. In the case of patients, they would be also reflected in attitudes towards those *potential* patients who made up the viewing and listening public.

5
From Needs to Wants: Restructuring Audiences, Restructuring Patients

I From needs to wants

Restructuring audiences

In her discussion of the medical programmes of the 1980s, media historian Anne Karpf wrote:

> The media's long standing obsession with health and medicine has swelled in recent years into an obsession. Pages and programmes are crowded with patients offering up their illnesses, physical and emotional for the viewers' gaze; doctors parading their novel skills and micro-instruments; philosophers pondering medico-ethical conundrums; and testimonials from ex-hedonists renouncing their former ways and flaunting their healthy new routines.
>
> (1988: 1)

As she identified four approaches to medical programming vying for dominance across the airwaves – the *'look after yourself'; medical; consumer* and *environmental* approaches – she observed convincingly the ways in which these were mapped on to shifting social attitudes. Broadcast programmes address a wide audience, but each of these categories conceptualised its audience in a particular way.

The *'look after yourself'* approach had been in vogue since the 'keep fit' and 'eat sensibly' programmes of the 1940s. Partly due to the rigours of the Second World War, they ran alongside campaigns like 'digging for victory' and 'grow your own vegetables', and imagined their listeners taking responsibility for their personal well-being. The approach was, to a certain extent, displaced by the post-war explosion of scientific research and technological advance. This meant that a focus on personal behaviour was replaced by a heavily *'medical'* approach, in which doctors reigned supreme and the interest was in illness and its cure rather than healthy living and prevention. Viewers and listeners now tended to be seen as potential 'patients'. However, by the 1960s, there was a change in the tone of many broadcasts. They became much more critical and assertive, encouraging individuals to see themselves as demanding *consumers*. Perhaps it is not surprising that an *environmental* approach, which subjected easy assumptions about health and illness to a thorough-going critique and looked for explanations within a wider social, political and economic context, was by far the least common of Karpf's four categories. The other three 'emphasise illness as individually experienced and caused, playing down its economic and environmental origins', but for programmes with an 'environmental' approach, the audience would be addressed as critical and enquiring citizens (pp. 70–71).

All four categories would make an appearance within the context of the contentious politics and changing broadcasting environment of the 1980s. And they were linked to changes within the NHS itself.

Restructuring patients

> The founding ethos of the NHS is, of course, wholly alien to Thatcherism...In the NHS 'the patient is to be seen not as a consumer, deciding what he (sic) wants, but as a passive recipient of whatever the all-knowing powers on high decide that he ought to have'.
>
> (Letwin 1992:204)

Shirley Letwin's chapter on the NHS was headed 'Invalids or Consumers',[1] and in it she argued that even someone who was unwell could be treated as a 'consumer' with a right to insist on what they 'want' rather than being prescribed what they 'need'. Although this chimed with many of the left-wing critiques of arrogant professionalism, for Letwin and Thatcher's advisers in the Centre for Policy Studies, it entailed moving away from a publicly funded service. Letwin rejected

---

[1] Parts of the chapter were based on a Centre for Policy Studies pamphlet written in 1988 by Letwin's son Oliver Letwin, a member of the Prime Minister's Policy Unit from 1983–1986, and here described as 'an adviser on privatisation to overseas governments', and MP John Redwood, Head of the Policy Unit from 1984–1986.

the argument that 'buying health care is nothing like buying a car or a house because the consumer of health care cannot know what is good for him'. 'Wants' can be 'decided by each individual in accordance with his personal circumstances and tastes' (p. 206). 'The Thatcherite understanding of Britain [is] as a nation of individuals who could and should run their own lives and whose self respect would be violated by bureaucrats or doctors who ordered them about like children being forced to do what is good for them' (p. 207).

In the booklet *A National Health Dis-service*, Arthur Seldon, of the Centre for Policy Studies, asserted that the NHS *must* fail, because it prevents people from expressing 'their elemental instinctive urge' and paying for themselves or their family (Seldon 1980:145). 'If it were not for the *politically* controlled NHS we should have seen new forms of medical organisation and financing better reflected in *consumer* preferences, requirements and circumstances' (p. 10 italics in original).

Clearly responding to 'wants' rather than 'needs' meant pushing aside the sort of 'environmental' approach to health care, which identified problems beyond individual preferences. However, in the early 1980s, environmental explanations retained a powerful presence, both in the arguments of campaigners and in parts of the broadcast media. Policy documents published in the first years of the Conservative government illustrated conflicting approaches, as the mood of the critical 1970s negotiated with the increasingly monetarist 1980s.

II   Putting patients first?

Patients First

The early months of the Conservative government saw the publication of three significant official documents on the NHS. A long-standing Royal Commission reported in July 1979; the new government's policy statement, *Patients First*, followed in December, then amid a great deal of controversy, a much-delayed report of a working party on *Inequalities in Health* was published on August bank holiday 1980.

The title of *Patients First* made clear the government's declared intention to prioritise the *users* of the NHS above those who worked within it. However, the document had little to say about the actual experiences of patients or the daily relationship between health workers and those in their care. It focussed on streamlining the NHS and 'reducing bureaucracy', and it indicated a shift to a more managerial culture within hospitals and the service at large. The 'strengthening of management' was described by the *British Medical Journal* (*BMJ*) as 'perhaps the most important change of all'. Forms of democratic representation were not looked on favourably, whether from the community or from workers: the lay Community Health Councils, 'may need to be reviewed' (eventually they were abolished) and 'the Government does not feel it right to have staff representatives as members of authorities' (*BMJ* 15 December 1979:1605; Iliffe 1985:63–65).

To put patients first, according to the document, doctors would be encouraged to leave the health service. The Secretary of State declared that 'it has been my aim to provide doctors with substantially improved opportunities for private practice', and – note the language – to '*free* private practice from the restrictions imposed by the previous government's legislation' (*BMJ* 1979). Full-time NHS consultants would now be able undertake private practice on top of their NHS work and controls over the private sector were reduced. Sale of NHS land to private buyers was made easier, and private hospitals could be larger. This was a topic which would be taken up with considerable venom by the scriptwriter G.F. Newman in his biting television dramas *The Nation's Health* broadcast in 1983 (see Chapter 6).

In the drive to prevent a deterioration through funding cuts, alternative revenue through fund-raising and lotteries was encouraged, and hospitals would increasingly look to charities, voluntary workers and the labour of relatives (Illife 1985:57–58) (see *Your Life in Their Hands* Chapter 6). These shifts in attitude, as well as in organisation and structure, were met with a great deal of resistance, not only from those working within the service, but also from many users and potential users within the local communities. Some potential patients were determined to be participatory activists rather than passive consumers, and they found some outlets on the broadcast media. In November 1979, under the subtitle 'Health: Who cares?', the series *Grapevine*, produced by the BBC's Community Programme Unit, investigated the ways in which ordinary people could influence decisions made about the health service. It included contributions from the Patients' Committee of Aberdare Health Centre, the Birmingham Community Health Council and the Hospital Action Campaign in Brent (17 November 1979).

Inequality: The Black Report

> 'I don't like the idea of an egalitarian society,' declared Margaret Thatcher. 'We believe in equality of opportunity... that means the opportunity to be unequal.'
>
> (quoted in *The Secret History of 'Analysis'* BBC Radio 4 25 October 2010)

The Report of the working party on *Inequalities in Health*, known as the Black Report after its Chair Sir Douglas Black, appeared more concerned with the experience of patients than *Patients First* had been. Its focus was strongly on the environmental conditions which promote good health and on access to health provision. And it deployed the language of class, so unwelcome to the Conservative government. Sir Douglas's Introduction asserted: 'We have no doubt that... in the last two decades of the twentieth century a new attack upon the forces of inequality has regrettably become necessary and now needs to be concerted... Greater equality of health must remain one of our foremost national objectives' (Black 1980).[2]

The 1979 Royal Commission had also noted that 'the position of those in social classes four and five appears to have worsened relative to those in social classes one and two since the inception of the NHS in 1948' (Merrison 1979). The Black Report documented in harsh detail this continuing, and in some respects, increasing, inequality in a number of areas, including life expectancy, frequency of illness, child poverty and general health and well-being. It made numerous recommendations which tended to be concerned as much with social welfare and community provision as with the NHS itself. The Report was deeply unwelcome to a government committed to rationalising health provision and cutting state expenditure. However, as an official Report, it fell to the Secretary of State for Social Services, Patrick Jenkin, to write the Forward – which he did with clear distaste. He distanced the government from the Report's tone as well as its recommendations. The expenditure required is 'quite unrealistic in the present or any foreseeable economic circumstances, quite apart from any judgement that may be formed of the effectiveness of such expenditure in dealing with the problems identified'.

The government was accused of covering up these inconvenient facts by publishing on a bank holiday. The major current affairs series, *Panorama*, *TVEye* and *World in Action*, which all had substantial track records in investigating and exposing problems of poverty and inequality, were on their summer break. Even so, a considerable press furore followed, led by the weekly *New Society*, which had been campaigning on the issue for a number of years (especially with articles by Richard Wilkinson, later to become celebrated as an author of *The Spirit*

---

[2] The original text of the Report can be found at http://www.sochealth.co.uk/public-health-and-wellbeing/poverty-and-inequality/the-black-report-1980/. The website also contains information about the history of the report.

Level[3]). The report became a 'media event'. On 17 September, *File on Four* responded with what Hugh Chignell describes as 'a particularly revealing edition'.

Hugh Chignell writes:

> The focus was on Liverpool and the problems of the health service in a deprived area. A maternity hospital was visited and described as 'drab' and like a 'conveyor belt'. The reporter, Michael Cooke, then visited a working-class housing estate with very poor housing conditions, broken windows and damp homes. Doctors refused to use the stairs or lifts for fear of being mugged. The residents talked about the effect of these conditions on their children's health and the high levels of depression and anxiety.

In many ways this edition was typical of a *File on Four* on the health service in this 'crisis' period with its reports on a demoralised and under-funded NHS. However, the programme also contained criticisms of the patients themselves. Cooke mentioned the high rates of infant mortality but he also referred to the problems of 'apathy' and 'ignorance' among the local women. In the Liverpool borough of Toxteth, Cooke described the vandalised houses with crumbling facades (Toxteth would be the site of serious rioting a matter of months after this broadcast). The health service was failing the district because GPs could not give enough time. However, young parents were often ignorant about their own and their babies' health and the reporter described them as part of the problem. 'A lot of the parents are, of course, not highly motivated are they? That seems to be the focal point of the problem...Mothers in the doctors' clinic who had just given birth couldn't wait to carry on smoking'. Cooke talked to a young mother in a waiting room of the maternity hospital: Mother, 'Well I've always smoked haven't I? Some nurses say you shouldn't smoke but I like smoking so...' Cooke: 'Persuading women like that to change their ways may seem like a forlorn hope.'

This edition of *File on Four* contained familiar ingredients; a northern city, working-class deprivation and the voices of people in difficulty, but at the same time there were echoes of a burgeoning right-wing critique of the 'underclass' with implications of welfare dependency and irresponsible behaviour. This is significant because as has been

---

[3] Richard Wilkinson's influential article from 16 December 1976, 'Dear David Ennals', can be found at http://www.sochealth.co.uk/Black/ennals.htm.

suggested, *File on Four* seemed to possess the structural qualities of a left-wing programme but clearly also had room for a right-wing analysis expressed by its own reporter.

The contradiction between promoting energetic consumerism, depending on 'personal circumstances and tastes', and conveniently blaming 'women like that' who stubbornly refuse to eat healthy food or give up smoking, is easily overlooked. But it was more in tune with the government's approach to blame the feckless individual than to consider the environmental issues raised by the Black Report. The 1979 Royal Commission had also addressed the question of personal responsibility, and it too had argued that attention should be paid to 'environmental and occupational hazards as well as personal behaviour. We were concerned that local authorities should not let standards of environmental health slip' (para. 22.14).

Health is a political term: Need *should* be the sole criterion

The 1980 Reith Lectures took up the issue and pulled no punches (BBC Radio 4 5 November–10 December 1980).[4] The lectures were (and are) a prestigious annual event, named after the BBC's founder and delivered by prominent thinkers on social and political topics. In 1980, under the title *Unmasking Medicine*, Ian Kennedy delivered a series of spectacular challenges to the institution of the NHS, but from a very different perspective from that of the Centre for Policy Studies. Kennedy was an academic lawyer who had founded the Centre for Medical Law and Ethics at King's College in London. Delivered in calm and even tones, his lectures developed a critique even more radical than that of the Black Report. 'It's hard to avoid the grave conclusion that the NHS has failed us,' he stated (lecture 3). The NHS accepted a view of health care which focused on illness and its cure, instead of a society which promoted well-being and the social conditions for good health. He firmly rejected the priority given to hospitals and to expensive technology rather than the environmental circumstances which the Report had documented, and he launched a thorough-going denunciation of the institutional, social and political power invested in the medical profession. Doctors are 'the new magicians'. They have the power to define what counts

---

[4] The BBC has published an archive of the Reith Lectures. The 1980 lectures can be found at http://www.bbc.co.uk/search/?q=Ian%20Kennedy%20Reith%20Lectures%201980%20Unmasking%20medicine.

as illness, and they treat their patients as 'an ambulatory assemblage of parts', paying no attention to their environment.

'Health', he stated, is a political term, and 'the present political climate is a further obstacle to improvement'. Its preoccupation with costs suggests that money is the only value. In diametric opposition to the view put by the Centre for Policy Studies, he argued that 'need should be the sole criterion of the receipt of a service'. Echoing the Royal Commission and the Black Report, he deplored poor nutrition, unsafe workplaces, inadequate housing and social inequality, and called for priority to be given to abolishing child poverty. 'Modern medicine has taken the wrong path' (lecture 2). 'The extent of the re-examination and re-orientation of values called for is breathtaking' (lecture 3). Health should be seen as a positive state, not just as the absence of illness.

Kennedy's views may not have accorded with those of the government, but he was not a marginal figure. In 1986, he would become Dean of the Law School at King's College London. He was also a member of the General Medical Council, and as Sir Ian, would go on to Chair and contribute to numerous government commissions. He also had a second career as a host on Channel Four's *After Dark* discussions.

The themes of inequality and the problems of poverty and the environment would continue to surface in different spaces within the broadcast output. In 1982, Central TV produced a series of documentaries which took up the concern that high high-tech medicine is prioritised over local provision. *The Best of Health?* (29 July–2 September 1982) followed life in a health centre based in a deprived area of Birmingham. It observed the daily activities of its GPs, health visitors, consultants and others, including running a baby clinic, helping mothers to give up smoking and dealing with patients whose problems ranged from depression to broken limbs. And it interleaved captions, statistics and archive film to review the history of the NHS with all its contradictions and compromises, as the original proposal for health centres to serve the community had never been fully realised. Statistics on doctors' training demonstrated that half will become GPs, but the bulk of the training is geared to hospitals. 'I prefer to be in the community, dealing with people,' says trainee GP, Dr Jane Gilby, 'but half the students wanted to be heart surgeons and do dramatic things.' She added, 'if you look at television, you see the more sensational aspects of medicine; you don't see the run-of-the-mill practitioner' (programme 1). The Centre emphasised prevention and environmental issues. Health visitor Joan Horton explained, 'When I have students I like to show how the physical, emotional, social and psychological factors all fit together' (programme 5). But Dr Ivan Cox is more pragmatic. 'Doctoring for me is not to change society but to provide solace and care for the individual and the individual's family – that's as far as I would extend it' (programme 2). The programmes began with, and returned to, a quotation from David Ennals, Labour Secretary of State for Health and Social Security from 1976–1979:

> The purpose of the National Health Service is to enable people to live happier, richer and fuller lives, freed from preventable pain and anxiety.

III   Everyday broadcasting: Self-help or challenge?

From 'look after yourself' to a consumer approach

It was in the off-peak hours that approaches which 'emphasise illness as individually experienced and caused', tended to find a slot. And the off-peak hours were being extended. Morning television arrived in 1983, with the BBC's *Breakfast Time* and *Good Morning Britain* from TV-AM, a glamorous new company based in a postmodern building adorned with giant breakfast egg cups. More hours to fill meant increasing space for the everyday informality which had been a developing characteristic of 1970s programming (see Chapter 3). A flow of 'everyday television' suited the off-peak schedules, and this was where numerous programmes directly addressed the experiences of viewers and listeners as patients or as potential patients. There was also a recognition that more women would be watching during the daytime, and a sense that this area of programming should be more concerned with personal, 'feminine' issues, including health care. In these spaces, programmes could be comfortable and reassuring rather than spiky and critical.

This was where many of the programmes described by Anne Karpf as 'look after yourself' found a home. These were programmes which helped the individual solve their own problems through, for example, giving up smoking and eating healthily. The 'look after yourself' approach would gain official support as the NHS came under pressure and broader environmental explanations were rejected. From the mid-1970s, the government had issued a series of reports and consultative documents, such as *Eating for Health*, which discussed 'the diseases of affluence' (Karpf 1988:16–17). Official bodies became involved in sponsoring or supporting educational programmes. The Health Education Council ran a 'Look after yourself' campaign and co-funded eight one-hour plays on Radio Clyde, in which 'the hapless heroes became alcoholics and heroin addicts, suffered heart attacks and contracted sexually transmitted diseases'. BBC Scotland's daily soap *Kilbreck* was funded by the Scottish Health Education Group and commercial radio's twice-weekly *Devon Lanes* by the Exeter Health Authority. They were part of what Anne Karpf described as a 'whole new genre: the "look after yourself drama"' (pp. 205–206).

However, by the early 1980s, there was a tendency for programmes which offered advice on medical matters to turn their attention to the health service itself, and to point out its inadequacies. This was the 'consumer approach', and Ian Kennedy made it his topic for his sixth Reith Lecture. To claim the status of 'consumer', he argued, is to challenge the ways in which doctors infantilise their patients. It rejects doctors' claims to exclusive knowledge and demands that they become accountable. The assertion that one role of consumerism was to 'discipline bad doctors' was a strong theme in programmes which dealt with discontent about medical practices. The rhetoric of 'patients first', and patients' rights seemed to fit in with the consumer mood. Patients were less patient. They were visibly asserting the right to complain, to be awkward, to demand information and involvement. Consumer programming on medical topics could venture into dangerous territory. It could make space for the users of the NHS to question its arrogance and opacity, and raise concerns about medical mistakes and prescribed drugs which caused damage to their users.

Just as libertarianism had its left and right poles, so 'consumerism' saw an overlap between those promoting a market in health care and the broader aims of grass-roots campaigners. There was a huge political gulf between a demand for consumer choice and the 'humanist' consumerism of democratic accountability. For Ian Kennedy, 'a wholly separate method of supervision and sanction must be created' in order to ensure accountability (lecture 6). This call for regulation implied a version of consumerism utterly different from the government's aim to '*free* doctors from restrictions' or Milton Friedman's world in which 'self-interest will produce public welfare' (programme 2). Nevertheless, the two approaches shared a sense of personal entitlement and a distrust of professionalism and authority.

An important outlet for a new committed programming style would be the long-awaited fourth channel. The establishment of Channel Four by the Conservative government in 1982 would be one of the strangest contradictions in any account of broadcasting in the 1980s.

IV Channel Four: Adjustments to the idea of public service

From Open Broadcasting to Channel Four

The structure of both the BBC and ITV was reaffirmed in the early 1980s: the BBC's Royal Charter was renewed and the new ITV contracts granted in 1980. Some franchises changed hands, but the 1981 Broadcasting Act reasserted ITV's public service contribution, requiring the Independent Broadcasting Authority (IBA) 'to provide television and local sound broadcasting services *as a public service* for disseminating information, education and entertainment' (Section 2 my italics). The shape and the regional basis of the network continued as before – but change was in the air. Across the decade, both television and radio would expand: gaining both longer hours and more channels. A radically different set of conditions of possibility was on the horizon and would change the relationship between broadcaster and audience. Brian Wenham, at the time Controller of BBC2, wrote that a 'third age of broadcasting' was imminent (Wenham (ed.) 1982) (see Chapter 7). As broadcasting extended its scope there would be significant consequences for both the concept and the practice of 'public service'.

Despite differences between the various groups, campaigning for the fourth channel had intensified in the run-up to the 1979 election. A new umbrella group, the Channel Four Group, had been set up and as the Conservatives seemed set to win, they played up the aspects which would appeal to the right, and 'decided to re-brand themselves as a free-market in ideas' (Lambert 1982; Darlow 2004). The Campaign's prime mover, Anthony Smith, went to see Keith Joseph, who was running the Centre for Policy Studies. 'I explained this was by way of introducing competition and enterprise into the broadcasting system but keeping the notion of public service dominant,' he told Maggie Brown, the channel's historian (Brown 2007:18). The first Broadcasting Act of the decade (1980) enabled the setting up of the new channel, but it did not establish an independent Open Broadcast Authority, as the Annan Report had recommended. Instead, the channel would be a wholly owned subsidiary of the IBA.

Campaigners who had set their sights on an independent Authority outside the old duopoly were disappointed, but the principle of a different type of channel had been accepted by Home Secretary William Whitelaw. Channel Four would be a 'publisher' rather than a producer and would commission programmes from independent production companies. It would have a remit 'to encourage innovation and experiment in the form and content of programmes, and generally to give the Fourth Channel a distinctive character of its own' (Broadcasting Act 1981: Chapter 68, s. 11(c)). It would provide innovative material and cater for minority audiences not reached by the other channels. It would be funded by advertising, but instead of selling its own advertisements, the ITV companies would sell them and pay a subscription to cover its costs. It was a formula in the spirit of Annan's favoured plurality of funding, and it guaranteed the channel's independence from direct commercial pressure.

Channel Four is a prime example of the patchy and uneven nature of ideological shifts, and the ways in which they may be embedded in institutions and reflected in ambivalent cultural forms. As a 'publisher', the channel's structure was close to the market model favoured by the neo-liberals. It commissioned programmes from newly established independent companies and opened the airwaves to both aspirant outsiders and business entrepreneurs. At the same time, the new channel was knitted into the public service ecology of British broadcasting. Above all, its brief was to serve interests not catered for by the existing channels and this arrangement gave it a great deal of freedom to experiment. Its first Chief Executive, Jeremy Isaacs, stated: 'We want a fourth channel that everyone will watch some of the time and no-one all of the time' (Isaacs 1989:20), and in its first year of broadcasting its content was startlingly original. The Broadcasting Act had enabled a channel that accommodated diverse groupings whose conflicting ideologies and interests were not immediately apparent. At the same time, the conditions of possibility for producing content were vastly expanded.

Ambivalent radicalism: The expansion of the public?

The arrival of Channel Four posed a high-profile challenge to the concept of public service in broadcasting – and indeed to concepts of 'the public' itself. It brought significant changes in each of the three aspects of television broadcasting: production, content and audiences addressed. There was an unprecedented expansion of voices and viewpoints, both as producers and as a visible presence on the screen. As audience, the channel sought out multiple *publics*: plural, fragmented and differentiated.

Channel Four had 'a licence to be different' and in its first years was the home for left-wing campaigners, feminists, black and Asian filmmakers, extreme political views, avant-garde filmmaking styles, challenging drama, auteur films, art films and amateur filmmakers. Liz Forgan was in charge of news and current affairs, even though she had no previous television experience. She told Maggie Brown, 'they'll forgive us crap programmes. They will not forgive us for playing safe' (2007:41). Many of the programmes were made by established filmmakers, but the channel was also able to bypass the entrenched professionalism of the BBC and ITV companies. Under a special agreement, the broadcasting union, the Association of Cinematograph and Television Technicians (ACTT), waived its closed-shop requirement to enable some Channel Four programmes to be made by radical film and video workshops, including many who had campaigned in the 1970s. These were usually groups of non-professionals or independent filmmakers, who frequently shared their skills rather than sticking to the established craft demarcations (Baehr 1987; Nigg and Wade 1980).

This broadening of possibilities and the unapologetic radicalism of the output was likely to be deeply unsympathetic to the mood and ethos of the Conservative government. However, Margaret Thatcher saw a different potential for the channel. For her, its structure demonstrated a success for market forces and the promotion of an entrepreneurial spirit. The promotion of small independent companies was a blow against trade unions (Hood and O'Leary 1990:207). In supporting small businesses, Channel Four was taking a first step towards the competitive, multichannel broadcasting system advocated by neo-liberal policies. 'Stand up for free enterprise, won't you Mr Isaacs,' she urged its Chief Executive (Isaacs 1989:107). Later, she wrote in her memoirs: 'I wanted to see the widest competition among and opportunities for the independent producers – who were themselves virtually a creation of our earlier decision to set up Channel Four' (quoted by O'Malley 1994:70; Cockerell 1998:333–334). It is striking that this structural factor was far more important to her than the challenging content, which she, like her supporter Mary Whitehouse, was inclined to deplore. Lord Nugent of Guildford declaimed in the House of Lords: 'the reports I have show that a whole new perspective of obscenity and bad language has been introduced' (McSmith 2011:212). And the channel was greeted by the tabloid press as either 'Channel Bore' or 'Channel Swore'.

Nevertheless, in the long run, it was the structure which came to shape the character of the channel. The increasing clout of independent production companies would prove to be a Trojan horse, smuggled in to transform the broadcasting landscape. In the early days of Channel Four, the independent companies, organised by the producers' group PACT, included small informal groupings, some of them set up to make a single programme, as well as established producers. However, as time went on the companies consolidated. The smaller groups would drop out and the major independents would expand until they became as powerful as the broadcasters themselves. By the early 2000s an unnamed Channel Four executive told Georgina Born: 'the independent sector is becoming concentrated on about 10 suppliers...I find that really sad...It's sad for the indie sector that we're not really there for most of them. There's a carve-up happening.' It was a move towards what Born described as 'the commercialisation of public broadcasting in the UK' (Born 2003:799).

C4 and medical programmes: Campaigning consumerism

> Channel Four has generally and specifically irritated, stimulated, delighted and disgusted its audiences.
>
> (Hobson 2008:28)

The first night of Channel Four was extraordinary by any measure. Because of an actors' strike, the new channel was unable to show any commercials. Despite this and many other problems due both to inexperience and to too little time for checking and editing, that first evening set the tone (Brown 2007:53). It kicked off with a celebratory three-minute montage and a taster of programmes to come: promising exotic parts of the world, wild animals, clowns and dancers, as well as talks on philosophy, a new soap opera, documentaries on art, and *The Tube* with rock music and reggae bands. Later came *The Body Show*, half an hour of leotard-clad workout with dancer Yvonne Ocampo. But its main feature was a challenging drama directed by Stephen Frears. In *Walter*, Ian McKellen played a lonely man with learning difficulties, just about coping and dependent on his mother and his pigeons. When his mother died he was taken to a degrading institution. The *London Evening Standard* described it as 'one of the most shocking films about mental illness ever shown on British TV' (28 October 1982). It was not easy viewing and clearly signalled that Channel Four would not play down to its audience, and that issues of health, sickness and disability would be dealt with very differently from the other channels. Established institutions would be challenged. The mood was one of non-conformity and dissent.

Well Being: Speaking in an ordinary voice

The new team of commissioning editors set out to radicalise every genre, among them, medical programmes. 'As Channel Four comes to the end of its gestation period, in a studio just off Soho, a GP and a team of journalists and cameramen are putting together a new kind of health programme,' reported the trade paper, *Medical News* in October 1982.

Commissioning editor Carol Haslam had produced a discussion paper in which she declared that she would broaden the range of health programmes, and an off-peak 'health slot' was planned for Friday evenings at 10.30 (Karpf 1988:25). Its first series, *Well Being*, will concentrate 'on health rather than illness', and on primary care, low-tech medicine and 'the illness from which large numbers of people are known to suffer – arthritis, depression, diabetes and backache'. However, it will not outrage the establishment, because 'the establishment in the form of the Royal College of General Practitioners is collaborating to produce it' (*Medical News* 7 October 1982[5]). The series will be fronted by Dr Simon Smail who was not only expert in the field but 'knew one of the most important things about television which is that you have to speak in an ordinary voice'. The series was part of the expanding genre of informal consumer programming, creating an easy relationship between the doctor/presenter and the audience. However, Producer Robert Eagle added that he also aimed to 'understand outside pressures...poverty and unemployment [which] make individuals much more vulnerable to stress and depression. We don't blame individuals for their health problems, nor, I hope, do we preach at them.' The second half of each edition allowed viewers to participate in a studio discussion and phone-in.

Kill or cure

Thirteen weeks of *Well Being* was followed by an interview show titled *Predicaments*, then, more challengingly, by *Kill or Cure* (1983) made by the independent company, Meditel. This was a series about injury from prescribed drugs, and *New Scientist* compared it favourably with the usual 'half baked critiques of modern medicine and the drugs industry' (19 May 1983). Producer Joan Shenton was a journalist and television presenter who specialised in medical issues. She had herself suffered from an iatrogenic (medically induced) condition and her sceptical approach to health and medical professionalism came out of that experience (Shenton 1998:1–2).

'Today we're going to look at what you yourself, as an individual, can do if you've been injured by a drug without being adequately warned of the risks in taking the drug,' she told the audience for her first series (29 April–2 June 1983). Questions about drug companies and pressure from drug salespeople had been a recurring feature in current affairs

---

investigations. The Thalidomide scandal of the early 1960s, when a drug prescribed for pregnant women caused serious birth defects, including limbs which were malformed or completely missing, had been a high-profile example. The campaign for compensation from the manufacturers and the distributors of the drug was taken up by broadcasters and journalists in the 1970s (Karpf 1988:102).

In her Channel Four series *Kill or Cure*, Shenton went beyond individual scandals. One edition asked: 'Are there too many drugs? Are all 6,500 available preparations needed?' (programme 4 20 May 1983). Others in the series explored the difficulty of getting compensation. There was no legal right to redress, and a victim of drug injury must prove negligence. An edition on the 'watchdogs', the Committee on the Safety of Medicines, alleged links to the drug companies (27 May 1983).

Channel Four was thorough-going in its educational approach to its audience. It did not assume that its engagement simply lasted for the half-hour of transmission, but offered carefully prepared back-up. In the illustrated booklet which accompanied *Kill or Cure*, Shenton wrote of complainants' distress and confusion, as well as their sense of injustice since the drug companies acted as judge and jury in their own case. Her programmes were themselves a form of activism, and readers were referred to activist groups and the (soon-to-be-abolished) Community Health Councils, 'acting on behalf of patients'. The booklet sold out after the first showing of the series. It was retransmitted a year later with updates, and, according to the press release, 'triggered a sequence of questions in the House of Commons, a review of one drug by the Committee on the Safety of Medicines, and inquiries into links between the pharmaceutical industry and the nation's drug watchdogs'. It brought 'increased awareness of potential drug damage and the failure of drug monitoring systems'.

The approach of the Meditel team was forensic, scientific and factual. It was partly in the mode of an established, but not very well-known or prestigious tradition of scientific documentary making in the UK which aimed for clarity of explanation and an innovative use of graphics and animation, rather than going for impressionism and emotional empathy (Boon 2008). *Kill or Cure* was updated and made several reappearances, although at off-peak times, 5.15 p.m. in 1984 and 11.30 p.m. in 1987. *The Health Services* journal wrote that that the series 'demonstrates higher level of informed comment than most other documentary programmes on medical topics' (20 May 1983). This was campaigning consumerism.

V   The irreducibility of dependence

Going gently?

Within the political rhetoric around empowering patients as 'consumers', very little consideration was given to the times when coping was just not possible: to the experience of pain or sickness, or to those unwelcome moments when, in Margaret Thatcher's scornful words 'people' become like children and have no alternative but to 'cast their problems upon society'. A discussion of 'empowerment' can overlook the physical and mental experience of sickness itself; of times when bodily discomfort becomes a dominating obsession; when pain, fever, debilitation or mental illness takes over consciousness, bringing a separation from habitual everyday activities. These are experiences which all of us pass through to a greater or lesser degree, at some point in our lives. They inevitably involve dependency and call on social resources. While questions about resources were at the centre of political debates and continually reflected in current affairs and factual programmes, the *experience* of sickness was much more difficult to address.

Those dramas and comedies which did approach this difficult topic were able to explore the charged relationship between professional and patient, the routines and those trapped within them, the experience of the sufferer and the power of the institution. Comedy could bring flashes of insight – but was in drama where the patients' experience could be most powerfully presented, in plays like Trevor Griffiths's 1975 *Through the Night* (see Chapter 3).

On BBC2's *Playhouse*, *Going Gently* (5 June 1981) was a rare exploration of the awful truth for terminal cancer sufferers. As in *Only When I Laugh*, incompatible patients share a hospital room. But Fulton Mackay and Norman Wisdom are in a hospice, and what they have in common is their illness and their impending death.[6] Here is no easy critique of the institution; and there is no way in which these two, individual, incommunicable journeys could have been made easier. This play is about illness and dying, and its focus is on that dreadful experience. A huge outburst of anger is not directed at the institution, but against that fate. It was not until Dennis Potter's *The Singing Detective* was commissioned by the BBC in 1986 that the full subjectivity of being a patient in hospital would be explored in such painful extremity.

---

[6] The play was adapted by Thomas Ellice from the novel by Robert Downs, with unobtrusive directing by Stephen Frears, who would later direct *Walter*.

By the mid-1980s, there were fewer outlets for the authored single play, making less space for original playwrights and difficult topics. But Anne Karpf noted a different way in which the 'consumer critique' was bringing a change to the popular dramas of the time. 'Cosy doctor shows had all but disappeared,' she wrote, and 'a new generation of medical drama was emerging'. American series such as *St Elsewhere*, with its naturalistic acting style and dysfunctional doctors incorporated 'aspects of the consumer critique, and the chief way in which it differed from its predecessors, was by introducing a new character, the doctor as a human being' (1988:193).

The effect was to broaden the possible ways in which professionals were presented, while the 'onerous citizenship' of a suffering patient remained far more difficult to explore.

In this chapter we have seen how the pressure for the health service to adopt a 'consumer'-centred approach, to move from identifying social needs to responding to individual wants, meant overlooking or rejecting the sort of unwelcome information contained in the Black Report and the Royal Commission. However, as Ian Kennedy's Reith Lectures demonstrate, in the early 1980s, broadcasting, both through the BBC and the independent companies, created a significant space for a critique from a broad environmental perspective. Meanwhile, the conceptualisation of the public addressed was changing. Restructuring was taking place. Viewers and listeners, as well as patients, were beginning to be treated as 'consumers' – and we have seen the sometimes contradictory inflections of the idea of 'consumerism'. Meanwhile, Channel Four was enriching the concept of 'public service' as it set out to address multiple, diverse 'publics'. New possibilities were opening up, and, during Margaret Thatcher's first term in office it was not at all clear which of the conflicting ideologies would come to dominate.

As we go on to look at the restructuring of professionals, the third group who make up the medical encounter, we will observe these tensions in an even starker form.

6
Your Life in *Whose* Hands? Restructuring Professionals

I Professionalism: Pimp or magician?

Challenging professionals

In 1948, Aneurin Bevan told the doctors and surgeons:

> My job is to give you all the facilities, resources and help I can, and then to leave you alone as professional men and women to use your skill and judgement without hindrance.
>
> (*The Lancet*)

But Margaret Thatcher had a different view of professionalism:

> The most obvious hallmark of her reign was a relentless war – partly rhetorical, but partly through state intervention – against the cultural and professional elites that had once sustained authority in society and the state.
>
> wrote historian David Marquand (*New Statesman* 14 April 2009)

The relationship between the medical establishment and programme makers had never been entirely respectful. Undermining arrogant surgeons, giving them a taste of their own medicine, mocking their authority, had entertained the nation through the *Carry On* and *Doctor* films. The tradition continued with Richard Wilson's tactless and hung-over surgeon in *Only When I Laugh*. Such moments could be seen as a safety-valve, a carnivalesque expression of fears, which served to confirm rather than attack established relationships. However, by the beginning of the 1980s the medical professions were being subjected to more serious challenges.

Margaret Thatcher's description of professionals as 'powerful interest groups' disguising their self-interest as 'high-minded commitment to some greater good', echoed the views of many who were campaigning for greater democratic accountability in the NHS, as well as those who were demanding more control over the management of their bodies and their health. For Reith Lecturer Ian Kennedy, doctors were the 'new magicians' with the power to define what counts as illness (see Chapter 5). Both investigative journalism and the rising genre of consumer programming were scrutinising claims to superior skills and esoteric knowledge. And as the policies of the new government began to take shape, the centrality of medical professionals would indeed be undermined – but not in the way that many campaigners had argued for.

In the worldview of Milton Friedman and the Centre for Policy Studies, it was money that should act as the driving force: it would prove both a discipline and a liberation. If professionals were redefined as *sellers* of services, they would respond to the demands of their 'customers' rather than work to their own internally defined standards. (A similar proposition was being fought over in relation to broadcasting.) In many ways this was a moral position, reflecting a strongly held belief that such a system would indeed bring about the best outcome for all parties. But for many, a monetary approach would mean an abandonment of the public service ethic. 'You'll be a surgical pimp for wealthy hypochondriacs' was the accusation from the dedicated doctor in *General Hospital* (see Chapter 3).

Despite, or perhaps because of, this multifaceted challenge to professionalism, a major concern of both the medical and broadcasting establishments was to ensure that the audience's trust was not seriously undermined by critical programming. Anne Karpf identified a need for reassurance as an important feature of what she described as the 'medical' approach, which focussed on professional expertise. Crudely put, current affairs was for when things went wrong, as with the Thalidomide scandal, or *TVEye* on tranquillisers (21 February 1980), while programmes in the 'medical' mode showed things going right. Its heyday had been the 1950s, which had 'bubbled with therapeutic optimism' boosted by the arrival of the NHS (Karpf 1988:52). In the medical approach, 'health' tends to be equated with diagnosis and cure. Programmes 'describe a world largely rational and ordered, where science increasingly dominates nature, where medical knowledge is incremental, cumulative and systematic' (p. 13). The medical approach celebrates the specialisms of surgeons and other highly trained medical experts; it takes for granted their ability to define the needs of their patients, and their patients' implicit trust in their expertise. The doubts and questioning which came to the fore in the sceptical 1970s challenged, but did not eliminate, this approach.

Your life in *whose* hands?

Back in the 1950s, a pioneering series on BBC television had offered audiences an unprecedented view of developing technology and surgical expertise. With the significant title *Your Life in Their Hands*. It was launched in 1958 and centred on that climax of medical intervention – the operation. The programmes showed in unflinching close-up, albeit in 1950s black and white (or rather, shades of grey), the details of an operation: the incisions, the glistening organs, the array of instruments, the swathes of drapery which concealed the patients and, of course, the skilful hands of the surgeon. 'The visual grammar reinforces the doctor's centrality,' wrote Ann Karpf. 'Viewers were addressed as potential patients, implicitly telling us "this is what medicine can do for you".' The message was reassurance. Operations followed by the death of the patient may have been filmed but were never shown. The BBC said that this was for the benefit of relatives, but on one occasion when the relatives gave permission, the episode was still not screened (p. 12).

Leaving aside the focus on the details of the procedure, the dramatic potential of the series was unparalleled. Here was a classic narrative structure: the life-threatening condition, the trepidation at the very real dangers involved and the build-up to the climactic incision. Here was the horrific imagery, featuring blood, sharp instruments and internal organs – subject matter otherwise only permissible in the horror genre. And, of course, here was a brave and heroic central figure with near-magical skills and power over life and death – the surgeon.

When the series launched under the urbane guidance of surgeon Charles Fletcher, it had been highly controversial within the medical profession. Some doctors were upset that the mystique surrounding their profession was being broken down. The *British Medical Journal* (*BMJ*) warned that 'doctors and nurses appear as mummers to provide entertainment for the British public' (quoted by Karpf 1988:51). The *BMJ* continued to condemn the programme in four successive editions. However, by the time the second series aired in 1961, the medical establishment had largely become reconciled to what was, in effect, positive publicity. Nevertheless, it continued to keep a wary eye on media coverage. From 1976 the *Journal* carried a regular 'Medicine and the media' page. 'Doctors are without doubt the most sensitive to criticism of any profession with which a television producer has to deal,' wrote producer Paul Bonner (quoted by Karpf 1988:169).

There continued to be considerable nervousness about public reactions to medical programmes, both in relation to the accuracy of their informational aspects and their potentially distressing content. (Newspapers reported suicides among worried viewers following the first *Your Life in Their Hands* (Karpf 1988:51).) It was hardly surprising that journalists and producers routinely turned to knowledgeable sources. Karpf wrote that programme makers prided themselves on 'a close association with the medical establishment' and showed a great deal of deference (p. 257). Medical programmes, including dramas, employed advisers, who were allowed to preview and revise and there was a call for 'articulate and telegenic' doctors to act as spokespeople and to front the programmes (pp. 115; 111–112). Broadcasters were guided by very little specific policy, but one statement from the regulator, the IBA, emphasised that 'medical programmes should be based on competent professional advice and give a hearing to more than one opinion on matters of potential controversy'. It was an approach accepted for most topics across current affairs and factual programming (p. 22).

The BBC brought back *Your Life in Their Hands* in 1980, after a gap of 16 years (BBC2 22 May–21 June 1980), its full colour made the series even more startling than the 1950s black and white, while the medical technology displayed was even more advanced. But the position of the expert was less secure. Although an attentive viewer could find traces of all four of Anne Karpf's approaches in the series, by focussing on cost, and hinting at the Centre for Policy Studies' favoured discipline of money, it offered a subtle undermining of the position of the professional.

'I now have the tumour in my hand'

The surgeon draws his scalpel across the skin. The suspense is tangible as the camera peers into the wound. 'I now have the tumour in my hand,' he finally announces (programme 1). It was May 1980, and this was the first of six programmes which featured skilled and caring surgeons making use of impressive technological advances, and achieving results which seemed almost impossible. In programme 1, viewers watched an operation to remove a cancer; in programme 2, they observed the very moment when a heart is stopped in order to create a bypass. This seemed like the quintessential medical approach. However, the series explicitly invited a style of viewing which would move beyond admiring observation, as it posed a number of dilemmas around questions of cost.

In his 1980 CPS pamphlet, *A National Health Dis-service*, Arthur Seldon quoted a 1970 British Medical Association report, 'there's little prospect of tax revenue matching the increasing costs of providing health services at even at the *current* inadequate quality. And there is no prospect that tax revenue can ever provide the *rising* standards which science makes possible and which should be the aspiration of us all' (p. 100 italics in the original). Now, in the context of the high drama of the operating theatre, the same questions are asked: can this treatment be afforded? *Should* it be afforded? From programme 1, viewers were made aware that costs would be debated, and this may or may not have affected the ways in which they followed the stories of the six patients and their treatment. The final programme, 'A question of cost', was set up as a series of discussions, involving the patients, their doctors/surgeons and Minister of Health Gerard Vaughan, who had himself been a hospital consultant. A form of 'environmental' approach, which looks more broadly than the illness itself, had shifted its focus, from the social and economic causes of ill health, to the political and economic context of treatment and cure.

The title sequence for the new series offered a familiar medical montage, but this was presented slowly, with great solemnity: hands carefully washing; a surgical mask tied into place; surgical gloves pulled on. Each programme was introduced by Robert Winston, at the time a registrar at Hammersmith Hospital, London, where the series was filmed. His easy manner linked to his personal expertise would later make him a celebrated television figure, but this was his first presenting role. In *Illness as a Metaphor*, Susan Sontag identified cancer as a symbolic expression of 20th-century affliction, and programme 1 did indeed deal with this focus of so many dreads. Speaking from the operating theatre, dressed in a blue cap and mask, Winston set up the drama: for some, the operation we were about to witness could improve the quality of their lives. Others, like Mrs McGowan whose experience we will follow, would die without it.

As the operation proceeded, Winston questioned the surgeon, Chris Wood. Why was bowel cancer on the increase? Mr Wood replied with a 'look after yourself' explanation, 'it's the increased meat and fat we eat... and we have too little fibre... this leads to constipation so it has more chance to spread'. Then, turning away from the camera he asked, 'Can I have the stapling instrument, please, sister?' The tumour had been removed, but the climax of the operation was the procedure of repairing the bowel using a special instrument recently developed in the USA. 'The cancer has been caught in time,' he told viewers, and 'she's lucky, because we can use the "American gun" ' which is expensive. The programme then left the operating theatre and demonstrated the stapling process using a plastic tube. Viewers were reminded how costly it was. Finally, they learned that six months later Mrs McGowan was able to go about her normal life, and they met her again in programme 6, alongside Ken Hill who had a coronary bypass, Margaret Batten who donated a kidney to her daughter, Yan Chu Civil who was unable to conceive and Marilyn Ross whose premature baby had spent seven days in intensive care. In a version of the 'consumer' approach, this final programme gave a voice and personality to the patients. As examples of calls on late 20th-century medical expertise, the cases selected had not all been 'illnesses' to be cured; infertility was a social and personal problem with a possible medical solution.

'Many say the National Health Service and particularly its hospitals are currently in a state of crisis,' this final programme begins, 'so you may have been surprised at the degree of surgical excellence we were able to feature. But the question some now ask is, can we afford it and also can we go on affording it?' The cases selected had been studies in the dilemmas of costing: Chris Wood had borrowed the staple gun at a cost of £50 per staple; Ralph Sapsford, who had carried out the coronary bypass, argued that his operation was cost effective because the patient was now back at work and did not need any more expensive drugs; the kidney transplant surgeon usually operated at night and spent his days on an awareness campaign, fundraising for the research. Finally, the equipment used for Mrs Civil's operation, undertaken by Robert Winston himself, had been paid for privately. 'Patients come from all over the UK, and the specialist equipment is paid for by its earnings.'

The issues have a political dimension. Should surgeons have to spend their time fundraising? Should they have to provide own equipment? The Minister of Health offered the opinion that it 'makes them realise the value of what they're doing, the cost of what they're doing'. In the studio, the surgeons were unanimous, declaring that the operations they conducted were absolutely necessary. 'Patients and cancer don't usually wait,' stated Chris Wood. 'You have to do what you feel is best.' When Robert Winston explains that they were not able to do precise costings, the Minister declared himself 'horrified'. The process of commodification, of breaking down a service into quantifiable segments which could be separately priced, and potentially sold (as Colin Leys would explain in *Market-Driven Politics* 2001:84) was not yet in place.

Gerard Vaughan concluded with the government's approach to health care: three-quarters should be provided by the state; one-quarter by private companies. Private provision brings *standards*, he argued. However, it was Charles Fletcher, the pioneer surgeon/presenter from the 1950s who had the last word. He was unequivocal on the commitment of the NHS. 'Medicine should come out of the market place,' he stated. It should serve 'needs rather than people's idea of needs'. The stress on 'needs', as we have seen, and will see again and again, proved a crucial site of contest. Fletcher echoed Ian Kennedy in his Reith Lecture: ' "Need" should be the sole criterion of the receipt of a service' (see Chapter 5). The two political positions could not have been staked out with greater clarity: 'standards' which it was claimed, would arise naturally from a commercial interaction, versus a professional attention to 'needs'.

The issue of funding continued to be explored across current affairs and factual programming – away from the glamorous world of high-cost medical technology. On 9 April 1980, *File on Four* had looked at 'Financing the NHS' and visited a hospital at Ashington in Northumberland, a coal-mining town with a tight community and a long tradition of solidarity, trade union activism and working-class self-education.[1]

Hugh Chignell writes:

Once again the emphasis was on a health service in crisis. Tight budgets were insufficient in the face of inflation and there was a serious problem of understaffing. The views of nurses were given particular prominence, 'they [patients] can't even die with dignity because you haven't got time to help them', stated one nurse and another claimed, 'I'm overworked and I'm tired. I come off the ward in the morning in tears.' To address the issue of underfunding these staff were also involved in fund-raising and they organised bingo sessions and other charity events. This was information which strongly underscored the depth of the financial crisis in the NHS.

Privatisation or 'safe with us'?

Privatisation was on the agenda. On the one hand, it was argued that 'private facilities draw on other sources of finance...and...help to

---

[1] Ashington was the home of the 'Pitmen Painters', a group of coal miners who became artists in their spare time, celebrated by writer Lee Hall in the play of that name (2007).

bridge the gap between the demand for health care and its supply' (DHSS circular February 1983 quoted by Riddell 1987:137). On the other, Health Minister Vaughan could proudly describe health care as 'one of our biggest growth industries' (*TVEye* 'Going Private' 5 February 1980). In 1982, a document from the government's Central Policy Review Staff considering options for the total privatisation of health care was leaked to the press. It was greeted with a public outcry and led Margaret Thatcher to insist, in her speech to the Conservative Party Conference later that year, that: 'The National Health Service is safe with us...the principle that adequate health care should be provided for all regardless of ability to pay must be the foundation of any arrangements for financing the Health Service. We stand by that' (8 October 1982). (Perhaps it was a cultural echo of *Your Life in Their Hands* that gave rise to the persistent mis-remembrance of that declaration as 'The NHS is safe in our hands'.) In her 1992 analysis of Thatcherite policies, Shirley Robin Letwin repeatedly stressed the pragmatism of Thatcher's approach, and commented that she intended to protect the NHS 'not as a holy relic but as "the most suitable arrangements for current circumstances"' (1992:208). At Yorkshire Television, John Willis produced *Sick in Sheffield, Broke in Beverley Hills* (8 February 1982), in which doctors and patients from California find that their system based on private insurance does not match up to the NHS.

The question of whether health care should be paid for directly remained central to the debate. The issue was not new. The right granted to GPs and surgeons to market their skills had been the compromise which had enabled the National Health Service to be set up in 1948, and more concessions had been made in the 1970s. When Gerard Vaughan declared his preference for 25% of health care provision to move into the private sector, it was not a new move, but a continuation of an existing trend (Iliffe 1982:30). In itself this double role potentially brought their professionalism into question. Privatisation, as we have seen, was also an important tool for re-structuring class relations as well as relationships within the medical encounter.

II The Nation's Health

Drama on Four

Many of the changes to the NHS paralleled changes in broadcasting policy, but the situation in broadcasting in the early years of the Conservative government was rather different. While the public service role of the NHS appeared to be under attack from the promotion of the private sector, public service in broadcasting was enriched by the arrival of Channel Four; within the private sector but managed and regulated. The new channel would create, as we have seen, substantial space to debate the politics of health, and to push beyond the cautious boundaries of political consensus. Its factual programmes on health issues were longer and more radically questioning than on the other channels, and drama, too, took up the theme. The channel had been on the air for barely a year when it became the outlet for a savage attack on the NHS as an institution, and, in particular, on its insensitive and self-serving professionals. Four linked plays, under the series title *The Nation's Health*, were transmitted in October 1983.

As the BBC and ITV companies felt under greater pressure to move to more popular formats, critics were lamenting the decline of the single play and the disappearance of the radical tradition. However, Channel Four gave new life to the genre. Commissioning Editor for Fiction, David Rose, had headed the BBC's regional drama production at Pebble Mill in Birmingham, where he had been relatively free to innovate and experiment. At Channel Four he continued the policy of commissioning original dramas from new writers, as well as presiding over the expansion of 'drama' to include films which had a cinema distribution and short films in experimental styles. Channel Four's fictional output saw 'innovation, experimentation and sheer diversity', wrote Lez Cooke.[2]

The Nation's Health

The screening of *The Nation's Health* was a major event (6–27 October 1983). Its author, G.F. Newman, was an established writer who had already provoked controversy with a BBC series portraying corruption as endemic throughout the British legal system (*Law and Order* BBC2 1978). Channel Four commissioned the new series from Euston Films, an arm of the ITV company, Thames Television, and the plays were transmitted on consecutive Thursdays at the peak viewing time of 9.30 p.m.

The Nation's Health was a bleak and uncompromising attack on institutionalised medicine, portraying a world in which unfortunate patients were helpless in the hands of arrogant professionals and an uncaring system. It drew on the campaigning of libertarians like Ivan Illich, and on critiques of an over-bearing, paternalistic professionalism. The attack on

---

[2] Thanks to Lez Cooke for giving us access to his comprehensive list of drama on Channel Four.

the system was so thorough-going that a nervous Independent Broadcasting Authority commissioned a survey among viewers to find out if their trust in the health service had been reduced after seeing the plays (Wober 1983). (Despite the extreme situations portrayed, it had not.) In addition, each of the plays was followed by a probing 50 minutes of reflection, using studio discussions and documentary sequences. *Follow the Nation's Health* was commissioned from Meditel, the company set up by presenter Joan Shenton to deal with medical issues, and was chaired by Shenton herself.

The Nation's Health was *Your Life in Their Hands* turned upside down. Just like *Your Life*, the drama began with that most feared of conditions, cancer. Just as in the earlier series, the climax of episode 1, *Acute*, was the operation. But this was the horrific underside. In the play the surgeon was not the hero, but was blinkered, supercilious and determined to demonstrate his skill in order to publish and gain prestige among his peers. ('The old man's making a name for himself hacking out malignancies,' muttered a junior doctor.) In a graphic and disturbing sequence, the patient was subjected to 'heroic surgery' and the major part of his face was removed. Newman multiplied the damage done by the disease with the damage done by the treatment, a theme which echoed across the four plays. It was a perfect exemplar of the distrust of professionals shared by right and left libertarians, and it was underpinned by Newman's own rejection of conventional medicine. Watching the plays is a gruelling experience.

Gordon Newman and his team carried out their own practical research for the plays. Like Paula Milne and her colleagues for *Angels* he spent time as an auxiliary 'nurse' on a ward and worked in the hospital kitchens, where painters were, in fact, getting in the way of the cooks, just as they do in *Acute*. 'I wrote what I saw,' he said (personal communication). He also worked in a mental ward, an experience which is reflected in the final play, in which the democratically run ward, with participation by the patients, was the only humane environment viewers encountered.

'I was very aware of politics,' he said, 'whether you spoke to doctors, nurses or trade union people, the cuts were all they talked about' (personal communication). In the third play, *Chronic*, nurses and ancillary workers demonstrated against the closure of a geriatric ward. The imagery, as they waved their 'Stop the cuts' placards, echoed scenes familiar from the news bulletins. But the style of the plays remained low key: 'I was aware how exhausted everyone was all the time – they were on the point of falling asleep,' he says (an experience echoed by the nurse in *File on Four's* Ashington programme (see p. 106). The underlying theme of the plays was that institutionalised medicine was itself the problem. In *Acute* a doctor consoled a patient and recommended visiting a healer, because 'you have to understand the source of your illness'. In the fourth play viewers learnt that the doctor has been suspended for 'unethical behaviour' (in other words, for recommending 'healing').

Below, Sherryl Wilson discusses the series, drawing on her own experience as a psychiatric nurse in the 1980s. Against the background of Thatcherite policies, she interprets the plays in relation to concepts of the public and public service. Quoting Jason Jacobs on the 1970s 'conflict' medical dramas, which he described as reflecting 'a desire to map social anxieties onto the body' (Jacobs 2003:7), she argues that in *The Nation's Health* the body is the critically ill health service itself.

Sherryl Wilson writes[3]:

> G.F. Newman states that his drama series, *The Nation's Health*, was intended as a critique of the 'arbitrary power' held by the medical profession. He was also critiquing the dehumanising effects of the total institution. The result is a drama that situates the medical and other NHS staff as operating a system in which patients are alienated rather than as central to the proper concerns of a public service institution. The effect on the viewer (this viewer anyway) is rather a dislocating experience. Nonetheless, the series presents an early commentary on the impact of Thatcherite policies on the health service, the staff who work in it and those served by it. *The Nation's Health* marks the moment of transition when the service, already destabilised through spending cuts by Labour governments, reached what Martin Gorsky calls a 'true turning point' 'with constrained expenditure, promotion of the private sector, [and a move towards a] market economy' (2008:441).
>
> Newman was not only concerned with Thatcherite policies governing health care provision. His intention was to show how the arbitrary power accorded to doctors leads to abuse (Newman 2008).

[3] Sherryl Wilson's contribution is based on research for the AHRC-funded project ' "There's No Such Thing as Society?" A Study of Broadcasting and the Public Services under the Three Thatcher Governments, 1979–1990' at Bournemouth University. She has expanded on this research in 'Dramatising Health Care in the Age of Thatcher' *Critical Studies in Television* 7(1) Spring 2012 13–28.

He was echoing views like those of Ivan Illich who argued in 1977 that doctors (and social workers) gain legal power that by law they alone will be allowed to satisfy...They turn the modern state into a holding corporation of enterprises, which facilitates the operation of theirself-certified competencies (Illich 1977:16).

Nonetheless, *The Nation's Health* offers a commentary on the wider political picture concerning health care policies and the new cultural environment determined by the market economy endorsed by the Thatcher government. The four plays present an NHS dehumanised by powerful but incompetent medical staff (nurses are barely present), indifference to patient suffering, an ineffective managerial system and resource starvation.

Across the four dramas, *The Nation's Health* presents a kaleidoscope of political issues, illnesses, fatalities, personal greed and professional vanities. This is a landscape in which bleak hospital wards, unsympathetic nurses and doctors, careless portering and kitchen staff combine to produce harsh conditions that would deter all but the very needy. The ill are positioned symbolically outside of society, the Other against which the Thatcherite ideology of individual endeavour rather than dependence is measured.

The four episodes of *The Nation's Health* are entitled 'Acute', 'Decline', 'Chronic', and 'Collapse'. Each takes one area of the health care system using the vehicle of junior doctor Jessie Marvill (Vivienne Ritchie) navigating her way through her training, first as a surgeon and then on a GP training scheme. It is through her that we encounter a public-service institution diseased by corrupt and self-serving medical staff, strangulated by bureaucracy and starved through diminishing resources. While Marvill illuminates aspects of health care provision, the new NHS culture of the 1980s, identified by Martin Gorsky, is articulated through a parallel narrative that concerns Nightingale Block. Symbolically named after the pioneer of modern nursing, Nightingale Block houses wards for the elderly ill, and, like the people it supports, it is costly to maintain, a drain on resources. Despite the evidence for its ongoing need, the block is earmarked for closure. (This is emblematic of a wider context in which assets owned by the NHS were being sold off to raise capital, despite the shortage of accommodation experienced by a number of areas within the NHS.) Chris, the porter (who travels through all areas of the hospital and knows the topography well) is also the union rep. Speaking at a meeting he states:

What was put forward as a temporary panacea for a perennial complaint – shortage of finance – is now being offered as the final solution. . . . We've suffered cuts, cuts and more cuts, and these I have persistently fought . . . but by closing 120 beds, i.e. one quarter of St Clair's, which the closure of Nightingale Block represents, for the saving of £56,000, i.e. 1/20th of hospital expenditure, makes no logical sense (*Chronic* Episode 3).

Contributing to the debate is the Community Health Council which opposes the closure of Nightingale Block due to 'urgent geriatric need'.

As it is, there are 'very old people' at risk and who 'should be brought into hospital' but who remain at home. Finally, however, Nightingale Block is sold to a consortium 'with Arab money' which will develop it into a private hospital. Rationalised on the grounds that, in the face of massive cut backs, 'private enterprise' will be seen to 'make up the shortfall'; a member of the hospital management team argues: 'If we get our timing right, we'll be seen to be fulfilling a real need' (*Chronic* Episode 3). Earlier scenes indicate that family and neighbours will be tasked with the responsibility of caring for the elderly frail rather than the private enterprise initiative which will depend on those wealthy enough to pay for services. Having been sold cheaply 'because of its limited use' (*Collapse* Episode 4) the story of Nightingale Block culminates in the inelegant removal of the few remaining patients as they are shipped out of their wards into an uncertain future.

(We are left with the image of the ward being cleared so that no costs are incurred, an image which would be reflected in *This Week*'s 'The Closure of Ward 19' (10 April 1986, see Chapter 8)).

Disengaged, blunted to the sensitivities and anxieties of their patients, the medical and managerial staff in these plays embody a dehumanising institution that displays little of the public service ethos that the NHS was founded on. This embodiment of a detached institution illustrates what Richard Sennett calls 'the corrosion of character', where 'character' refers to 'the ethical value we place on our own desires and on our relations with others'. For Sennett it is our connection with the world. Developed through loyalty and 'mutual commitment', 'character' is the long-term aspect of our emotional experiences (Sennett 1998:10). With the erosion of 'character', our sense of mutual dependence corrodes along with the attendant notions of community. Based on his studies of working environments, Sennett argues that the neo-liberalism of the 'Anglo-American regime' corrodes character and repudiates dependency, a consequence of attacks on the welfare state. Those 'who are dependent on the state [are treated] with the suspicion that they are social parasites, rather than truly helpless' (p. 139). Bonds of trust, formed through crisis and the need for help, are threatened, furthering the sense that people are disposable.

Sennett's diagnosis can be mapped on to Newman's vision of the NHS and its individualistically minded staff. But I want to take this a step further by thinking through what kind of 'public' is being articulated here. Sennett offers us a model of selfhood in which community ties formed through mutual trust and interdependency are dissolved, disconnecting us from one another. David Marquand also links trust to the wider social body, and like Sennett, identifies trust as an essential component of a healthy, functioning society. Marquand's notion of the public domain is that it is a dimension of social life in which activities link with notions of public interest; citizenship, equity and service are its central values. It is a space protected from the adjacent market and private domains; a space for forms of human thriving that cannot be bought in the market place or in the tight knit groups of clan or family (Marquand 2004:27; 32–34). The public domain is fundamental to a civilised society. Its institutions and practices embody principles of equity and service and are a source of public trust. However, Marquand argues, since the 1980s there has been an 'aggressively interventionist state systematically enfeebling the institutions and practices that nurtured [the public domain]' putting it in crisis.

Incessant marketisation... has generated a culture of distrust, which is corroding the values of professionalism, citizenship, equity and service... For the marketisers the professional, public service ethic is a con... There is no point in appealing to the values of common citizenship. There are no citizens: there are only customers.

(Marquand 2004:2–3)

Sennett's and Marquand's formulations illuminate much of *The Nation's Health* but I want to focus on one episode in particular which juxtaposes the public domain with that of the market by drawing out what is at stake in the loss of the former when the latter becomes the paradigm for health care provision. *Collapse* (Episode 4) is the final and most allegorical of the episodes. Here, Jessie Marvill is coming to the end of her placement in Coldbrook, a psychiatric hospital, and is questioning her desire to be a doctor.

With its depiction of gloomy locked wards, padded cells and heartless nurses Coldbrook resembles the psychiatric institution of twenty years before, depicted in Ken Kesey's celebrated book and film *One Flew Over the Cuckoo's Nest* (1962). It is contrasted with Breacon Unit, the beacon of hope that is the hospital's therapeutic community operating along democratic lines, where patients are given a voice, and which is depicted as being successful in the rehabilitation of the seriously ill. The community is premised on public principles, in which debates concerning the functioning of the unit are held, enabling agency through concern for the self and for others.

However, Breacon Unit is struggling for survival in the face of spending cuts and stifling bureaucratic red tape. Patient-led initiatives such as buying food and cleaning the Unit are devised to develop a sense of autonomy, achievement and confidence. But, while these engage the sympathies of the District Manager, the plans are thwarted because of the contracts already in place to supply food and cleaning services. As one of the patients remarks in the group meeting, 'Going to the hospital management will be a waste of time. They won't listen to us'. ('*Collapse*' Episode 4). It is not just the hospital management that will not take the patients and their need seriously: the proposed project to re-house patients in the community is vociferously and successfully challenged by the affluent middle-class inhabitants of the area.

Worse still, funding cuts mean that Breacon is threatened with closure, the consequences of which are catastrophic. Bernice Attwood (Oona Kirsch), a patient whom we have seen flourishing in the Breacon community, suffers a severe regression, destroys her beautiful sculpture and sets fire to the art room. The episode, and series, ends with a shot of a forcibly medicated Bernice clinging to the wall of the padded cell in which she is locked. In silence, the credits roll over the image of entrapment and despair.

In the context of *The Nation's Health*, Breacon Unit resembles Marquand's notion of the public domain. The Unit's purpose is the enrichment and cultivation of civilised life, and it is governed by ethics of equity and service. It is a fragile oasis of sanity amidst the insanity that is, Newman implies, corroding our public health system. As an allegory of Thatcherite health care policies, *Collapse* juxtaposes the values of the public domain with the neo-liberal economic vision that places the 'rational, self-interested utility maximiser' at its core (Marquand 2004:91). In *Collapse*, the public domain is gasping for breath.

Follow the nation's health

It is *dangerous* to go to hospital with something like cancer...the NHS is run by doctors for their own benefit. More people are switching to alternative medicine.
(Brian Inglis in *Follow the Nation's Health* programme 4).

Surgeons were – and are – the acknowledged elite of the medical profession. 'Half the students wanted to be heart surgeons and do dramatic things,' said trainee GP Jane Gilby in *The Best of Health* (Chapter 5). In *Your Life in Their Hands* and *The Nation's Health* the drama of being a surgeon was staged in different ways. The real real-life surgeons displayed superb professionalism, but were challenged by the question of costs; the fictional surgeons reflected the worst fears of those whose lives may, ultimately, turn out to be in their hands.

The plays emphatically broke with the reassurance which underpinned the medical approach and which the medical establishment was so anxious to maintain. ('The medical profession will be very angry if an erroneous impression is given', a spokesperson had told the *London Standard* when the plays were trailed (*The Listener* 6 October 1983).) In the spirit of the IBA's advice to 'give a hearing to more than one opinion on matters of potential controversy' they were put into context. *Follow the Nation's Health* included discussions between practitioners, academics, trade unionists, charities, advocates of alternative medicine and patients' representatives, as well as short filmed reports. The package was completed by a richly illustrated 'study guide' prepared by the channel's back-up team. It gave advice on how not to let doctors get away with 'acting like gods', as well as posing some of the life and death decisions that doctors must take.

Doctors were being challenged, and some practitioners who took part in the discussions were critical of the extreme situations shown in the plays. In *The Listener*, television critic Michael Poole echoed their concerns. '*The Nation's Health* appears at a time when the NHS needs to be more stoutly defended than ever before,' he wrote. 'It requires a complex argument to offer a critique that doesn't extend to the NHS itself...In the present climate it may just serve to cloud the issue when major closures and cutbacks are in the offing' (6 October 1983). And Julian Barnes wrote in *The Observer*: 'My only worry...is that BUPA will secretly buy up the gorier slices and run them as ads for private medicine' (16 October 1983).

But for Gordon Newman, the films were a contribution to a 'revolution in self-awareness' (*The Guardian* 5 October 1983).

A note on genre and generic possibilities

Social roles can be constructed across the broadcast genres, and it has been important to consider who appears in which type of programme and on what terms. In the staging of the public and private roles involved in the medical encounter, factual and fictional genres offer different, but related possibilities. In programmes ranging from *Hospital in Crisis* to *Your Life in Their Hands* and *The Nation's Health*, we have seen presentations in which both real-life and fictional 'characters' appeared as surgeons, nurses, cancer sufferers and others. These on-screen 'characters' have a dual presence, their visible appearance backed up by an invisible hinterland which makes an important contribution to the ways in which they are presented and received. In a factual programme, such as *Your Life in Their Hands*, Mr Wood is present in his role as a surgeon, but viewers will be aware that he is also a unique individual whose other interests, activities and qualities are not visible on screen. They may or may not be relevant to his performance in the medical encounter. Mr Thompson in *The Nation's Health* also demonstrates a convincingly possible way to inhabit the persona of a surgeon. This time viewers learn a great deal about his individuality and attitudes, but the fictional format makes it clear that these are derived from his creator, G.F. Newman. In all his arrogant certitude, Mr Thompson is the vehicle of Newman's powerful critique of the medical profession.

Viewers may reflect, compare and consider as perspectives are mobilised across the different genres. A rich spectrum of possibilities takes into account both on-screen and off-screen roles. From the point of view of the audience, the range of generic possibilities enables multifaceted, sometimes conflicting, empathies and understandings. Spaces for reflection and argumentation – as in *Follow the Nation's Health* – reflect on and expand impressions and opinions. This range of generic possibilities potentially makes a valuable contribution to the public debate.

However, for real doctors, nurses and others who are part of the daily routine of the medical encounter, the situation is more problematic. Documentaries, discussion programmes and current affairs open up a possibility for individuals to 'give an account of themselves', to claim a 'voice' in Nick Couldry's sense. Yet, their self-presentation on the airwaves is inevitably constrained by the necessity to represent their *role* as well as their individuality, to balance their public and private personae. In a *public* forum, an individual must be aware of his or her responsibility as spokesperson: a nurse must speak *as* a nurse; a doctor *as* a doctor. The interaction between public role and private individuality is inevitably complex and must be carefully managed. A decision to take on a certain role, especially one which carries the historical weight and public service significance of nurse or doctor, remains a crucial part of a personal narrative. And, in the programmes we are reviewing, we will see those roles, which are at the same time public and personal, increasingly put under stress. Across the programmes of the 1980s, it is possible to observe a visible attempt by doctors, nurses, ambulance workers and others within the NHS, to cling to their own understandings of their commitment, while being pressed to adopt a persona of a different kind. Professionals, in particular, would face even greater challenges later in the decade (see Chapter 8).

By tracing the major roles within the medical encounter – workers, patients and professionals – through the broadcast output, the last three chapters have demonstrated how attitudes towards the NHS were changing. At the same time, broadcasting itself was changing, and restructuring broadcasting will be the topic of the next chapter. While the public service commitment of the NHS was being re-evaluated, the challenge to the concept of 'public service' in broadcasting was intensifying.

Chronology and Programmes: 1983–1987

1982 *The Third Age of Broadcasting* published, edited by Brian Wenham.

1983 Broadcasting hours extended:

17 January **BBC Breakfast Time** launched.

1 February **TV-AM** launched with *Good Morning Britain*.

8 February 'Talking Point: Hospitals for women run by women: are they something to fight for or an anachronism?' *Woman's Hour* BBC Radio 4.

Rupert Murdoch launches pan-European **SkyTV**.

June **General Election**. Margaret Thatcher becomes Prime Minister for a second term.

2 August 'Cuts in the NHS' *File on Four* BBC Radio 4.

NHS prescription charges are raised. Charges introduced for eye and dental checks.

Breadline Britain LWT/ITV series about poverty.

11 November *Auf Wiedersehen Pet* Central Television/ITV. Comedy drama in which a group of self-employed builders travels to Germany to find work.

Open Space: Community Programme Unit makes 'The Consultant's Tale'; 'The Doctor's Tale'; and 'The Nurse's Tale' BBC2.

1984 20 January Margaret Thatcher appears in a special edition of *Yes Minister* with Mary Whitehouse, to mark 20th anniversary of Whitehouse's National Viewers and Listeners Association, which campaigns against sexual and violent material on television.

26 February *Spitting Image* Central/ITV starts a 12-year run. Satirical puppet show lampoons Margaret Thatcher and her Cabinet.

Griffiths Report *NHS Management Inquiry* implemented. General Managers introduced: NHS hospitals must invite competitive tendering by private companies for cleaning, laundry and catering services.

Cable and Broadcasting Act establishes a Cable Authority to grant franchises.

March Miners' strike begins. Continues to March 1985.

Adam Smith Institute publishes *Omega Report: Communications Policy* arguing that the BBC should be broken up.

British Telecom privatised.

Reports of 32 hospital closures in London planned or completed.

11 October *TVEye* 'No room for sentiment' Thames/ITV. On the need to ration treatment, focussing on kidney failure.

Heathrow Conference. The Association of Independent Radio Contractors lobbies for public service programming obligations to be relaxed.

12 October Brighton bomb. Conservative Party Conference in the Grand Hotel, Brighton, bombed by the Irish Republican Army (IRA).

1985 Green Paper on the future of **Family Practitioner Services**.

Mail on Sunday 'Doctors have had their way for far too long . . . now Mrs Thatcher prepares her own prescription'.

18 January *The Practice* Granada/ITV (1985–1986). Drama series on life in a health centre.

7 February 'Consultants on the Make' *TVEye* Thames/ITV.

19 February *EastEnders* begins on BBC1. The soap opera would deal with many issues concerned with sickness and health.

May *The Thatcher Phenomenon* six programmes BBC Radio 4 (5 May–9 June 1985).

Doctors' Dilemmas BBC2 five programmes exploring ethical issues.

June *Who Cares?* Meditel for C4. Four programmes comparing health care in the UK and the USA.

The Public Service Idea in British Broadcasting: Main Principles published by the Broadcasting Research Unit.

Inner-city riots.

September *Howard's Way* begins BBC1 (1985–1990).

1986   January Rupert Murdoch moves the production of his papers overnight to a new plant at Wapping, partly to reduce the power of the print unions. Pickets and demonstrations continue to February 1987.

10 April *TVEye* 'The Closure of Ward 19' Thames/ITV.

'If you see Sid, tell him!' television advertisements for British Gas shares.

Yes Prime Minister BBC2. Jim Hacker is promoted and Sir Humphrey becomes Cabinet Secretary.

3 July **Peacock Report** *Report of the Committee on the Financing of the BBC* published. Envisages an eventual 'full market' for broadcasting.

Privatisation of British Gas and British Airports Authority.

The Health Education Council publishes an update of the Black Report. *The Health Divide* demonstrates increasing class inequalities in standards of health.

17 September 'AIDS is a four letter word' *Diverse Reports* for C4.

23 and 30 October *This Week* 'AIDS – The Last Chance' Thames/ITV.

December Public information advertisements about AIDS. *Don't Die of Ignorance.*

December IBA awards the contract for Direct Broadcasting by Satellite (DBS) to British Satellite Broadcasting (BSB).

Health Education Council is abolished and replaced with the Health Education Authority.

1987   7 January *AIDS – The Facts.* LBC Radio; syndicated to all Independent Local Radio stations across the network.

27 February–5 March **AIDS Week.** 26 programmes on all television and radio channels.

9 April 'The toughest job in medicine' *This Week* Thames/ITV. The first AIDS-specific ward opens in Middlesex Hospital, London. A survey documents hostility to AIDS sufferers.

Nightline – special AIDS edition. Late-night phone-in show, between 10.00 p.m.–1.00 a.m. featuring Dr Philip Hodson, one of the first agony 'uncles'. LBC Radio.

Government Green Paper on Radio published. *Radio: Choices and Opportunities,* proposed expanding commercial local radio.

7
The Third Age and the Fresh Winds of Market Forces: Restructuring Broadcasting

I The end of rationed television

Thatcherism in the early 1980s: The limits to public service

The monetarist economist Samuel Brittan declared that

> 'Public service' represents 'puzzling and embarrassing words for liberal economists who assume that all provision for the consumer on a competitive basis in a non-distorted market is a public service'.
>
> (quoted by Pratten 1998:399)

And the concept of 'public service' continued to provoke anger, as well as embarrassment for the Conservative government.

Accounts of the three Thatcher governments point to the less confident nature of her first years of power. There was the battle between the free-marketeers and the 'wets' in the Cabinet, the slow progress towards her favoured economic policies, and her own, sometimes contradictory concern with moral as well as economic values. However, the Prime Minister made sure that the economic departments were controlled by monetarists who believed in 'making sure there's no more money unless we earn it' and that 'it's not the job of government to ensure full employment'.[1] This led to the public spending cuts which, as Gordon Newman found, obsessed those working within the health service at every level, and to some deeply unpopular budgets. The years 1981 and

---

[1] Cabinet Minister John Nott and the government's economic adviser Patrick Minford in programme 2 of the retrospective series *Tory, Tory, Tory* (BBC 4 June 2006).

1982 saw inner-city riots in Brixton, Liverpool and Bristol, while January 1982 saw unemployment rise to three million for the first time since the 1930s. Numerous strikes included several in the health service. Margaret Thatcher resisted pressure to use government spending to ease the economic situation as her Conservative predecessor Ted Heath had done, and announced 'the lady's not for turning'. In those same years a series of Acts was passed, notably in education, transport and housing, which promoted private provision and marked the first steps in the government's attack on the publicly funded parts of the economy. As an illustration, an often repeated BBC television news item shows her celebrating the sale of the millionth council house and greeting the new home owners.

The changes in the NHS were part of this pattern, and in broadcasting the setting up of Channel Four could be seen as a similar move. Encouraging independent filmmakers to become entrepreneurs was not dissimilar to encouraging surgeons to conduct private practice. Together these changes began to undermine the principle of universal provision, as well as abandoning the aim to promote equality, even though, in the NHS, both the Black Report and the Royal Commission had both demonstrated that this was desperately needed.

Already, in the first years of the 1980s, a tangible change in atmosphere and attitudes was reflected in the culture, and those who sought to support public service were growing increasingly anxious.

> If we look towards the next decade of British TV it would seem that the 'economic' wing of the 'cultural class system' is about to go on the rampage ... [this makes] the cultural wing look positively progressive ... [with] a hostility to a second group of gangsters – the national and multinational corporations without whom no modern 'cultural class system' would be complete.
>
> wrote Andrew Goodwin in a short-lived left-wing magazine
> *Prime Time* 1982 (quoted by McGuigan 1992:127–8).

Popular programmes and the enterprise economy

A move towards 'popular' genres may have been closing down spaces for radical playwrights, but it did not mean an abandonment of inventiveness and social comment. On television screens across the nation, comedy and popular drama continued to provide a rumbling undercurrent, some of which bordered on the subversive. At the BBC, *Yes Minister* (1980–1982) reflected the widely held suspicion of both politicians and civil servants, as Minister Jim Hacker and Private Secretary Sir Humphrey

Appleby engaged in a hilarious dance of mutual deceit and manipulation (Oakley 1982). But *Yes Minister* lampooned politics in a way that did not radically undermine the consensus – it was one of Margaret Thatcher's favourite programmes and she even appeared in a specially scripted take-off of the series to mark the 20th anniversary of Mary Whitehouse's National Viewers and Listeners Association (Whitehouse 1993:90–94). Meanwhile, other comedies reflected Thatcherite Britain from below. For all the talk of transforming workers into consumers and home owners, many popular programmes reflected the cynicism of working people who were on the sharp end of the changes – including low pay and poor working conditions. In 1983 Granada, based in industrial Manchester, produced *Brass*, an exaggerated satire on Thatcherite values. Set in the 1930s, an entrepreneurial boss tramples over the rights of his workers and they respond with suitable cap-touching and deference. 'If it's a crime to have initiative and enterprise...I plead guilty,' announces Timothy West as Hardcastle, echoing the Conservative election broadcast of 1979. 'I can't stand here talking all day. I've got men to lay off.' When he grants his workers a lunch hour, he explains that it's so he can deduct food money from their wages (ITV 1983–1990).

The sitcom format was able to open up unexpected perspectives. Irony could be tinged with bitterness, especially from companies based in the Midlands and the North, areas which were feeling the brunt of the economic cut-backs. Following the reallocation of franchises in 1981, Central Television had taken over from the more entertainment-driven ATV in Birmingham and in 1983, as unemployment hit the industrial areas, the company offered *Auf Wiedersehen Pet*, produced by the independent company Witzend for the ITV network. The comedy-drama followed a disparate group of unemployed builders as they travelled to Germany to find work – often in dodgy circumstances (1983–1984, 1986). Like the much bleaker *Boys from the Blackstuff* it played off the working-class humour, rivalry and the camaraderie of male groups. But while *Blackstuff* portrayed a dying culture (with its most painful metaphor in *George's Last Ride* (see Chapter 4), *Auf Wiedersehen* reflected the spirit of Thatcherite enterprise. This was non-union labour, wheeling, dealing and cutting corners. And the validation of work through tough, manual labour could be replaced by an alternative working-class image: the duck-and-dive, rely-on-yourself enterprise economy. In *Only Fools and Horses* (BBC1), which began its 15-year run on 8 September 1981, the comradely gang was replaced by the family firm of Del

Boy and Rodney, devising get-rich-quick schemes from a Peckham council block.

Meanwhile, the arrival of Channel Four in 1982 would not be the only way in which the broadcasting ecology was changing. New technologies were causing considerable excitement among neo-liberal campaigners. 'The era of "rationed" TV will soon be over,' declared Cento Veljanovski of the Institute of Economic Affairs (1983:11). For Brian Wenham, at the time Controller of BBC2, Channel Four was 'the final chapter in the old story and the first paragraph in the new' (Wenham 1982:15). The 'Third Age of broadcasting' was about to begin.

The Third Age: Freedom and technological change

> Those who care passionately for freedom in communication and publishing... need now to gird themselves for a prolonged struggle against old habits and vested interest to ensure that the new freedoms, which the technology will make technically possible are in fact translated into real freedoms for both producers and consumers under law.
>
> (Peter Jay: speech to Edinburgh Television Festival 1981, quoted by O'Malley 2009:63)

As the fourth channel was preparing its launch, in 1982, the government set up a Committee under Lord John Hunt, to investigate the expansion of cable broadcasting. It also granted a licence to the BBC for two satellite services, one funded by subscription, to start broadcasting in 1986. Wenham celebrated the expansion of choice through these and other new technologies: video cassettes would allow 'each man (sic) to be his own scheduler' and cable could be expanded and tailored to local needs (Wenham 1982). These were clear benefits for what he described as the 'citizen-viewer'.

The government's emphasis was different. The brief of the Hunt Committee was to find 'opportunities for new forms of entrepreneurial activity' under a 'looser regulatory regime'. With cable technology, Hunt argued, viewers would be freed from the planned schedules of the BBC and ITV and would eventually be able to purchase their viewing programme by programme (Hunt Report 1982). The resulting 1984 Cable and Broadcasting Act claimed to bypass 'public service' by creating what would be 'in essence a private relationship between a subscriber and a cable operator'. For Tom O'Malley, the Act marked the 'first significant break with the tradition of establishing new radio and TV services as public service broadcasters' (O'Malley 1994:6). For the Institute of Economic Affairs, Veljanovski hailed a 'watershed in broadcasting policy' (Veljanovski and Bishop 1983:11–13). Significantly, cable would come under the Department of Trade and Industry. From 1974, responsibility for broadcasting had been with the Home Office. Thatcher's first Home Secretary, William Whitelaw, had been instrumental in launching Channel Four and was known to be sympathetic to the BBC. However, in 1983 the Prime Minister combined the Departments of Trade and of Industry and ruled that broadcasting *as an industry* would come under the new DTI. The Department became 'the seat of radical Thatcherite industrial policy in the early 1980s', allowing her to bypass the Home Office and develop the approaches she favoured (O'Malley 1994:70, 123).

In the event, the cable experiment did not take off. The cost of laying cables across the UK proved too great for private companies, and, despite the energy of some local activist channels, the initiative was not a success (Goodwin 1998:54–68). However, the government continued to encourage forms of broadcasting which could be outside the public service structure, and this included satellite.

In the excitement of the moment, it seemed that satellites were the future (Leapman 1986:154–169; Goodwin 1998:38–53). In 1977, an international agreement had allocated an orbital position for a high-powered satellite to serve the UK, and a private consortium was set up to build a satellite to carry two BBC channels. Internationally based channels broadcast from low-powered satellites were already available, and a station which covered most of Europe was launched in 1982 by the ambitious Australian media mogul, Rupert Murdoch.

In the early 1980s, Murdoch was already an influential player in the UK media field. In 1981, he acquired the most prestigious of British newspapers, *The Times* and *The Sunday Times*. This aroused a great deal of controversy since he already owned two influential tabloids, *The Sun* and *The News of the World*, and the purchase, by Murdoch's News International, was not referred to the Monopolies and Merger Commission, as would have been expected. Recently released government documents have revealed the unusual haste with which the deal was done, and the role of the government in facilitating the sale (BBC Radio 4 *The Media Show* 22 December 2011; Travis 2012:15). Murdoch was one of Thatcher's favourite businessmen and had had several private meetings with her prior to the purchase. He was an interfering proprietor, a supporter of the government and strongly committed to a market-based politics. He was deeply opposed to the publicly funded BBC, and the editorial policy of his newspapers would play an important role in the developing debate (Evans 1984; Milne 1988). In 1987, he took over the middle-market tabloid *Today*, which meant that that he controlled 33% of the UK newspaper readership. His papers gave him both political influence and substantial funds, which he was able to plough into his satellite venture.

Back in 1982, Brian Wenham and the eminent broadcasters who contributed to his book, were expressing a degree of foreboding about the coming Third Age. There was concern that the technological developments would undermine rather than expand public service in broadcasting. 'The greatest danger is that of gradual disenfranchisement by stealth' (p. 27). New channels, even when run by the BBC, would lead to increased costs to the viewer, and the 'citizen-viewer' may be deprived of 'what he or she now receives' (pp. 17–18). Even the BBC's projected satellite channels would be paid for by subscription, and this would create two classes of viewer. 'If we do not look very carefully at how we set up the new technologies we are in grave danger of widening the national divide' (p. 102).

The changing mood had clear implications for the Corporation and its funding by a universal payment, the licence fee. The attitude of the government, backed up by both the popular press and the 'top peoples' ' papers, set the terms of the debate.

II The BBC in the early 1980s: Fresh winds?

BBC: The licence fee and unctuous impartiality

> Margaret Thatcher's adviser, Tim Bell, stated baldly 'I want the BBC to fail because I don't want that system to work. It only works now because it has a monopoly'.
>
> (*Media Week* 26 July 1985, quoted by O'Malley 1994:28)

> The day that the BBC announced its bid for the renewed licence fee, Thatcher's press secretary briefed journalists that the Corporation was 'over committed, over staffed, and inefficient. It should no longer be protected from the fresh winds of market forces. Advertising was the answer'.
>
> (O'Malley 1994:76–77)

Margaret Thatcher had what one executive described as a 'visceral hatred' of the BBC (personal communication). Its success challenged the economic model she favoured, and it created a space for some uncomfortably critical programming. She deplored the arrangement by which it received its income from a special fee rather than from general taxes. The licence fee went to the heart of the BBC's independence and its public service commitments. As well as securing a non-commercial relationship with viewers and listeners, it underpinned the Corporation's ability – and what many journalists in the 1970s and 1980s saw as its duty – *not* to toe the government line, and to take a critical stance across a wide range of issues.

For Margaret Thatcher, the BBC's vaunted 'independence' was not a contribution to an open, democratic debate; it was a cover for its anti-market bias and subversive tendencies. Despite the criticisms of radical activists and examples of right-wing programmes such as *Analysis*, for Thatcher and her allies, the BBC was a buzzing hive of leftist conspiracies. In particular, its news and current affairs coverage were attacked for what Norman Tebbit described as 'the *unctuous* "impartiality" of the BBC's editorialising' (O'Malley 1994:55, my italics). 'Impartiality' was a particular problem at times when the nation was embroiled in armed conflict, which meant that the Falklands War of 1982 and the Northern Ireland 'troubles' were particular flashpoints. Thatcher was determined to 'make Britain great again' and any hint that government policy may be open to question brought down the wrath of Tebbit and some very public attacks.

In the face of overt government hostility, the public service status of the BBC became a preoccupation within the Corporation, particularly as the licence fee was due for renewal in 1985 with a level to be negotiated with the Home Office. Despite the role of the fee as a guarantor of independence, the BBC was (and remains) totally dependent on the government of the day to set the level and hence determine the Corporation's income. Licence-fee renewal was a moment of particular vulnerability for the Corporation, and a time of intensified attacks from pressure groups who wanted to shift it away from its publicly funded position. In a widely quoted pamphlet, *The Omega Report*, the Adam Smith Institute argued that it was an inappropriate and unpopular tax and its workings were not transparent. It should be reduced and the BBC forced to make up its funding with advertising (1984).

The BBC faced a central dilemma: if it did not appeal to a broad audience the licence fee would not be justified. If, on the other hand, it gave too much priority to 'popular' programmes it could be accused of abandoning public service principles and competing with ITV at its own level (Sutherland 2007:23,60; Leapman 1986:91). Within the Corporation, the need to maintain this balance meant that the *practice* of public service must reach beyond the prestigious, if contentious, news and current affairs, and across the genres.

Light Entertainment and public service-ness

> The absurdities and frivolities of the human condition as well as its more serious aspects are worth celebrating. A good belly laugh can also be life-enhancing.
>
> (BBC internal document quoted by Sutherland 2007:326)

From the early days, genres had varied in their prestige and in the ways in which they had been assessed.[2] At the early BBC, John Reith had only grudgingly added 'entertainment' to his famous triad of requirements, and the suspicion lingered. 'It was not that it wasn't the most respected department, it was that entertainment *as a genre*, to some compared less favourably,' James Moir, Head of Light Entertainment (1987–1893) told researcher Heather Sutherland (11 March 2005 my italics). Within the Corporation some continued to think that 'popularity' was at odds with a 'public service' role, and that entertainment should be left to the commercial channels.

Successful programmes could be described, perhaps tongue-in-cheek, as 'distressingly popular' (Sutherland 2007:285, 230). However, in 1977, the BBC had challenged the hierarchy of genres by appointing Bill Cotton, the successful Head of Light Entertainment, as Controller of BBC1. He would subsequently become Managing Director of Television (1984–1988). Light Entertainment had become a 'core terrain' in the contest over the meanings of public service.

At the beginning of the 1980s, competition was with ITV alone, but this was a time when the companies were producing flourishing popular sitcoms, such as *Only When I Laugh*, as well as numerous well-loved variety and entertainment formats. To maintain its 'public service' role, the BBC sought to differentiate its output. Internal papers stressed the aim for 'quality' in production values: high technical standards, accomplished performers and what was described as 'a "classy" not "brashy" or "vulgar" "presentation"' (p. 326).

---

[2] This section is based on research by Heather Sutherland at the BBC Written Archives Centre for *Where Is the Public Service in Light Entertainment? An Historical Study of the Workings of the BBC Television Light Entertainment Group, 1975–1987* (PhD thesis, University of Westminster 2007). The references are to internal BBC papers to which she was given access.

The Corporation also had the advantage of no commercial break, which was 'a visible and indisputable difference between "public service" and "commercial" programmes' (p. 253). The extra five minutes and the unbroken format allowed writers to pace the development of their characters and plot lines. 'We could write lines about character, whereas they couldn't afford to. They had to be funny and good on page one, as it were,' writer John Howard Davies told Sutherland (p. 256). Despite reservations about the status of the genre, the Corporation saw itself as 'doing public service light entertainment' with an emphasis on 'added value' and quality elements. There was a continuing rhetoric 'around the visibility of a "public service-ness"' (p. 326).

Another aspect of 'public service-ness' 'revolved around the idea of the long-term, of evolution, of having faith in potential, securing and conserving enduring talent'.

> There was an accommodation for failure, which was recognised and accepted as an intrinsic part of the craft of producing light entertainment...the BBC Light Entertainment Group had within its ethos the idea of 'nurturing' talent, of producing and shaping talent to suit the Corporation's aims, ultimately recognising that long-term commitment to talent would allow the BBC to bask in the reflective glory of the high quality broadcasts that would be the result. (p. 329)

The BBC made much of its reliance on audience research, and stressed the importance of measuring appreciation as well as numbers, since 'any claim to be serving the public must rest on reliable evidence that all sections of the public are indeed receiving a service' (internal document quoted p. 269). Yet, some still rejected this as an accommodation to 'wants' rather than 'needs'. 'Knowing too much about the audience would ultimately affect the programme output and...this instilled a fear within the Corporation that the BBC's entire programme policy would come to rest on audience tastes' (Briggs 1965:247).

But the broad and unified audience envisaged by the early BBC had already been thrown into crisis by the libertarian debates and demographic changes of the 1960s and 1970s. The coming of Channel Four meant a different sort of positioning would be necessary. Aware that the new channel would aim to attract younger audiences, the BBC pre-empted its launch and became the first to bring 'alternative' comedy to the screens. In *The Young Ones* (1982–1984), four outrageous teenagers shared a flat. For the reviewer in *New Musical Express* it was, 'good old market forces [which had] kicked the BBC and television comedy into some sort of contemporary shape' (4 December 1982 Sutherland 2007:235).

The *real* nature of public service broadcasting

> BBC Director General Alasdair Milne described what he called 'the real nature of public service broadcasting: its vitality depends on offering the widest cultural choice and on addressing itself to the whole community, not to a part singled out by education or class'.
>
> (McDonnell (ed.) 1991:87)

The Third Age got under way. As Channel Four began offering a glorious hodge podge of independent filmmakers, animation, extremist views, late-night experiments (*After Dark* discussions started at midnight and ran until the participants were exhausted), as well as programmes that *looked* different, dilemmas around the nature of public service became more urgent. Libertarian arguments for self-expression and a rejection of monolithic structures seemed to be overtaken by the market ethos of entrepreneurialism and consumerism. Meanwhile, the new technologies promised to change everything. It was a contest between public service and the market, argued Nicholas Garnham in a response to the Hunt Report (*Screen* 1983: Vol. 24, No. 1, pp. 6–27).

The ways in which the concept of public service was mobilised would have significant consequences for future policy. They included:

Is 'public service broadcasting' synonymous with 'publicly funded'?

Before the advertising-funded ITV arrived in 1955, it would have been possible to describe 'public service broadcasting' as equivalent to 'publicly funded broadcasting', in other words to the output of the BBC. Viewers and listeners paid an equal amount for free access to the entire output. And the commitment remained. When Director General Alasdair Milne was asked by the Peacock Committee which parts of the BBC's programming he considered to be 'public service', he replied 'all of it' (Seaton and McNicholas 2009:124). However, the legislation which set up ITV in 1955 and Channel Four in 1982 had made it clear that broadcasting *as* a 'public service' would not be confined to the publicly funded channels. The 1981 Broadcasting Act required the Independent Broadcasting Authority (IBA) 'to provide television and local sound broadcasting services as a public service for disseminating information, education and entertainment' (Section 2).

Giving evidence to the 1986 Peacock Committee, John Whitney, Director General of the IBA, argued that the current system, 'brings benefits which outright commercial systems...cannot and will not provide'. It supports creative people and makes space for what is 'counter, spare, original, strange' (Whitney 1986:94). 'The essence of public-service broadcasting is that it is not determined by market forces alone. The IBA ensures that programmes are sufficiently insulated from advertising pressure' (p. 6). The IBA is 'not the censor but the gardener'. It does not play a negative role, but offers 'positive nurture'. Echoing the Annan Committee in the mid-1970s, he stressed the importance of the separate sources of finance (p. 92).

Public service and public funding were not the same thing. However, it could be argued that the commercial companies were granted an implicit public subsidy when they won the right to broadcast freely on the radio spectrum. And the notion that the concept of 'public service' *ought* to equal 'publicly funded' – or at least publicly subsidised – remained politically convenient. It could then be argued that such institutions could be described as 'public service broadcasters', subject to restrictions and limits which did not apply to fully commercial ones. Throughout the 1980s, the Thatcher government grudgingly accepted the fact of a 'public service system', but energetically encouraged the development of technologies, including cable and satellite, which would be outside that system.

Is it a type of programme? A genre?

The term 'public service *content*' began to be used in the 1980s, with the clear suggestion that not all broadcast content could be considered to be a service to the public. In John Reith's triadic formulation, perhaps only the first two categories, 'inform and educate', should count. Certainly, Reith himself thought so, as did the Pilkington Committee in 1962 which had condemned ITV for too many programmes which were mere 'candy floss'. The ITA then 'mandated' certain genres to ensure the public service commitment of the ITV companies. However, in both the BBC and the ITV companies the rich diversity of formats which developed in the 1960s and 1970s had led to cross-influences between the genres, a great deal of inventiveness and what many have described as television's 'golden age'.

By the 1980s, the context was different. The Peacock Committee would argue that 'public-service programmes' should be complementary to those types of programmes shown in the marketplace. Such programmes would compensate for 'market failure' (Peacock 1986, para. 580). It was arguments of this sort, with their influence on government policy, that forced those working at the BBC into much soul searching, as they felt the need to justify 'light' entertainment on the BBC channels. Should the Corporation confine itself to the 'weightier' genres? The question would continue to be debated.

Needs or wants: The role of the 'popular'?

So, when a programme becomes 'popular' – when audiences *want* to watch in large numbers – does it cease to be 'public service'?

Pilkington had been clear about the importance of 'needs' on all channels:

> If viewers – the public – are thought of as 'the mass audience' or 'the majority' they will be offered only the average of common experience and awareness… they will be kept unaware of what lies beyond the average of experience: their field of choice would be limited. (1962)

This was the opposite of the neo-liberal argument, in which going beyond expressed 'wants' is 'authoritarian', depriving the viewer/consumer of 'freedom to choose'. In neo-liberal economics it was assumed that 'wants' are facts, but the term 'needs' 'is merely a statement about what the people *ought* to want', as Friedrich Hayek had asserted (Pratten 1998:384, 395, 403–404, my italics).

If 'public service broadcasting' was on hand to deal with 'needs', it was easy to take the next step and argue that a 'commercial' service had no obligation to look beyond apparent 'wants'. Such a step had not been accepted by Pilkington with his strictures on ITV, nor by the 1981 Act which referred to ITV '*as* a public service'. Lady Plowden, Chair of the IBA, even sent a memo to the BBC asking it *not* to refer to ITV, independent television, as *commercial* television (*Michael Grade on the Box* BBC Radio 3, April 2012). The issue would be much discussed by the Peacock Committee (see Chapter 8).

Quality?

Finally (for the moment), was public service defined by *quality*? Did it, as the BBC's Light Entertainment department argued, involve a certain approach to programmes *within* a genre rather than a differentiation between genres? Bill Cotton, Controller of BBC1, stated that the BBC's

biggest achievement was that 'it applied to popular contemporary entertainment the same values it applied to everything else', and a member
of the Board of Governors added, 'If the BBC, with its public-service
responsibility, did not maintain those standards, who would?' (minutes from a Governors' meeting 17 January 1985, quoted by Sutherland
2007:10:285).

But, for the free-marketeers in the government, the BBC's 'quality' was
the antithesis of commercial television's 'popular'. Douglas Hurd, at the
time a minister in the Home Office (Home Secretary (1985–1989)), was
concerned when these values appeared to be reversed. He briefed lobby
correspondents that the BBC could not expect an increased licence
fee when it ran the popular US drama series, *The Thorn Birds*, while
Granada was winning critical acclaim for its quality series, *Brideshead
Revisited* and *Jewel in the Crown*. This was different from other government criticisms. They had concerned news and current affairs, those
very programmes recognised as 'public service'. This new critique went
to the heart of the BBC's aim to deliver a balanced output and to compete with ITV. It was part of an increase in government attacks in
the run-up to the Peacock Inquiry (Leapman 1986:191). The debates
around 'quality' would intensify towards the end of the decade (see
Chapter 12).

These discussions were woven through many different fora – between
programme makers, in newspaper comment, in pressure groups, in political think tanks, among government policymakers and, increasingly,
among academic writers. Many of those who had campaigned for the
reform of broadcasting in the 1970s were based in academic institutions, where a broader social theory was influencing theorising about
the media.

III   Public service and the public sphere

The public sphere

> By 'public sphere' we mean first of all a domain of our social
> life in which such a thing as public opinion can be formed.
> Access to the public sphere is open in principle to all citizens.
> A portion of the public sphere in constituted in every con-
> versation in which private persons come together to form a
> public.
>
> (Jurgen Habermas in Marris and Thornham 1996)

From the mid-1980s, broadcasting scholars began to characterise broadcasting as a 'public sphere'.[3] The argument was that a stark division between 'public service' and 'the market' did not cover the potential of broadcasting structures and did not adequately address the media's role in a democratic society.

The concept, derived from the writings of the German philosopher, Jurgen Habermas, described a neutral space – either literal or conceptual – to which members of a 'public' have equal access, where information and ideas can be freely exchanged. For Habermas, such a space was made possible with the rise of the bourgeoisie and a market economy in the 18th century. In a rather optimistic interpretation of history, he pointed to the coffee houses and the liberal press of 18th-century London, where debate could flow freely, independent of the state and feudal obligations. For Habermas, this unfettered, face-to-face communication was being lost with the rise of modern mass communications and large-scale organisations.

Although Habermas was scornful of the popular media, in an influential article Nicholas Garnham argued that broadcasting did have the potential to act as an effective 'public sphere'. Despite the scale of broadcasting organisations and the lack of reciprocity between programmes and their audience, it nevertheless gave access to a wide range of knowledge and skills necessary for a properly informed democracy. Just as a public sphere enhances citizenship through participation, broad and diverse programming on the broadcast media can encourage critical thinking, questioning and debate. In this book we have been arguing that the diverse presentation of aspects of the health service was, in fact, offering such a space.

The next step was to relate this concept to public service broadcasting:

> The necessary defence and expansion of the public sphere as an integral part of a democratic society requires us to re-evaluate the public-service model of public communication...and while being necessarily critical of its concrete, historical actualisation, defend it and build upon the potential of its rational core in the face of the existing and growing threats to its continued existence.
>
> (Garnham 1986:53)

---

[3] Jurgen Habermas' *The Structural Transformation of the Public Sphere: An Inquiry into a Category of Bourgeois Society* was published in Germany in 1962 and translated into English in 1989.

In this spirit, many who had been bitter critics of 'public service' and the BBC in particular, began to seek out new definitions.

Principles of public service broadcasting

In academic journals – including the relatively new *Media, Culture and Society* (launched 1979) and *Screen*, the long-established mouthpiece for radical theory (originated in 1952) – and in think tanks like the British Film Institute and the Broadcasting Research Unit, there were increasing attempts to move beyond the pragmatics of public service and to formalise its underlying principles. The project became more urgent as, in 1985, the government set up an enquiry into the funding of the BBC, headed by economist Professor Alan Peacock.

The Broadcasting Research Unit sought contributions from a wide range of eminent broadcasters, regulators, critics, MPs and academics, and published them in a booklet decorated with a peacock feather. Contributors' concerns moved between the economic (questions of funding and competition), the social (a commitment to universality and appropriateness of provision), the cultural (high-quality, cater-for-all tastes and interests) and the ethical (impartiality, responsibility). Eight main principles were derived from the responses:

- Geographical universality. Broadcast programmes should be available to the whole population.
- Universality of appeal. Broadcast programmes should cater for all tastes and interests.
- There should be special provision for minorities, especially disadvantaged minorities.
- Broadcasters should recognise their special relationship to the sense of national identity and community.
- Broadcasting should be distanced from all vested interests, and in particular from those of the government of the day.
- Universality of payment. One main instrument of broadcasting should be directly funded by the corpus of users.
- Broadcasting should be structured so as to encourage competition in good programming rather than competition for numbers.
- The public guidelines for broadcasting should liberate rather than restrict broadcasters. (Broadcasting Research Unit 1985)

'Public service', argued the editors, did not merely depend on a scarcity of broadcast channels as its detractors like Peter Jay had claimed. Instead, it was based on principles which served important democratic aims. The arrival of new technologies, and new outlets for broadcasting in the Third Age, did not mean that these principles should be abandoned.

In this chapter, we have looked at some of the debates among broadcast practitioners and other supporters of public service in broadcasting, making clear the breadth and flexibility of the practice as well as the concept in the early 1980s. But, when Margaret Thatcher was returned for a second term of government, the restructuring processes we have been observing intensified. In the middle years of the decade the challenges to 'public service' were supported by major government reports in both broadcasting and health. These will be the topic of our next chapter.

8
Griffiths, Peacock and Restructuring Public Service

I Popular capitalism

The conquering army and the myth renewed

'It was like being part of a conquering army,' proclaimed Edwina Currie. The future Junior Minister of Health (1986–1988), with immaculate make-up and glistening red lips, positively glowed when, 23 years later, she recalled the Conservative election victory of 1983 (*Tory, Tory, Tory* programme 3 2006).[1]

In a dramatic reversal from being the most unpopular Prime Minister since records began, Margaret Thatcher's Conservative Party had won the biggest parliamentary majority any party had enjoyed since the Second World War. The myth of Thatcher had gained a new patriotic dimension with the warrior images from the Falklands War. The Prime Minister visibly revelled in the myth, and it was exploited with relish by the popular press. On the front cover of the *Daily Express* her face was enclosed in a celebratory 'V' for victory (Holland 1982:119–126). Analyses of Thatcherism and of Thatcher herself accumulated. She was a 'phenomenon' to be explored and explained. Six programmes on BBC Radio 4, *The Thatcher Phenomenon* (1985), set about the task by interviewing every relevant associate, from her childhood class-mates to the American President. And, as in so many accounts, the phenomenon seemed beyond easy explanation. 'Nobody has more voraciously dominated a peacetime government with their personal impact and commitment,' stated Hugo Young in his introduction to the series. Programme 3 was given over to a debate on her thought processes,

---

[1] Quotations in this section come from this three-part series which reviewed Thatcherism through the eyes of Margaret Thatcher's supporters (BBC4 8–22 March 2006).

with most of her associates refuting the charge of a rigid ideological commitment. Her Permanent Secretary from her time as a minister in the 1970s reflected that 'everything she did...sprang...from her own character...from innate prejudices and preferences' (Sir William Pile in Young and Sloman 1986:12).

As her second term of office developed, her political self-confidence grew. To outsiders it seemed that the direction was already clearly laid out, but for her colleagues this election marked a new start. 'I had a blank sheet of paper,' recalled John Redwood, in the 2006 BBC retrospective. He had been Head of her Policy Unit and claimed that 'privatisation was something new'. Important changes had been introduced in the Conservatives' first term but a much more radical programme was about to be launched and it would gather in speed and intensity.

For Margaret Thatcher, following her 'innate prejudices and preferences', privatisation was part of the restructuring of society which we have traced in the previous chapters. It was a way of 'transforming the soul' and changing what was 'true, possible and desirable', particularly in relation to social class and class consciousness (see Chapter 4). One way of achieving this transformation would be through 'popular capitalism'. 'Popular capitalism is nothing less than a crusade to enfranchise the many,' she declared. 'We Conservatives are returning power to the people.' The privatisations of the second half of the 1980s used television, press advertisements and huge posters in dramatic publicity campaigns which offered shares in publicly owned utilities to the population at large – and, for once, people were addressed in their capacity as workers.

The first television advertisements for shares in British Telecom in 1984 showed some rather stiff men with middle-class accents asking 'common-sense' questions 'but how much will it cost?' 'How can I find out more about it?' However, these were soon replaced by visions of building workers, shopkeepers and bus drivers. The message was how easy it is to become a shareholder. 'Just walk into a post office and pick up a form.' By the time of the 1986 sale of British Gas shares, a dynamic campaign from the agency BMP was featuring an invisible 'Sid', an everyman with a plebeian name. Some searched for Sid in remote locations – a Scottish loch, a windblown mountain – but others featured people at work: a bus conductor, a painter up a ladder, office workers, postmen, a dentist, a window cleaner. 'Did you know? Pass it on!' and 'if you see Sid, tell him!' As the message passed from person to person, incredulous recipients fell off their bikes in amazement or walked blindly into lamp posts. As well as becoming home owners and consumers, these people in ordinary jobs could find a new identity as 'popular capitalists'.[2]

In such an atmosphere the pressure intensified on the publicly funded NHS as well as the BBC. A new pressure group, 'No Turning Back', named after Thatcher's already legendary 'lady's not for turning' speech of 1980, was founded in 1985 by Ralph Harris, director of the Institute of Economic Affairs. It aimed to 'defend' (sic) the government's free-market policies, and argued for a thorough-going privatisation of all public services. For the health service, the group supported 'free-standing hospitals competing against one another' (MP Neil Hamilton on BBC4 2006).

The rest of the decade would be fateful for the public services. The mid-1980s would see major government reports reviewing both the BBC and the NHS. These would lead to White Papers on health and on broadcasting, followed by ground-changing Acts of Parliament. The concept of 'public service' would become subject to further challenge as moves towards a market-dominated economy gained strength. At the mid-point of the decade, the Griffiths Report on NHS management (implemented 1984) and the Peacock Report on funding the BBC (published 1986) were both oriented to efficiency, financial management and marketisation. In both reports there was an embrace of commercial values, but also a rhetoric of populism and an appeal to democratic choice. As well as becoming 'popular capitalists', users of the services were encouraged to become discriminating consumers, 'people who look to themselves first'.

II Griffiths: A challenge to the ethos of the NHS

'Health is a business': But where's the puss and blood?

> 'The consultants and the surgeons have a duty to live in the real world ... health is a business as is every other sphere of human activity that involves resources,' declared Tory MP Piers Merchant in a 1986 *TVEye*. But consultant surgeon Brian McEvedy of Newcastle's Royal Victoria Infirmary had a scornful response. 'You can't see how much puss and blood there is on a bit of paper. All you get is how many patients are being seen.'
>
> ('The Closure of Ward 19' 10 April 1986)

---

[2] In *Spitting Image*, Sid was found with his head in a gas oven in despair at his high bills (Central/ITV 1986).

Historians of the NHS are unanimous that the Report of the enquiry into NHS management, led by Sir Roy Griffiths, represented a defining moment in the Thatcherite changes. It created a potential conflict of interest between management and employees as it recommended a move from consensus to executive direction along the lines of the private sector (Klein 2010:120; Langan 1998:111). The new managers would provide a strategic policymaking leadership, with tighter criteria of efficiency and stricter accounting. They would be 'recruited from industry, commerce and the armed services', and the incentivising role of money was called on, as their salaries would be linked to performance. Implemented in 1984, the changes challenged the clinical autonomy of doctors and surgeons, and affected working lives throughout the service. 'Porters, nurses and consultants were no longer beyond reprimand in their own sphere but were subject to correction from the manager in charge,' crowed Shirley Letwin (1992:212). She praised the Report's blunt language. 'Unlike Royal Commissions [it] did not try to represent and reconcile all parties.' For historian Charles Webster, the fact that 'important changes were brought about in the face of professional opposition [was] a major precedent' (1998:20). Conflict between managers and professionals would be a feature of the following years.

TVEye's 'The Closure of Ward 19' was structured around this deep challenge to professionalism, and the gap between clinicians and newly recruited managers was laid out with great clarity. 'What price efficiency?' asked reporter Julian Manyon, as the dry language of business clashed with the demands of daily medical care. Brian McEvedy had been on Ward 19 for 25 years, but, as he rushed between patients, he explained that he had been given no prior information about the proposed changes. Efficiency experts from Birmingham University were introduced. They described two key measurements: 'turn-over interval' and length of stay. 'Do these indicators... reflect the real values that the Health Service should be aspiring to?' asked Manyon. McEvedy replied, 'They can't. They can't.' But the Chair of the local Health Authority was clear about the intended relationship between doctors and managers: 'You can't have clinical judgement dictating how much resource goes into the National Health Service.' The programme ended as porters began to clear Ward 19. The hospital got a rebate on the rates if the furniture was removed. The desolate image of the empty ward, without its beds, had been pre-figured in G.F. Newman's drama *The Nation's Health*, in which the significantly named Nightingale Ward had been emptied and sold off. The manager concluded that for him, 'It's a question of efficiency...the quality of the output, the serving of the client.'

Together with the restructuring of management and moves towards marketisation, in a clear parallel with the attack on the BBC's licence fee, a third plank of the government's strategy was to cut NHS spending back to below the growth of its estimated needs. In an effort to deliver the same for less, this meant reducing services or outsourcing. As we have seen, the NHS had been subject to incremental changes for a number of years, and lower-paid workers had been particularly affected as hospitals were encouraged to contract out ancillary services (Leys 2001:168). This had given rise to a 1982 laundry workers' strike. Now, from 8 September 1984, NHS hospitals were obliged to invite competitive tendering from private companies for cleaning, laundry and catering. For Ron Keating, Assistant General Secretary of NUPE, this was 'a sword of Damocles hanging over 250,000 support jobs in the NHS' (*The Times* 8 September 1983). For those working in the hospitals, the changes caused considerable disruption and a breakdown of the sense of teamwork – as well as dirtier wards (dirty wards were discussed by *Woman's Hour* BBC Radio 4 11 October 1989). 'From the point of view of the staff, work got harder while conditions got worse,' writes Colin Leys. 'Consultants were overridden; nurses did not have enough time to give the patients the care they thought necessary; support staff like cleaners and cooks found themselves transferred to private firms on lower wages and inferior terms of employment, typically non-unionised.' Between 1981 and 1991, the number directly employed by the NHS fell by more than 40% (Leys 2001:168).

Looking back, historian Rudolf Klein remembered Roy Griffiths's background, as managing director of the supermarket chain Sainsbury's:

> If supermarkets provide a good symbol for the 1980s it is because they can be seen as the embodiment of individual choice and the supremacy of the consumer...If management in the NHS was all about satisfying customers instead of keeping doctors happy, then the implications were indeed profound.
>
> (Klein 2010:121)

Shirley Letwin was more blunt: 'By assuming a good manager is obliged to deliver a good product to the consumer, the Griffiths Report for the first time directly challenged the ethos of the NHS.' 'Businessmen have a keen sense of how well they are looking after their customers' (Letwin 1992:213).

Investigative programmes about the NHS were also patient/consumer-oriented, but were less sanguine about the supermarket effect. When *TVEye* investigated issues which would disadvantage potential users of the service, the moves towards marketisation and privatisation provided examples which raised the spectre of a two-tier health system. 'Why are 1,500 people suffering from kidney failure allowed to die each year without hope of dialysis or transplant, when those who can afford £14,000 to have the operation done privately can be guaranteed a new kidney in four weeks?' asked reporter John Withington ('No Room for Sentiment' 11 October 1984). And in 'Consultants on the Make' (7 July 1985), monetary values had clearly won out over professional ones. Researcher Dave Perrin uncovered ways in which certain consultants were making money, not only by taking private patients in National Health hospitals, which was legal, but by avoiding the fee that was due to the NHS. In the programme, Dr Paul Noone spoke of a 'twilight' world between the NHS and private provision.

It was rare for programmes like these to accuse clinicians of abusing their power (that was left to dramas like *The Nation's Health*). Instead, as facilities were cut, wards were closed, and doctors and surgeons increasingly forced to question their role and their status, factual programmes tended to stress their professional commitment and to empathise with their loss of influence. BBC2 ran a series of five programmes, fronted by Ian Kennedy, exploring the difficult decisions doctors faced as a consequence of government policy. Echoing the title of Bernard Shaw's biting satire written 80 years earlier,[3] in *Doctors' Dilemmas* financial limits were transmuted into ethical dilemmas.

As the tension between a traditional commitment to public service and an approach measured in cost-effectiveness became more stark in the NHS, there were parallel changes in broadcasting. When the Committee on the Financing of the BBC was set up in January 1985, its chair, Professor Alan Peacock announced, 'our goal is of course derived from aims much wider than any applying to broadcasting alone'.

---

[3] Bernard Shaw, *The Doctor's Dilemma* (1906). Published together with a long essay condemning the self-interest and financial obsessions of turn-of-the-century doctors.

III   Do we need the BBC?

Anything but the licence fee

'In the next few weeks the government has the opportunity to begin the process of redefining public service broadcasting' declared the leader in *The Times*.

(16 January 1985)

Alan Peacock was a Professor of Economics. He had been a government adviser and was one of the group of radical economists who followed in the footsteps of Friederich Hayek at the London School of Economics. He and the committee's other most influential member, Samuel Brittan, brother of Home Secretary Leon Brittan (1983–1985), were associated with the Institute of Economic Affairs. Both were advised by the declared monetarist journalist Peter Jay. The setting up of the committee was the culmination of the government's aim to move the BBC to a more market-oriented position. The previous year the Home Secretary had insisted the Corporation call in management consultants Peat Marwick Mitchell (PMM) to conduct a 'value for money' assessment. Similarly to the NHS, the consultants recommended cost-cutting and contracting out various BBC departments.

But while the government and its supporters in the national press were cautious in their public pronouncements on the NHS, there had been no restraint in regard to the BBC. When the Peacock Committee was announced, in the words of Director General Alasdair Milne, '*The Times* thundered three times.' Its attack was uncompromising. 'Do we need the BBC?' a leader demanded. On three successive days (14–16 January 1985) the paper ran editorials arguing that sections of the Corporation should be auctioned off and the rest financed by advertising. 'The BBC should not survive this Parliament at its present size, in its present form and with its present terms of reference intact' (14 January 1985). And Peacock's brief seemed to confirm that this would indeed be the outcome. It was 'to assess the effects of the introduction of advertising or sponsorship on the BBC's home services', and also 'to consider any proposals for securing income from the consumer (sic) *other than through the licence fee*' (Peacock 1986, para. 1, p. 1 my italics). Although the BBC's public service status was put under question, unlike previous broadcasting committees, Peacock was not required to consider the social and cultural aspects of broadcasting.

To combat this critical barrage, Alasdair Milne led a high-profile campaign, generating stories for the media with specially commissioned research, interviews, speeches to meetings and other tactics. He stressed the importance of a full licence fee and attacked the coverage in *The Times*, whose recommendations 'if acted upon would have the practical effect of enabling its owner Rupert Murdoch to acquire some of the most valuable broadcasting action in the UK'. Murdoch's *News of the World* hit back with 'British Bonkers Corporation' and allegations about corporate overspending (14 April 1985) (Leapman 1986:217, 232; Milne 1988:129).

Inside the BBC, the strength of the press hostility was having a catastrophic effect. Producers and executives felt they were 'living in a bunker and having the stuffing knocked out of them'. Between the attacks from the government and the press, the feeling was that the BBC 'just could not win' (Horrie and Clarke 1994:22–23). Janet Morgan, an adviser to the Director General, described the atmosphere as a mixture of arrogance, defensiveness and secretiveness. In its efforts to preserve the licence fee, there was 'panic plus a degree of paranoia' as the BBC tried to please three constituencies: the public, government ministers and treasury officials, who 'mouth what they believe to be (and in some cases are) ministers' beliefs: that it's not fair for consumers who have a right to spend their money as they wish' (McCabe and Stewart 1986:25).

Against this background, the BBC was granted a licence fee at a considerably lower rate than it had calculated it needed, £58 per annum rather than £65. And Norman Tebbit set up a Media Monitoring Unit: 'We're taking the message direct to the BBC,' he declared at the 1986 Conservative Party Conference, adding ominously, 'they will be hearing from us soon' (Cockerell 1988:310–312).

The Peacock Report and market failure

Sir Alan Peacock assumed that his committee would indeed recommend that the BBC should be funded by advertising (O'Malley 1994:96). In the event, evidence showed that this was not economically feasible. Increasing the broadcast outlets for advertisers would disadvantage ITV and Channel Four, and the proposal was rejected; a conclusion which, allegedly, disappointed Mrs Thatcher. For Peacock and the free-marketeers, however, advertising shared certain problems with licence-fee funding, as it supported the entire output. Viewers and listeners – or rather 'consumers' as the Report preferred to call them – could not purchase programmes one by one, hence there was no direct relationship between a product (a single programme) and its user, which was what the Hunt Report had hoped that cable would provide. Instead, the final report laid out a longer-term and arguably more radical strategy.

It foresaw a 'full market' in broadcasting which would become possible when the appropriate technology was available. The BBC will continue to exist, but not in its present form. In the short term the Report proposed that the Corporation should begin to shift to subscription funding, and that Radios 1 and 2 and local radio stations should be privatised right away. In the committee's view, broadcasting should not be an accessible open space, like a park, into which anyone could wander at will. In order to turn such a public good into a commodity, there must be ways of *excluding* potential users. There must be fences, turnstiles and a charge for entry. In other words, the Report envisaged a time when the service of broadcasting would not be available to all, but would need to be paid for, programme by programme.

Rather than ignoring the cultural connotations of public service, the Report dealt with them indirectly – and narrowed them down. It accepted that, unlike the service of telephony, in which those who owned the wires were not responsible for the messages transmitted on them, broadcasters did provide content. Peacock conceded, 'there will always be a need to supplement the direct consumer market by public finance for programmes *of a public service kind'*. Having 'wrestled with the definition of public-service broadcasting', Peacock emphatically endorsed a version which gave priority to the market. Once more, money would be the driving force. 'Public service' is anything that 'broadcasting entrepreneurs' cannot monetise. Instead of the broad and vibrant system, envisaged by Alasdair Milne and described by John Whitney of the IBA (see Chapter 7), the meaning of 'public service' was *both* reduced to a genre – a type of worthy programme – *and* conflated with public funding.

> The best operational definition of public service is simply any major modification of purely commercial provision resulting from public policy. If a full broadcasting market is eventually achieved... the main role of public service could turn out to be the collective provision... of programmes which viewers and listeners are willing to support in their capacity of taxpayers and voters, but not directly as consumers.
>
> (Peacock 1986, para. 580)

The Peacock Report went beyond its original brief and made proposals not only for the BBC but also across the whole of the broadcasting structure. The ITV franchises, currently allocated by the IBA on the 'quality' of their proposals, should instead be auctioned to the highest bidder;

the BBC and ITV companies should take 40% of their output from independent producers, in order to 'increase competition and multiply sources of supply' (para. 110), and Channel 4 should sell its own advertisements. Samuel Brittan praised the Report with a horticultural analogy: 'It planted the idea of a broadcasting market...which will flower in time' (O'Malley 1994:117).

Historian Tom O'Malley points out that the proposals enabled certain *attitudes* towards broadcasting policy as well as actual policy options. What was possible began to shift what was desirable, as the redefinition of 'public service' changed the grounds of the debate. 'The decisions taken after 1986 gradually reshaped the whole framework of broadcasting policy,' he writes, in 'a world fit for money' (1994:126).

Independent radio throws down the gauntlet

Independent Local Radio (ILR) was subject to similar pressures.[4] At ILR's tenth anniversary in October 1983, the original rules remained in place: each company could own only one station and was required by the IBA to broadcast a wide range of music and speech programmes. However, the radio entrepreneurs, organised as the Association of Independent Radio Contractors (AIRC), were encouraged by the government's commitment to deregulation. They, too, wanted to throw off the shackles of 'public service' limitations, and began to lobby for greater freedom, both for commercial growth and for a relaxation of the programming obligations. The Chairs of the companies convened a special meeting in May 1984, which became known as the 'Heathrow conference'. Major changes were demanded, including a reduction in IBA 'interference' and 'a clear understanding that all forms of control will be reduced in accordance with the very much easier controls emerging for cable'. As well as sending their demands to the IBA, they circulated them to Home Secretary Leon Brittan and Industry Secretary Norman Tebbit. 'Independent Local Radio has thrown down the gauntlet,' they announced. According to Richard Findlay, Managing Director of Radio Forth and Chair of the AIRC, 'That's when the commercial momentum began. We could change things for our commercial betterment, and begin making money.'

In 1987, a Green Paper on Radio: *Radio: Choices and Opportunities*, proposed expanding commercial local radio, and Home Secretary

---

[4] For information on ILR, thanks to Tony Stoller and researcher Emma Wray. Their contributions can be found on the project website at http://www.broadcastingnhsbook.co.uk/

Douglas Hurd announced that a new separate radio regulator would be appointed. The IBA was deeply opposed to the move, but the 1990 Broadcasting Act, which set up the Radio Authority, also abolished the IBA. In the view of Tony Stoller, Chief Executive of the Radio Authority from 1995 to 2003, 1984 had been 'the moment when the politics of the Thatcher era finally began to have their effect on independent radio in the UK, and to redirect it towards its commercial incarnation'. He adds: 'Independent Local Radio (ILR) provides as good an illustration as you could hope to find of how the social liberal aspirations of the Seventies were subverted by the rise of market liberalism in the Eighties, before being confirmed under Major and Blair in the Nineties' (Stoller 2010).

Dumbing down?

As the conditions of possibility changed, so programming changed. All channels felt the commercial pressure to attract large audiences and to adopt a more populist approach, even though the BBC had been bitterly criticised for doing so. The pressure was deeply resented by broadcasters who had been part of the 'golden age' of the 1960s and 1970s. Denis Forman, the outgoing Chair of Granada Television (1974–1987), used his Richard Dimbleby lecture to attack 'media mercenaries' and the 'international brigade' who broadcast by satellite. And he reasserted the value of 'positive' regulation. 'Our masters have come to see television as an *industry* ... this is something new. Until now broadcasting in Britain has been first and foremost a service to the public' (BBC 1987).

At the BBC, Michael Grade had been invited to become Controller of BBC1 in 1984, partly because of his grounding in popular television. Looking back in April 2012, he noted that this was when the 'viewer' became the 'consumer'. There was a rise in consumer programming across the channels, and the 'daytimisation' of the evening schedules. Formats which had been in the mainstay of the daytime schedules, cookery, gardening, lifestyle, 'were suddenly mid-evening. You're pitching at consumers, because you want them to buy something' (Grade 2012).

The history of 20th-century media had seen numerous critiques of 'dumbing down' – if not in those precise terms – from the arrival of the mass circulation press in the 1900s to the launch of ITV in the 1950s. But the moment of the 1980s was qualitatively different. 'Dumbing down' was, in this case, a *political* move. It was a necessary consequence of the commercialisation of broadcasting; entailed by the definition of the audience as consumers rather than citizens, and the move away from the obligations which ensured that broadcasting remained a public service.

The content of broadcasting would no longer seen as a cultural contribution, responsible to society as a whole, but a commodity to be packaged and offered for sale to those who could afford it. Media, like health, was a business, and its job was to be economically viable and turn a profit. In the words of the Chair of the AIRC, 'We could change things for our commercial betterment, and begin making money.' 'Dumbing down' became not only politically acceptable, but also, in the 'Third Age' of broadcasting, inevitable. Satellite technology and deregulation would bring 'Wall to Wall *Dallas*' predicted media critic Chris Dunkley (1985).

Although the glitzy American soaps featuring the lives of the rich and glamorous topped the charts for popularity, for domestic programme makers the search for popular formats could give rise to a great deal of creativity. Lifestyle formats built up a more intimate relationship with their audience, while soap operas and sitcoms could deal with the daily problems of life in an intricate and practical way (Hobson 1982; Brunsdon 1987). In 1985, Michael Grade commissioned *EastEnders*, as a London-based soap to compete with Granada's well-loved *Coronation Street*, already 25 years old, and Channel Four's Liverpudlian *Brookside*. In its long life, *EastEnders* would deal with many issues concerned with sickness and health, and, in the early years, local GP Dr Legg was an important part of the community, offering advice and support alongside his medical role.

Meanwhile, in the mid-1980s, social unrest was filling the news programmes. 1984 had been dominated by the major confrontation of the miners' strike, and the autumn of 1985 saw more inner-city riots. In January 1986, Rupert Murdoch moved the production of his papers overnight to a newly equipped plant at Wapping, sacking the printworkers, establishing a non-union workforce and provoking pickets and demonstrations, which would continue to February 1987. In an early exercise of citizen journalism, an independent company documented the picketing in a video, *Despite the Sun*. Unlike Ken Loach's *Questions of Leadership*, which was effectively blacked by Central and Channel Four (see Chapter 4), this was never intended for broadcast, but was shown to activists in East London as the pickets were continuing.

In 1986, a Finance Act changed the way the Exchequer levy on ITV was organised, allowing the companies to keep more of their domestic profits. A Building Societies Act allowed the societies to behave like banks, and on BBC2 Jim Hacker was promoted. *Yes Prime Minister* (1986–1988) took over from *Yes Minister* on BBC2.

At Channel Four, Jeremy Isaacs, who had done so much to establish the lively independence of the channel, resigned to run the

Royal Opera House, Covent Garden, and Michael Grade left the BBC to replace him. His departure contributed to some significant changes in the top management of the Corporation.

IV   BBC Management

The last days of the Beeb? Management changes

> Today, enfeebled by what seems a chronic lack of purpose, the Beeb can find no effective defence against the sniping of a government ideologically opposed to the concept of a large publicly-funded corporation embracing a liberal philosophy.

This was how journalist Michael Leapman introduced his book *The Last Days of the Beeb*, written in the mid-1980s and published at the heart of the crisis in 1986 (p. 3).

Just as the Corporation was celebrating the 50th anniversary of its pioneering television service, it seemed to many that it was, indeed, nearing its end. Over the next few years, media scholars, historians, journalists and participants would publish a number of studies which, like *The Last Days of the Beeb*, traced the positioning and infighting as the Corporation coped with incessant financial, political, ideological and technological challenges. In 1988, ex-Director General Alasdair Milne gave his side of the story, and by the early 1990s there was a positive outpouring of publications. Their titles and subtitles were apocalyptic: *Closedown?* (O'Malley 1994); *Fear and Loathing at the BBC* (Horrie and Clarke 1994); *British Broadcasting Conspiracy* (Barnett and Curry 1994).

We have been drawing on these books, many of them written before the full extent of the changes had taken effect, for our own brief account of this key moment. All shed light on three structural ways, identified by Tom O'Malley, in which the government set about undermining the BBC from the mid-1980s: the reduction of the licence fee, the changes to the broadcasting environment brought by the 1990 Act which followed many of the Peacock recommendations, and, crucially, the changes in top management (O'Malley 1994).

Going against the long-standing tradition of political bipartisanship, the government had already begun a policy of appointing Conservative sympathisers to the Corporation's Board of Governors. They included Margaret Thatcher's enthusiastic supporter, ex-editor of *The Times*, William Rees-Mogg, even though he had been a bitter critic of the Corporation. (Rees-Mogg was Deputy Chair of Governors (1981–1986).) These were very different Governors from those interviewed by

Caroline Heller in her study of accountability in 1978. The relationship between Governors and management had never been clearly spelt out, but by 1987 the BBC's top management would also change, bringing a considerable shift in 'corporate culture' (O'Malley 1994:168).

In 1986, the Chair of the Board, Stuart Young, died after a long illness. Home Secretary Douglas Hurd appointed Marmaduke Hussey who had been Managing Director at Thomson Newspapers and had overseen the sale of *The Times* and *The Sunday Times* to Rupert Murdoch in 1981. Hussey's job at the BBC was 'to make it bloody clear that things have to change', was 'the word from Norman Tebbit's office'. 'He is to get in there and sort it out – in days and not months,' wrote Michael Cockerell (1988:312).

Soon after Hussey took over the Chairmanship, the Corporation once more came under attack from the government over a series which investigated official secrets. The security services called in the police, who raided the journalist Duncan Campbell's home and were filmed carrying his filing cabinets out of his BBC office in Glasgow. This time, Director General Alasdair Milne 'resigned against his will' and Hussey let it be known that in future the powers of the DG would be curbed. And, for the first time the new Director General would not be a programme maker. Michael Checkland, whose background was in accountancy, was appointed, with John Birt as his Deputy. (Tim Bell, who had been Margaret Thatcher's adviser, became the BBC's PR consultant (Horrie and Clarke 1994: Part 2).)

Together Hussey and Checkland were anxious to reorient the Corporation, and, it seemed, were prepared to accept that its scope should be reduced. Checkland declared that:

> The BBC must be seen to be adapting to competition and change as many other organisations and companies have had to do in this country, and doing it with enthusiasm and not with regret for the passing of our imperial role.
>
> (*The Guardian* 16 June 1987)

However, the most influential new appointment – and the most controversial – would be that of John Birt.

John Birt

John Birt had run London Weekend Television's current affairs series *Weekend World* in the early 1970s, when it became notorious for its dry, austere style (Tracey 1983). He had coined the phrase 'the mission to explain' in a series of articles in *The Times* co-authored with Peter Jay, a main presenter on the series (*The Times* 28 February and 30 September 1975; Holland 2006:91–93). Their argument had been that television journalism had been seduced by attractive images and filming techniques, which were a distraction from their pure informational role. Although in more recent years he had been Director of Programmes at LWT and had been more concerned with the company's lighter output, at the BBC he was given the task of reorganising news and current affairs. He brought them under one directorate and declared that BBC journalism should be more 'authoritative'. Coming from his *Weekend World* background, Birt had little sympathy for journalists who simply set out to nose out a story. He established a system in which scripts must be prepared in advance of shooting and there was less freedom for journalists to follow their instincts – much to the dismay of many of the more experienced reporters. He antagonised them by arguing that he was increasing 'professionalism' by bringing in specialists on topics such as economics and social affairs, and keeping a tighter control of the structure of programmes (Lindley 2002:321–330). Coming on the heels of the acrimonious disputes between the BBC and the government, journalists were afraid that 'a straightjacket was about to be imposed which would at best cramp and at worst stifle completely any innovation or creativity in BBC journalism – particularly journalism in awkward political areas' (Barnett and Curry 1994:81–85; Horrie and Clarke 1994:96–127). There was the dilemma. The BBC had been criticised when it moved in a more populist direction – but it was its dedicated investigations which infuriated the government.

On the one hand John Birt aimed to build better relations with the government by moving the BBC in a more market-friendly direction, but at the same time, taking his cue from the Peacock Report, he aimed to define the BBC's role as providing those 'high quality' programmes that the market could not, or would not, provide. In an article called 'Tuning in to Thatcherism', a contemporary writer commented that John Birt 'has already courted the charge that he is acting solely in the interests of the presently established power' (A. Foster *Management Today* February 1988, quoted by O'Malley 1994:156). For Michael Grade, Birt 'turned BBC upside down'. He did some positive things 'but his manner broke the Corporation's spirit... he sure as hell took the fun out of working for the BBC' (BBC Radio 2 30 April 2012).

The BBC had tacitly agreed to the terms of the Peat Marwick Mitchell report on management and financing, in return for Home Office defence of the licence fee (O'Malley 1994:127). Now, the new management of Hussey, Checkland and Birt set about carrying out the recommendations, including cutting back on expenditure, cutting jobs and outsourcing. On 3 January 1988, the BBC celebrated this new incarnation with an extraordinary three hours of programming at prime time on a Sunday night. *See for Yourself* (a title suggested by publicist Tim Bell) was a report on the BBC in 1987, and was intended to mark its shift in values (Horrie and Clarke 1994:147).

See for Yourself

See for Yourself assumed that the BBC1 audience was as obsessed with costs and value for money as the new regime itself. There was no agonising over the nature of public service here. Marmaduke Hussey introduced the programme: 'Before I became Chairman I often wondered how much everything cost and whether they really looked after money...' In what one caller described as 'a glossy brochure for the BBC', *See for Yourself* worked methodically through the genres and the BBC departments, quoting costs and explaining contingencies. There was nothing in this show about simply sitting back and enjoying the output. The audience were treated as cynical shareholders, probing and questioning. Those viewers who stuck with it were informed that a rainy day in Jersey while filming *Bergerac* could cost an extra £12,000. And it was raining spectacularly when the relevant sequence was filmed. There was little appreciation of the skill and commitment of the programme makers; instead the concerns were about how many people were employed and how long it takes: 'food is provided on site to save time and money'. Managing Director Bill Cotton adopted an almost apologetic tone as he explained that the costs for a BBC drama were less than for a similar cinema film or an American series. The glossy *Howard's Way* cost £240,000 per hour, 'a fraction of *Dallas*'. 'It's reasonable in economic terms.' Although the debate on whether the BBC should focus on its 'core purposes' was raging, there was acclaim for Light Entertainment. 'The BBC is the largest producer of LE in the world.' In 1987, there were more than 1,000 hours of variety and comedy. And Michael Checkland soberly reminded his audience that supporting the arts was one of the most important things the BBC does.

For two hours, *See for Yourself* covered the cost of satellite hours; told viewers how many staff covered the uprising in the Philippines; the cost of a new BBC centre in Newcastle; the cost of a 30-minute sitcom; how many assignments the BBC had offered freelance musicians; and how much of the schedule was given over to bought-in programmes (15%). And there was a moment of reassurance. Director General Michael Checkland stated: 'if the size of the audience were the only measure of its value this studio would be closed down. But it's not, and the reason is that the market-place cannot be the only yardstick of value.' Like a methodical company report, the presentation did indeed give an effective overview of the Corporation and its activities in the context of rising costs and a pegged licence fee. And there were some clear pointers of the changes which were under way. John Reynolds, Head of Co-production, stated: 'No substantial play or documentary is possible without co-production money.' The target was to double this in the next five years.

The programme was preceded by a brief sequence from *Open Air*, a daytime audience phone-in programme produced by BBC NW, and an *Open Air Special* made up the third hour of this Sunday evening event. Viewers were invited to put their questions to the Director General and the Chair of the Governors. Host Pattie Coldwell introduced 'Mike' and 'Duke', as they insisted on being called, sitting rather stiffly apart in their suits and ties, on a pink sofa.

A democratisation of the airwaves had been part of the BBC's output since the Community Programmes Unit had been created in 1973. Programmes like *Open Air*, involving audience members, had maintained a careful balance between democratic participation and the promotion of assertive consumer rights. Now, it seems, 'popular capitalism' was added to the mix: viewers were treated as shareholders. But in *See for Yourself* the 'company report' collided with the conversational style of *Open Air*. While Hussey and Checkland were anxious to make it clear that licence-fee payers get value for their money, the callers seemed less concerned with 'why is so much spent on programmes' as 'why are star performers paid so much'. A map showed the location of the callers, and the most cogent question came from the distant Orkneys. A young woman demanded why the BBC did not stand up for itself in the face of government pressure. She was told that it did, and that its independence was paramount. However, in a rather ominous conclusion, 'Mike' announced: 'I'm most pleased that we're facing up to the need for change.' (*See for Yourself* would become a regular feature, but later presentations were less austere. In 1990, the South and East region produced an engaging review of its activities and personnel, this time presented as 'an independent look' by critic Chris Dunkley (BBC1 8 January 1990).)

By 1987, following the Griffith and Peacock reports, in addition to a more managerial culture, both broadcasting and the NHS were dealing with reduced funding and the ideological attacks on the concept of public service mounted by government and the popular press. And this was the year when both services needed to find new ways of offering a service to the public, as they were challenged by the threat of AIDS.

9
AIDS and 'the Public' at Risk

I 'The public' at risk

'The public' in danger

A volcano shoots fire across the screen in a terrifying explosion. The voice is that of actor John Hurt. 'There's now a danger that has become a threat to us all. It is a deadly disease and there is no known cure.' A pneumatic drill thrusts dangerously into a rock. 'The virus can be passed during sexual intercourse with an infected person. Anyone can get it, man or woman. So far it has been confined to small groups, but it is spreading.' A tombstone is raised in a misty landscape worthy of a Hammer horror film. The carving has one word, 'AIDS'. 'So protect yourself and read this leaflet when it arrives. If you ignore AIDS it could be the death of you.' The tombstone falls back and a bunch of lilies falls beside the leaflet.[1] This public information advertisement ran on all television channels in December 1986 and marked the beginning of the government's AIDS-awareness campaign on television and radio.

'It is hard to overstate the overwhelming and extraordinary effect of HIV and AIDS on the NHS in the 1980s,' states the official history of the health service (Palmer 2008). The NHS was at the centre of a calamity which, apparently, threatened the whole of society and radically challenged the concept of 'the public'. Apocalyptic imagery abounded; no metaphor seemed too extreme. Suddenly, in the mid-1980s, the narrative we have been tracing – in which a drive towards privatisation and marketisation was forcing a reassessment of the meaning of public

---

[1] To be found on the website of the AIDS charity Avert at http://www.avert.org/AIDS-history87–92.htm.

service – was disrupted by a completely different scenario in which service to the public was both urgent and necessary. With the coming of the AIDS crisis, for a brief moment between 1985 and 1988, there were new parameters to the debate, increased pressures on the NHS and changed conditions of possibility for broadcasters.

However, despite intense disputes and differences of opinion between policymakers, broadcasters, health professionals and educators, the dominant view of 'the public' which emerged showed little recognition of the diversity and multiplicity which had brought so many changes at the beginning of the decade. The appeal to unity itself legitimated a backlash against a more differentiated view. Divisions between an imaginary 'public' at large and significant minorities, in particular male homosexuals, were exacerbated. Especially in parts of the popular press, prejudices were unleashed.

The arrival of AIDS

When the Acquired Immuno-Deficiency Syndrome (AIDS) was identified in the early 1980s, it seemed that this was a disease confined to the homosexual population. First occurring among the partying and high-living gay communities in California and New York City, this strange wasting illness, in which sufferers lost the ability to resist infections and ultimately died, was originally described as GRID, Gay Related Immune Deficiency. By 1982, the name had changed to AIDS and cases were beginning to be reported in the UK, including among haemophiliacs, who had received transfusions from infected blood. In the imagery and the discourse, the possibility of infection by blood and other fluids would join the dread of infection through sexual activity.

A fear of venereal diseases (VD), in which infections passed from person to person through sexual contact, was not new. VD had been seen as a dreadful punishment for promiscuity and as evidence of the polluted and pariah status of prostitutes, seen as the carriers of disease. Together with homosexuals, they had been subject to legislation, regulation and social exclusion. But, partly drawing on the writings of philosopher and historian of sexuality, Michel Foucault, feminist and gay historians had been revisiting the moral purity movements of the 19th and early 20th centuries, and re-evaluating the sexual economy in relation to gender inequalities and women's subordination (Weeks 1981; Coote and Campbell 1982). This body of work, together with a more complex understanding of sexuality itself in all its forms, had developed alongside activist campaigns by feminists and gay organisations. It had contributed to the changes in attitude and behaviour which the right-wing press was pleased to condemn as part of 'the permissive society'. As news about AIDS began to arrive from the USA, originally through the gay press, there was a new attention to sexually transmitted diseases and a similar search for blame. While Margaret Thatcher's government was balancing its libertarian drive with its moral message, stigmatisation was renewed. 'That old scourge of the sexually promiscuous – VD – is hitting back at the permissive society with a vengeance,' wrote *The Sunday Times*. This was 'revenge on the swinging 60s'. Here was an opportunity to renew the moral campaign for monogamy and family values (5 December 1982) (quoted by Mort and Bland 1984:147).

Gay plague

In 1983, HIV (Human Immuno-deficiency Virus) was identified as the virus whose transmission was responsible for the syndrome. As increasing numbers of homosexual men became affected, headlines on both sides of the Atlantic evoked a 'gay plague': 'Spread of the Gay Plague' declared the *Mail on Sunday* (1 May 1983); 'Alert over "Gay Plague"' added the *Daily Mirror* (2 May 1983); while the *Daily Telegraph* announced ' "Gay Plague" May Lead to Blood Ban on Homosexuals' (2 May 1983).

In response to the crisis, charities and support groups were set up among the gay community. The Terence Higgins Trust (THT), named after one of the first to die of AIDS in the UK, was founded in 1983 and became a vocal advocate for gay interests in the media. But its spokesman Nick Partridge explained that many were reluctant to come forward for fear of being targeted. The paradox was that discussing discrimination may lead to more discrimination (Glasgow 1998:126). When a *TVEye* programme explored its effect on two gay men living with AIDS, one was unwilling for his face to be shown ('AIDS: The victims' 28 February 1985). A nurse in a later programme described how some of her patients had had their houses wrecked. It's 'a very sad reflection on society that we're so damn cruel to people when really we should be caring for them' (*This Week* 'The toughest job in medicine' 9 April 1987). And the prejudice spread to anyone connected to AIDS. 'Somebody had written "Beware of AIDS here",' said the father of an AIDS victim describing the daubings on the outside of his house. 'Our lives just changed...someone would look at you and walk away and cross the road. We used to come in and cry' (*First Tuesday* 'The fatal factor' 1 March 1988 YTV for C4).

In this case the young man who had died was a haemophiliac, and, although gays were far more likely to contract the disease, the coverage drew attention to those described as 'innocent' victims: haemophiliacs who had received infected blood and children born to infected mothers. (The 'face of AIDS' shown in ITN's *Review of the Year* 1986 was a newborn baby.) In its exhaustive analysis of the coverage, the Glasgow Media Group documented a 'de-gaying' of AIDS (1998:8, 48). This exclusion of gay men from the public debate, even concerning an issue which was literally a matter of life and death, was of great concern to the gay press and gay activists. It posed questions not only about their public visibility, but also about the nature of the 'public' addressed by the media.

Homosexual acts between consenting adults had been decriminalised in 1967, scarcely two decades previously, with the added proviso that such 'acts' should be in private. But the celebratory Gay Liberation Movement had asserted itself with an outrageous visibility. Its very public Pride marches flaunted make-up, cross-dressing and public kisses. Now *The Times* wrote with disapproval, 'conduct which, tolerable in *private* circumstances, has with the advent of "gay liberation" become advertised, even glorified as acceptable *public* conduct, even a proud badge for public men to wear' (21 November 1984 my italics). Gay activist and theorist Simon Watney took up the issue of public and private modes, and argued that the distinction was indeed challenged by a gay identity. This identity had a right to public recognition, while maintaining its difference *and* its privacy. 'In addressing "the nation" the government does not specifically address those most affected, gay men. We are not recognised as part of the "social"' (Watney 1987). Indeed, the categories of 'public' and 'private', he argued, were themselves being replaced by the government's appeal to 'the family'. But in a *Diverse Reports* programme (*AIDS Is a Four Letter Word* C4 17 September 1986), a spokesman for THT asserted the right to a gay lifestyle, which would include promiscuity. And campaigners challenged the media's language. Those with AIDS, they insisted, were not 'sufferers' or 'victims', but *people living with AIDS*.

Everyone is at risk: 'Government has got to govern'

By 1985, programmes about AIDS were beginning to sound more anxious. It was not just that 'the permissive society' was getting its come-uppance. AIDS was now perceived as launching an epidemic of gigantic proportions. 'The whole of society is an at risk group' (*Diverse Reports* C4 17 September 1986). The emaciated, hollow-eyed 'face-of-AIDS' became a recurring image, while the fear of infection and the possibility of an epidemic dominated current affairs programmes (Glasgow

1998:180). By 1986, pressure was building on the government to take action. 'We have lives to save and that overrides good taste and sensitivity...We're at war...Government has got to govern,' declared one expert (Dr John Gallwey, AIDS consultant at Oxford's Radcliffe Infirmary in *This Week* 'AIDS last chance' Part 2 30 October 1986).

When it appeared that the disease did not derive from 'immoral' lifestyles, but could be transmitted through 'normal' sex, the tone of the coverage changed. This was a major challenge to the role of government in relation to issues of health provision and public health. But the need to address a wide public about AIDS meant facing embarrassing issues of sexuality and sexual practices. Despite the more open approach of the 1960s, the broadcast media had remained cautious, and the influence of moral purity campaigners, in particular Mary Whitehouse's 'Clean Up Television Campaign', had brought something of a backlash. In 1975, when Peter Taylor had made a programme for *This Week* on sex education in schools, Thames Television had insisted on a balancing programme featuring Whitehouse herself (*Sex and the 14-year-old* 20 and 27 February 1975, Holland 2006:81–82). But now, Minister of Health Norman Fowler declared that 'public education was the only vaccine we had to hand', and, in 1986, the government set up a Cabinet committee to co-ordinate a campaign (Glasgow 1998:15). Although this was, as we have seen, a tense period in the relations between broadcasters and politicians, all the channels accepted that it should be, nevertheless, a time for co-operation. The crisis would become a major media event. The first official announcements appeared in the press in March 1986, and in December the apocalyptic imagery of tombstones, volcanoes and icebergs erupted onto the television screens. The advertisements promoted leaflets sent to every household under the slogan 'Don't die of ignorance'.

However, as the Glasgow Media Group discovered when it investigated the background to the campaign, there had been a great deal of conflict between the different organisations involved. Margaret Thatcher herself was said to have treated the subject with distaste. Many of her ministers were deeply embarrassed by the issue, and some were pushing for an overtly moral message. Responsibility for producing the advertisements and the educational material lay with the Health Education Council (HEC), which was not looked on favourably by the government. It had pursued an 'environmental' approach to health education, and had taken up the contentious issue of inequality. When its survey *The Health Divide* was due to be published, the Chair of its Council himself cancelled its press launch. (The report was eventually published in 1988, incorporating the now notorious Black Report (see Chapter 5) (Townsend and Davidson 1988).)

In 1987, the HEC was abolished and replaced with a Health Education Authority, monitored more closely by the government. Even so, there was tension between its AIDS unit, committed to putting out clear educational information, and the publicity department, which was convinced that the only successful campaign would be one which alarmed the public. The result was a great deal of confusion and imprecision. 'You can see how we ended up with icebergs and tombstones,' one researcher told the Glasgow group (p. 21). At the same time, despite the differences, the government's campaign remained committed to what the Glasgow researchers characterised as a 'liberal/medical line'. A clear decision was taken to address the public at large and to avoid a moralistic message. The focus would be on information and, above all, on protection through safe sex. Although the press continued with their mixture of homophobia and cynicism, the broadcast media followed the government's line. In December 1986, BBC's popular music channel, Radio 1, launched an AIDS education campaign, *Play Safe*, with documentaries and phone-in shows, and in early March 1987, 'AIDS week' ran across all television channels (27 February–8 March 1987). Targeted at a youthful audience, the programmes opened the door to an unprecedented frankness in the broadcast media.

AIDS week

In its 26 programmes, the move towards informality turned a week of education into a roller coaster of open discussion, exploration and an extraordinary flood of hitherto forbidden images and vocabulary. The IBA's rules on taste and decency were temporarily revised, to allow overt discussions of sexual practices and explicit language.

The week kicked off with *First AIDS*, hosted by Radio DJ Mike Smith, and featuring pop stars, doctors, comedians and an audience of 16–24-year-olds (ITV 27 February 1987). Treading a fine line between teenage flippancy and chilling warnings ('it could make the bubonic plague look like a runny nose...besides killing several members of the studio audience'), it was firmly directed at heterosexual activity. A mixture of songs, comedy sketches (Rik Mayall doesn't know what to do with a condom: Hugh Laurie and Stephen Fry swap roles as doctor and patient 'nothing to worry about – you'll only die') and discussions with the youthful audience ('Will you always use a condom?' 'Well...it's uncomfortable'), it took the 'safe sex' educational line recommended by the government ('The doctor will show you how to put on a condom...if

Mrs Whitehouse is watching, don't worry, he's going to use his fingers'). Sexual activity was taken for granted, and questions of sticking to a single partner and replacing sex with 'courtship' were presented as pragmatic, rather than moral choices. There was a general consensus that the onus was on the girls to carry the condom and to insist on its use. Boys were definitely let off the hook: 'men can't be relied on...there's this substance called testosterone' declared a psychosexual expert. There was no discussion of living with the illness, and no mention of homosexuality.

Condoms were all over the television screens. And the aim was to overcome embarrassment. An advertisement made the point. It featured an awkward young man, who, after deep breaths and several false starts, plucked up courage to whisper to the shop assistant. Unfazed, she yelled to an invisible colleague, 'how much are these condoms?' A decade before, the image of a teacher dangling a condom in front of a class of 14-year-olds had provoked outrage in the popular press (Holland 2006:81–82). Now they were passed from hand to hand, stretched, blown up into balloons, pulled on over fingers and bananas. The lesson was that condoms will protect you – not only from unwanted pregnancy (a risk that was hardly mentioned), but also from the deadly virus.

John Fairley, who co-ordinated the input on behalf of ITV said later, 'we became sort of evangelists for condoms...I, rather overall, regret it' (*Network* BBC2 23 January 1988). More seriously, perhaps, there were concerns about the wisdom of television appearing to be a government mouthpiece and a fear that this could be seen as a precedent (Glasgow 1998:95). Nevertheless, the question of AIDS threw overboard decades of restraint and moralising on the airwaves, and the change in iconography and language effectively undermined the 'moral purity' strand in Thatcherite values.

Programmes in AIDS Week included a drama from ITV, and numerous chat shows and audience-participation shows. The BBC's morning phone-in programme *Open Air* moved to a late-night slot with a series of special editions. It was broadcast live which, as the Glasgow study pointed out, created space for callers to indulge in the victim-blaming, which was largely avoided in the output (p. 97). However, the last edition dealt with the experience of living with AIDS (BBC 5 March 1987), and callers with the disease reported prejudice and discrimination, including from those who were supposed to care for them. 'You're treated like an alien,' said a caller from Cornwall. Especially outside London, it seemed that hospital staff were deeply unsure of correct procedures. 'I was in an isolation room: some nurses wouldn't come in to the room: my sheets were incinerated: the lab wouldn't handle my blood.' Apart from the specialist doctor, the panellists all had experience of supporting those with AIDS and, unlike the stark confrontation with death presented in *First AIDS* they were much more positive about the future. Terry Madeley, a panellist with AIDS, did not have the expected haggard look and was determined not to die. This was an insight into a completely different world from that predicted to Mike Smith's teenage audience.

On radio, LBC had been one of the first ILR stations to discuss the disease during its *Nightline* phone-ins.[2] In this late-night slot, medical experts and counsellors responded to listeners' concerns, and, as the months went by, researcher Emma Wray has noted a significant change in the language and tone of both broadcasters and callers; from shy and conservative to graphic and frank. Just as the proprietors of independent radio stations were fighting for less programme regulation, that very regulation and its requirement to provide speech programming meant that ILR was able to play an important role. The network became part of the awareness campaign and both LBC and Capital Radio made programmes which were distributed to all stations (Wray 2010).

Three phases: Challenge to the NHS

The media coverage of the AIDS crisis moved through three phases (Glasgow 1998). First, the early 1980s, the time of the 'gay plague'; second, the major government campaign of 1986–1987, when the general population was seen to be at risk; and third, a gradual decline in coverage, with the view that the epidemic was, after all, mostly confined to gay men. In 1989, there was a great deal of concern when Lord Kilbracken wrote an article denying that AIDS was ever heterosexually transmitted (November 1989). The special Cabinet committee was disbanded.

At the height of the coverage, between 1986 and 1988, the focus was almost entirely on heterosexual transmission. Predictions were on an apocalyptic scale. A *This Week* programme described it as 'a twentieth century Black Death' (23 October 1986). In *Diverse Reports*, expert contributors imagined an existential threat: 'Society itself may not survive if 60% of the population is infected' (Dr Willie Harris, Consultant venerologist, St Mary's London). At the time, there were only 500 cases of AIDS in the UK, but 2,500 individuals were HIV positive and the government

---

[2] A commercial radio sound archive is available for academic users from the British Universities Film and Video Council (BUFVC) at http://www.bufvc.ac.uk/.

estimated there were 40,000 carriers. A survey of *Diverse*'s own office showed that 27 respondents had had, between them, 63 sexual partners in the previous year. Extrapolate from that (17 September 1986). The language of war and battle was common. 'The worldwide war against AIDS has moved to a new battleground' (*Panorama* 'AIDS: The Fight for Control' 29 June 1987).

The anticipated epidemic brought a major challenge to the NHS. Since it was necessary to assume that an entire population was at risk, hospitals had to gear themselves up for a huge influx of patients. 'Like a field hospital being prepared before battle', was how reporter Margaret Jay described the Radcliffe Infirmary Oxford in October 1986 ('AIDS – The Last Chance' 23 and 30 October 1986). And, a few months later, *This Week* filmed for 10 days in the first special AIDS unit in Britain, at the Middlesex Hospital London, before it was opened by the Princess of Wales ('The toughest job in medicine' 9 April 1987). 'Such wards are a burden on an already stretched health service.' Case loads were climbing; there needed to be extra care in operating theatres and the mortuary was too antiquated to use for post-mortems. The workload had quadrupled because of the advertising campaign, exactly as the health authority 'suffered savage cuts'. In the all-important hospital laboratory, cuts in the budget had brought about a reduction in staff (similar to a situation envisaged in *Tishoo*, one of the last of the *Play for Today* series in 1982). Since the publicity campaign started, there had been more than 1,000 requests for AIDS tests. Dealing with AIDS was 'the toughest job in medicine'. Reporter Margaret Jay was daughter of Labour Prime Minister James Callaghan and recently divorced from economist Peter Jay. She fronted a number of programmes about AIDS, and that same year (1987) became the founding director of the National AIDS Trust, the charity set up by the DHSS.

Although the warning that 'we are all at risk' was regularly repeated in these programmes, reservations had begun to appear. Immunologist Professor Anthony Pinching pointed out, 'it's not a very infectious disease. In fact it's quite hard to pass on' (*TVEye* 28 February 1985). And the government's Chief Medical Officer Sir Donald Acheson put out a press release: 'It is important to put the risks of the spread of the AIDS virus into perspective ... apart from high-risk groups ... there's little indication of heterosexual spread' (*This Week* 30 October 1986).

Yet, the fear remained, reflected in dramas, such as the episode in the American series *Midnight Caller* in which a man with AIDS deliberately infects numerous unsuspecting partners (Glasgow 1998:109). Just

like the prostitutes of the 19th century, the 'victim' began to be seen as
the aggressor (Mort and Bland 1984). An audience poll reflected public attitudes: 31% thought carriers should be isolated; 72% thought
they should be confined to special hospitals; 75% thought it should be
illegal to have sex if you're infected; and 46% wanted laws to restrict
homosexual behaviour (*Open Air Special: AIDS the Facts* BBC2 5 March
1987).

II Dissent

Dissent

Constrained by the requirement for impartiality, broadcast news and
current affairs largely accepted the 'liberal/medical' consensus which
had been backed by government policy, and were careful to avoid the
moralism which continued in parts of the popular press. Those voices
which broke through on the audience-participation shows and phone-
ins tended to be seen as marginal. However, some programmes broke
with the consensus. On Channel Four, *Diverse Reports* had a brief to
reject neutrality and balance, and to express unorthodox viewpoints.
Its *AIDS Is a Four Letter Word* (17 September 1986) was a clear presentation of a moral approach. The programme traced the transition from a
'gay' problem to a general one, and laid out its recommendations. The
only solution was monogamy. Reporter Christine Chapman pointed out
that the derogatory term 'promiscuity' had been avoided in the official
publicity, despite the fact that 'the more sexual partners you have the
more at risk you are', and she challenged Chief Medical Officer Acheson:
'Why are you refusing to promote monogamy?' The programme ended
by creating its own advertisement. An assortment of individuals was
lined up: old and young, men and women, formally and informally
dressed. 'Who would you choose?' demanded a sonorous voice. 'You
can't tell by choosing. AIDS can choose *you*.' The slogan was: 'AIDS.
Make it monogamy.'

Programmes on both television and radio tended to highlight practical and experiential concerns: the fear of an epidemic; the search for a
cure; the lives and experience of sufferers; and the groups who were considered to be at risk. Some looked at the problems posed for the NHS, but
few considered the science, and especially the politics of science, which
underlay first the search for the cause, and then the search for treatment. The Glasgow study noted that science series, including the BBC's
Horizon, tended to focus on 'hard' laboratory science. 'The story of the

scientific response to AIDS was presented as a straightforward matter of scientific progression which reasonable sounding theories are tested and then abandoned if falsified' (pp. 105–106). Once HIV had been identified, even fewer dared question the orthodoxy that the deadly syndrome was brought about by this particular virus. An exception was Joan Shenton and her team at Meditel.

Since the beginning of the decade, Meditel had been asking difficult questions about the pharmaceutical industry and many aspects of commercialised medicine, probing political and financial interests behind health care. Now, together with director Jad Adams and advisers including a number of gay men, Shenton persuaded David Lloyd, Commissioning Editor for Channel Four's main current affairs series *Dispatches*, to commission a programme exploring alternative theories. She had to work hard to convince him. 'Visiting David at Channel 4 always reminded me of my university tutorials. There he sat with his monk-like fringe chopped across his forehead, throwing daggers of Jesuitical logic at you' (Shenton 1998:9). *Dispatches* was prepared to explore unpopular views and Lloyd gave the team some development money. It was during the research period that she and her collaborators came across an article by virologist Peter Duesberg, which demonstrated that HIV cannot kill cells. The consequent programme *AIDS, the Unheard Voices* (November 1987) argued that HIV could not cause AIDS, and that the syndrome was not, in fact, spread by sex. The dissenting voices in the programme included a number of immunologists, some gay activists and Duesberg himself who stated: 'AIDS is a whole bag of old diseases under a new name' (Shenton 1998:15). It was the third programme in Channel Four's new current affairs series *Dispatches*.

The programme was ignored by the medical press, but won a Royal Television Society award for journalism. It was vigorously attacked, not least by the gay community. 'I entered the AIDS debate with a certain journalistic campaigning innocence and zeal. Gradually I began to realise that the wall of opposition was unbreachable...the harder I tried the more sceptical and unbelieving anyone in a position to commission our work became,' wrote Joan Shenton (p. 3).

The project developed into a long-running campaign, backed by considerable scientific and medical arguments. 'Little by little the enormity of the AIDS cover-up would envelop us. The more we delved, the more we discovered the darker side of some of the world's scientists, and the ruthlessness and dishonesty that can surround "high science".' The group became activists, writing letters to newspapers and to MPs, and mounting a protest outside the Medical Research Council. Director Jad

Adams followed the programme with a book, *AIDS: the HIV Myth* (1989), which was well reviewed in both *The Lancet* and *Nature*.

Despite the opposition, this first programme gave rise to a number of follow-ups on Sky and an American PBS channel, as well as Channel Four. In a second *Dispatches*, Shenton blamed the pharmaceutical companies for promoting a drug, AZT, which it was argued, damaged the immune systems of patients and effectively caused rather than prevented deaths (*The AIDS Catch* June 1990). And she blamed the rival scientists who had identified the HIV retrovirus, and had subsequently become millionaires through patenting test kits (p. 47). But her scepticism came at a price. She wrote in the preface to her book,

> what I have learned [is that]...today science can be bought, and the individual dissenting voice is able to be silenced and dismissed because of the enormous sums of money involved protecting a prevailing hypothesis, however flawed it may be. Politics, power and money dominate the research field.
>
> (p. xxiii)

However, what she described as 'plague terror' continued to grip the country in the late 1980s, and to have a serious effect on the NHS.

And then.....

The Terence Higgins Trust felt it had been successful in ensuring that broadcast debates on AIDS were 'three-way'. Instead of just an interviewer and a doctor: 'we've always managed to make that a three-way debate with...somebody affected in some way or other by HIV' (Glasgow 1998:143). It had also achieved a franker discussion of sex on television, on programmes like *Open Air*: and 'Tony talking about masturbation on *Woman's Hour*.' But Nick Partridge felt the openness of 1987 had been a blip 'which has now been screwed down tight'.

Margaret Thatcher herself gave an interview to *Woman's Own* in which she insisted that 'there's no such thing as society'. And in 1988, Section 28 of the Local Government Act forbad the 'promotion' of homosexuality by local authorities.

The AIDS panic had forced a reassessment of the nature of 'the public' in relation to both health and broadcasting. On the one hand it meant a recognition of the gay community as a significant minority – evidence of the diversity that many critics of a universal public service had noted. On the other hand, the prominence given to fears that the entire population was at risk meant that the needs of that minority were not fully recognised, and even opened a space for discrimination and prejudice. Despite the wider range of subjects and approaches made possible by Channel Four, across the broadcast output the focus was on pressures towards popular consumerism rather than the needs of a differentiated public. It is to that move towards popular programming that we now turn.

Chronology and Programmes: 1986–1990

1986 6 September *Casualty* begins on BBC1. It would become the longest-running emergency medical drama series in the world.

9 October 'Nurses – Condition Critical' *This Week* Thames/ITV.

27 October Big Bang in the City: deregulation in the financial services market.

16 November *The Singing Detective*. BBC1 six-part series by Dennis Potter on the hallucinatory consciousness of a hospitalised crime writer.

11 December 1986 and 8 January 1987 'Who Lives, Who Dies?' *This Week* Thames/ITV 'The National Health Service is now stretched to a breaking point'.

1987 January Marmaduke Hussey becomes Chair of BBC's Board of Governors, Michael Checkland becomes Director General and John Birt Deputy Director General.

25 February **Choices and Opportunities** Green Paper on radio. Public service obligations are loosened for commercial radio, mergers are permitted.

March *Analysis* series on 'The Thatcher effect' BBC Radio 4.

7 April 'Nursing' *File on Four* BBC Radio 4: 'qualified staff are leaving the NHS in droves'.

1 June Broadcasting hours extended. *Jimmy's* ITV/Yorkshire. Docusoap based in St James's University Hospital, Leeds is commissioned to fill a daytime slot.

11 June **General Election**. Margaret Thatcher becomes Prime Minister for a third term. The NHS is an election issue.

Election Spitting Image 'Tomorrow belongs to us' Central/ITV.

13 September *The New Statesman* Yorkshire/ITV. Comedy drama series featuring Alan B'stard, a thoroughly amoral Conservative MP.

23 September Margaret Thatcher gives her 'No such thing as society' interview to *Woman's Own*.

20 December 'Rethinking the NHS: the end of a free service?' *Weekend World* LWT/ITV.

1988 3 January *See for Yourself* BBC1. The BBC's Director General and Chair of Governors present their case to the public. Followed by an *Open Air Special*.

15 January *This Morning* ITV. Richard and Judy's chat show begins, featuring celebrities, show biz and lifestyle items.

28 January 'Right Wing Medicine' *This Week* Thames/ITV. A report from the USA on the free-market models that are finding favour with Mrs Thatcher.

Kenneth Clarke becomes Health Secretary and pursues a policy of 'money following the patient' internal market.

500 NHS Trusts formed. Government initiates a review of the Health Service.

1 February 'The NHS: a terminal case?' *Panorama* BBC1. 'Is its disease so serious that the only remedy is dismemberment and a vastly boosted private sector?'

May *Kentucky Fried Medicine* Vanson-Wardle for C4. Three hard-hitting programmes comparing the US health system with the NHS.

June *A Very British Coup* C4. Political drama series on spin doctoring and conspiracy under a projected Labour government.

October The total number of hospital beds has fallen by 21% since 1977.

7 November. **White Paper on Broadcasting.** *Broadcasting in the 1990s: Competition, Choice and Quality* published. Recommends an 'auction' for ITV franchises.

Campaign for Quality Television set up.

11 December Astra satellite launched from Luxembourg to transmit 16 channels.

1989   February **Sky Television** launched, with four channels on the Astra satellite. The company loses £2 million per week in its first year.

The IBA relaxes rules on sponsorship (of weather forecasts, arts and instructional programmes).

Quality in Television: Programmes, Programme Makers, Systems published by the Broadcasting Research Unit.

Capital City Thames/ITV. Drama series about traders in a City merchant bank.

White Paper on Health Service *Working for Patients* published. Proposes the creation of an 'internal market'; hospitals should be self-governing.

13 March 'NHS PLC? What's in it for patients?' *Panorama* BBC1.

13 June 'Opting Out' *File on Four* BBC Radio 4. 'To introduce a competitive challenge into the NHS as a spur to efficiency, diversity and choice.'

1 July *After Dark* Open Media for C4. An edition on health issues from the series in which an open-ended discussion lasts into the night.

28 August *Stitching Up the NHS* Vanson-Wardle for C4.

Structural Transformation of the Public Sphere by Jurgen Habermas translated into English.

Surgical Spirit Granada/ITV (1989–1995). Comedy set in a busy hospital. A female surgeon deals with the old boy network.

A six-month ambulance workers' strike (1989–1990).

1990   2 March 'The Battle for Guy's' *The London Programme* LWT/ITV.

Investigation into plans for Guy's Hospital to 'opt out' and become a trust.

29 March 'What's Up Doc?' *This Week* Thames/ITV.

A major London teaching hospital is shutting down for six weeks to save money.

29 April **British Satellite Broadcasting** (BSB) launches on the Marcopolo satellite.

15 May-19 June *The Television Village* Granada for C4.

6 September *Jimmy's* Yorkshire/ITV. Hospital managers discuss the pros and cons of becoming a trust.

November **Broadcasting Act 1990** establishes competitive tendering for ITV franchises. Sets up an Independent Television Commission (ITC), a Radio Authority and a Cable Authority in place of the Independent Broadcasting Authority (IBA).

November BSB 'merges' with Sky to create **BSkyB**.

National Health Service and Community Care Act initiates an 'internal market' with a purchaser/provider split.

The Question of Quality published by the BFI.

22 November **Margaret Thatcher resigns**.

13 December 'Poor Kids' *This Week* Thames/ITV. On the link between illness and poverty.

10
Who's the Casualty? Popular Programmes

I Casualty: Generic possibilities[1]

Who's the casualty?

'In 1948 a dream was born: a National Health Service. In 1985 the dream is in tatters.' This was how Paul Unwin and Jeremy Brock began their proposal to the BBC for a hospital series based in an accident and emergency department. They pitched a document which 'read like a manifesto' (Kingsley 1993:4).

Casualty began its angry first season on 6 September 1986, and would eventually become the longest-running medical drama in the world. Controversy over the NHS was high on the public agenda, and *Casualty*, especially in its first three series, left no doubt that those who worked within it were unhappy with the way things were going. The pressures on the fictional characters who worked the night shift at Holby General A&E echoed those which were explored in the factual programmes of the late 1980s.

The commissioning of *Casualty* reflected in a striking way the confluence of the multiple strands we have been tracing throughout this book. A BBC under pressure commissioned a series whose main topic was the pressures on the NHS, at a time when the public service commitment of both services was being challenged. Both were being forced to cut back in favour of private provision and commerce, and it was argued that both should be subjected to the disciplines of the market.

---

[1] The section on *Casualty* draws on research carried out by Sherryl Wilson. Her interviews are indicated by (SW). She has expanded on her work in 'Dramatising Health Care in the Age of Thatcher' *Critical Studies in Television* 7(1) Spring 2012, pp. 13–28.

Money should be a discipline and an incentive. ('The payment of cash would focus the minds of both consumers and providers and make them more consumer oriented,' explained a *Panorama* reporter (1 February 1988).) In 1986, the implementation of the Griffiths Report was bringing considerable instability to the NHS, just as it was dealing with the extra pressures brought by the AIDS crisis. Its future would be a key issue at the Conservative Party's Annual Conference. As for the BBC, its confidence was undermined. The newly published Peacock Report contained a serious challenge to its very survival, and the government was publicly attacking the Corporation over its drama output as well as its news coverage. Unwin and Brock were part of a committed opposition which continued to critique the changes and sought to keep alive a democratised version of public service. 'We were passionate and left wing and both of us had recently been in hospital so we knew what stories there were to tell and how we wanted to tell them,' Paul Unwin told the *Radio Times* on the 25th anniversary (3–9 September 2011). *Casualty* reflected the BBC's need to develop new popular formats. It expanded what we have described as the 'generic possibilities' of the broadcast output. By working within the accessible genre of popular drama, it engaged with topical issues in a different way and for a wider audience than the more demanding dramas and factual programmes. In its first season, its very energy derived from its critical edge. And it, too, antagonised the government.

The series was commissioned to boost the ratings of BBC1 in peak viewing time on Friday and Saturday evenings which, during 1984–1985, had been in decline. Competition between channels was fierce and viewing figures for programming scheduled in the same slot on ITV were eclipsing those of the BBC. Historically, the BBC had screened drama in these slots, aiming to provide 'quality' programming and to stand as a point of difference with ITV's quiz and game shows. A part of this competitive thrust had resulted in the BBC developing *EastEnders* (1985–), designed to be gritty and 'bad tempered', according to Jonathan Powell, Head of Drama at the time (SW 19 May 2009). *EastEnders* aimed to rival ITV's long-running *Coronation Street* (Granada/ITV 1960) and, with its multiple, interweaving stories and varied cast of characters, it provided a template for *Casualty*. The 'flexi-narrative' approach developed by the soap-opera genre, with its fast editing and short dramatic sequences, was being taken up by a number of highly popular, fast-paced 'workplace' series from the USA, including the medical drama *St Elsewhere* (MTM, 1982–1988). 'We were obsessed with *Hill Street Blues* (another MTM series) and the idea of using multiple interweaving stories,' said Paul Unwin (NFT 2011).[2] The format meant that some stories could be resolved within a single episode while others continued across several episodes (Nelson 1997; Feuer et al. 1984).

On BBC1, when the police series *Juliet Bravo* (1980–1985) ended, Jonathan Powell believed that a new medical drama would plug the gap and approached Jeremy Brock, then a script editor at the BBC. At first he was unsure whether the accident and emergency setting which Brock suggested would really generate the stories necessary for an ongoing series. After all, patients don't spend much time in A&E, so where's the continuity between episodes? As well as this urban drama with its political edge, he also considered a proposal for a series based in a comfortable cottage hospital in a rural setting. He put both to Controller of BBC1, Michael Grade, who told him, 'trust your own judgement. I'll leave it to you'. Powell decided to take a risk with *Casualty* and appointed the experienced producer of *Juliet Bravo* Geraint Morris (SW 19 May 2009).

Casualty was based in the fictional city of Holby – easily recognised as Bristol, since the first episode featured a striking yellow car driven across the landmark suspension bridge. Its driver was Charlie Fairhead, the actor Derek Thompson, who would remain with the series for the next quarter of a century and is still on the wards at the time of writing. In 1986, Charlie was Charge Nurse on the night shift at Holby A&E. Cuts to the NHS meant that the shift was threatened with closure, and, despite his diffidence and calmness under pressure, Charlie was the young firebrand whose vocal opposition carried the writers' radical message. 'When we were researching it there was a rash of stuff about the NHS in the press…the NHS was beginning to explode through lack of resources. So we reflected all that assiduously and it was very exciting,' the Executive Producer later told Georgina Born (Born 2004:331).

As its long life continued into the 1990s and 2000s, *Casualty* moved closer to the well-established conventions of popular drama, highlighting personal relationships among the team and seeking out ever more dramatic plot lines. But the first series was more radical both in its politics and its dramatic register, which moved from pure comedy (Kuba, the Polish porter, was played for laughs, as was the superbly arrogant upper-class surgeon who descended to A&E with great reluctance) to moments of deep poignancy. It was held together by its overt political comment and its underlying medical realism.

---

[2] Quotations are taken from the programme notes and a presentation by Paul Unwin, Jeremy Brock and Peter Salt at the National Film Theatre season *The Nation's Health*. BFI Southbank 12 May 2011.

The team had visited Bristol Royal Infirmary to observe its A&E department, where Peter Salt was a Staff Nurse. 'During the shift [when the television team was present] the full spectrum of cases arrived,' he remembered. 'In particular I dealt with a fatal road accident involving a small boy, his attempted resuscitation and subsequently supporting his bereaved parents. I think these events had a significant impact on Jeremy, Paul and Geraint.' 'We were hampered by lack of knowledge,' said Unwin, 'and then we met Peter – he made it more like the real NHS.' Salt was invited to be the series medical consultant – and at the time of writing is still with the show. His input may have affected the unusual prominence of male nurses in the series. 'Charlie Fairhead's career basically followed my own,' he says. Peter Salt is glimpsed as the nurse in attendance in the title sequence of the first series, which evokes the experience of being rushed to A&E: an ambulance – blue lights flashing against anxious pulsating music; the faces of concerned staff – fuzzy images from the point of view of the casualty; a rush through the corridors and into an operating theatre. The agitated beat of a heart monitor superimposed, changes to jagged flashes of lightning. 'Everyone is levelled by pain,' says Jeremy Brock. 'When you smack through those doors, however much you earn, whoever you are, your need is the same as everyone else ... A casualty department is democratic.'

Under threat

In the first series of *Casualty*, the popular format was built around narratives which reflected the state of the NHS, and the hospital melodrama grew out of topical commentary. At the centre of the drama was a night shift under threat of closure. 'We've got just six months to prove ourselves,' Head of the Unit Ewart Plimmer (Bernard Gallagher) told the audience in the BBC's promotional video. The eight central characters made up a varied and sympathetic team, whose camaraderie developed with the need to present a united front against the cost-cutting management. It fell to Charlie to argue for action against cuts and privatisation, while the other characters found ways of living through and dealing with the dilemmas the writers faced them with.

Episodes dealt with issues that were paralleled by the current affairs and documentary programmes which ran across the broadcast output, producing a resonance back and forth between the highly serious factual presentations and the entertainment orientation of popular fiction. Topics included inadequate resources, work-related stress, bed shortages (a favourite), long waiting times for patients, private medicine and outsourcing. 'Crazies' (episode 8 25 October 1986) took up the issue of nurses' wages. Trish supplemented her low pay by working in a pub. When she was assaulted by a drunken customer, she decided to apply for a job in Australia. It was an issue which had been addressed in an edition of the relaunched *This Week* barely a fortnight earlier. In 'Nurses, Condition Critical' (9 October 1986), nurses spoke about the difficulty of coping on their income and viewers met a married couple, both nurses, who were reluctant to move, but had, indeed, been offered jobs in Australia.[3]

'Crazies' also explored the question of 'going private'. The husband of an elderly patient had saved up for private treatment ('What's the use of money if you haven't got your health,' he asked plaintively). But now his wife had come to Holby General following a misdiagnosis and numerous tests, which had been both costly and inappropriate. Baz, the ever-pragmatic doctor, argued with Charlie over the morality of private medicine. 'You shouldn't criticise them, they did what they thought was best,' she said. 'Am I supposed to tell people that they should *not* be frightened by NHS cuts; that the waiting lists are *not* too long?' In the previous episode, a cleaner had been found weeping by the nurses (episode 7 'Professionals'). She had been sacked then re-employed by a contract company, with a heavier workload and lower pay. In another thread, Head of the Unit Ewart misinterpreted an invitation to a plush restaurant from a glamorous business woman. But she was after a contract for her cleaning company and walked out on him when he insisted that outsourcing would break up the unit. 'The unit *works*.'

As Peter Salt points out, *Casualty* reflected the real conflict between the new breed of post-Griffiths managers and the clinical staff (DVD commentary 2006). Signalling this tension loudly, we first meet Ewart spluttering in fury having been admonished by his manager for taking equipment from other parts of the hospital:

> We're on the frontline damn it! We're under equipped . . . I started this shift because I saw a need for morale, team spirit, call it what you like. It's simple. Casualty gets more violent every night, the staff get paid a pittance and nobody thanks them because nobody wants to be there.
>
> (Episode 1 'Gas'; the original title suggested
> for the series had been *Frontline*)

---

[3] In 'Nursing', *File on Four* had depicted chaos in the NHS. 'London's struggling hospitals' are 'getting desperate'. 'The haemorrhage from the health service' means that 'qualified staff are leaving the NHS in droves' (BBC Radio 4 7 April 1986).

However, in the final episode the administrator himself appeared embarrassed and apologetic. The system is stronger than he is. Paul Unwin explains. 'The admins are under pressure, too. We tried to move away from goodies and baddies. It's too easy to make them a demon.'

Whereas *The Nation's Health* had depicted the NHS, its staff and its practices imploding under the weight of market-driven policies, the final episode of *Casualty*'s first series, 'Closure', showed the team defiant as it was announced that the night shift would, indeed, be shut down (27 December 1986). Despite saving lives, patching up broken bodies, intervening in patients' social problems, the team was to be disbanded. Charlie called for a strike but Megan was strongly opposed ('You know the RCN's code as well as I do'). Charlie was marginalised and walked out of the meeting. However, the compromise was a vociferous demonstration and overwhelming support from the rest of the hospital staff. In the final scene of the series, the sounding of a horn signalled the moment when banners demanding the night shift be saved were simultaneously dropped from hospital windows, and a boisterous crowd chanted outside the administrator's office.

Sherryl Wilson writes:

the team was willing to fight to retain its integrity, telling us that the public domain remains, embodied in the staff which perform its functions. Feedback from the Royal College of Nursing (RCN) after Season Five was that the series played 'no small part' in the recruitment drive especially for men. Peter Salt has 'interviewed countless people who went into nursing as a result of watching *Casualty*' (DVD commentary to 'Closure' 2006). Despite the onslaught of policies reshaping the NHS, this suggests that the stress experienced by the staff was mitigated by high levels of professionalism and the interpersonal relationships that developed amongst colleagues. Challenging old gender and sexual stereotypes of doctors as men and nurses as sexually available women was a part of *Casualty*'s political project, and the anti-Thatcherite shout articulated in the drama was apparently not a deterrent to aspirations towards working at the sharp end in the NHS. Whilst we see an endless catalogue of problems relating to shortages, difficult and demanding patients, threat of closure, they are mitigated by the public-service ethos the team embodies. 'The NHS... acts as a mechanism, and a symbol, of reassurance and social stability' (Langan 1998:112). In *Casualty* it is the team that provides the ultimate reassurance, the stable centre and buttress against the disruptive and corrosive elements that threaten from without.

Factual programmes, on the other hand, frequently told a story of disaffection and fragmentation.

Government attack: 'Contentious political reality'

Casualty was a dramatic hybrid. But, despite its moments of pure comedy, its conscious melodrama and its positioning as a popular format, the realism of the medical emergencies together with its naturalistic filming style, gave it a conviction which some observers interpreted as documentary reality. A debate about whether it was ethical for drama to use what were seen as documentary techniques, such as naturalistic acting and mobile cameras, had a long history, dating back at least to *The Wednesday Play* and the impact of dramas such as *Cathy Come Home* (BBC 1966). Audiences would be deceived, argued the critics, and critics included those who saw themselves under attack. 'Realism' in drama had, in itself, come to be seen as 'political', and this perception was echoed in the outrage expressed by various official bodies, including the government, as the first series of *Casualty* drew to a close.

The series drew complaints from the Casualty Surgeons Association and from the Royal College of Nursing. Brock and Unwin regretted upsetting the nurses and went to a conference of A&E nurses to make amends. 'In the end they saw we were sincere and wanted to tell us stories,' they said. The Conservative government was a different matter. Said Controller of BBC1, Michael Grade, 'the mood the Tory party are in at the moment they would find some political motive in *Bob's Full House*' (Kingsley 1993:17). In addition to criticisms of news reporting there was what Tebbit described as 'the lack of balance in the drama department' (O'Malley 1994:156). In August 1986, *The Monocled Mutineer*, a drama which claimed to tell the true story of a deserter in the First World War, was thought to be deeply unpatriotic, whereas a play which *was* patriotic, Ian Curteis's drama on the Falklands War, had *not* been transmitted. Now, just as the NHS was becoming the most sensitive issue for the upcoming general election, along came *Casualty*. This was not the licensed dissidence of Channel Four, but a *popular* drama which openly critiqued the Conservative's policy on the NHS.

'We were electrified by the vehemence of the Government's response, particularly as it was a fiction,' the Executive Producer told Georgina Born. 'We had Norman Tebbit and Edwina Currie ringing up the production office and shouting at us. They were so open!' He pointed out that Geraint Morris had produced 'loads of popular TV' such as *Juliet Bravo* 'with a terrible political bias the other way, presenting the police as nice, warm, festive people' (Born 2004:331). *The Guardian* quoted a Conservative Party spokesperson, saying: 'If you listen to *Casualty* it's like a Labour Party meeting. The general patois used throughout is so-called health service cuts' (3 October 1986; Karpf 1988:192). In *The Listener*, Paul Kerr commented on the confusion in interpreting hospital dramas as if they were documentary reports. 'Drama is biased by definition,' he wrote, what the critics really mean is that a drama like *Casualty* was 'smuggling contentious political reality on to our screens' (13 November 1986:30).

The first series of *Casualty* was not particularly successful, 'but the Tory government was so livid with the BBC Governors that, as I remember it, the reason *Casualty* had a second series was because the BBC couldn't be seen...to be being leaned on by the government' (interview with Georgina Born 2004: 331). (But, according to *Casualty*'s official historian, Hilary Kingsley, series 2 was already in production at the time of Tebbit's attack (Kingsley 1993:18)). Nevertheless, it could be argued that, despite the outrage of Norman Tebbit and of Junior Health Minister Edwina Currie, who was particularly critical of the staff being seen smoking and taking stimulants to keep them going (a step further than the 'untidy hair' criticised in *Angels* (see Chapter 3)), *Casualty* did not present a deeply radical critique. Unlike the total dissent of *The Nation's Health*, *Casualty* asserted that the current structure *could* work, and it suggested that the changes that were being introduced, as when the cleaner was sacked, made things worse. It posed the possibility of co-operation between a diverse team, including the porter and the receptionist as well as the doctors, nurses and head of unit; it displayed job satisfaction in the provision of a crucially important service; and it criticised the ways in which the positive qualities of this system were under attack. 'The team *works*,' as Ewart emphatically told the employer who was angling for business. (It was perhaps in that very cohesion and dedication that it lacked realism!) In addition, in its aim for a broad popular audience, *Casualty* could not afford to cause the viewers to distrust the service as the *Nation's Health* clearly aimed to do.

For Jonathan Powell, 'The Tebbit stuff was never serious. The public were with us. Hospitals *are* run down and underfunded. Mrs Currie may have had a point about smoking, so we cut down on that in the next series...we had truth on our side' (Kingsley 1993:17).

In the second series, the night shift was closed, but a nine-to-five A&E led to preventable deaths, so the shift was reinstated, with more layers of management. But the early politicised plot lines did not survive. In 1989, a new Producer, Peter Norris, was appointed. He told Hilary Kingsley, 'The first three series had looked at the politics of the NHS.

I cut back on that so I'd have the chance to go in harder on individual social issues; terrorism, football hooliganism, charity fundraising, racial violence, lack of understanding for mentally ill, child prostitution' (p. 25). But the political nervousness was not totally lost. In 1993, a manager was introduced who had come straight from industry, and there was a plan to close down the whole hospital (Kingsley 1993:43).

As the series developed over the years, as with earlier series like *Angels*, the focus turned to the fortunes of the staff and their personal relationships.

II Across the genres

Fiction and fact

A month after *Casualty*, the BBC launched a quite different hospital drama. *The Singing Detective* was transmitted in peak time, 8.00 p.m. on Sunday nights (BBC1 16 November–21 December 1986). The six-part series enacted the hallucinatory consciousness of a hospitalised crime writer. Author Dennis Potter himself suffered from psoriasis, a painful arthritic condition of the joints and the skin, which afflicted the protagonist, Philip Marlow, played by Michael Gambon. Here, in a rare dramatic experience, the illness itself was at the centre. In this complex drama, the interweaving mysteries of Marlow's novel, his childhood traumas and his relationship with his ex-wife are seen through the haze of attendant nurses, diagnostic doctors and the patients – some recovering, some dying – in his ward. At this level of extremity, the politics of the health service dissolve. Performing the role of 'patient', viewing the external world of the hospital through the subjective mind in a sick body, was beyond most hospital dramas.

Meanwhile, *Casualty* became an iconic reference point, and was strikingly echoed in contemporary factual programmes. The football hooliganism that producer Peter Norris introduced in the fiction, featured large when *This Week* spent a weekend in a real-life A&E department (25 May 1989). 'When Mrs. Thatcher finally retires to her home in Dulwich, if she should have an accident or suddenly be taken ill, an ambulance would take her to the Accident and Emergency department of King's College Hospital,' says the press release. The title *Casualty* was a homage to the series. And here the atmosphere was even more pressured than at the fictional Holby General, and demands on the staff from the constant inflow of patients all too real. As the day shift handed over to the night shift, dozens of patients were sitting in what appeared to be a dilapidated corridor used as a waiting room, while others were lying on trolleys shielded only by screens. The crumbling walls and peeling paint revealed more than writers of fiction would dare to show for fear of being criticised for exaggeration.

The passing hours were documented by observational filming. There was a severely injured eight-year-old, knocked down by a car as he ran across to an ice-cream van; an elderly woman waiting for transport to take her home (it arrived at 2.00 a.m.); and a man with a sprained ankle who thought he'd be seen more quickly here, rather than going to his GP. Hardly an urgent case, he was treated with immense courtesy by a doctor who had just dealt with an extreme emergency. There was tension among the staff as they waited for the dreaded moment when the pubs closed and the football crowds took to the streets. Young men came in to be repaired. Scarred heads, broken noses were all patched up by the patient staff. ('I gave him as good as I got,' declares an unrepentant fan with a serious head injury.)

In the 2000s, real-life hospital routines have become familiar to television viewers, with the intimate observation of programmes like *Junior Doctors* (BBC3 2011–2012) and *24 Hours in A&E* (which also follows the team at Kings (C4 2012)). But in 1988, despite the cinema-verité revolution of the 1960s, and the pioneering work of filmmakers like Paul Watson and Roger Graef, observational programmes on medical topics rarely made it to the screen. *This Week's* 'Casualty' departed from the more familiar, journalist-led style of current affairs. Viewers simply observed what was happening and were left, largely, to draw their own conclusions. Reporter Denis Tuohy sat with the record book and gave an account of numbers seen as the shifts progressed. 'Midnight Friday, with the register showing a near average total of 236 people seen during the last 24 hours'; 'Midnight Saturday, 235 people have been seen, 22 have been kept in hospital'; 'Midnight Sunday, 200 patients have been seen, 31 have been kept in hospital . . . three days that feed an annual flood of eighty thousand patients into the Accident and Emergency department of this one hospital.'

This Week still occupied its mandated peak-time slot on the ITV schedules, but the pressure to develop popular genres and the extension of broadcasting hours would soon bring another dimension to observational programme making. Less austere than the original, self-effacing verité style, the new 'docusoap' format would take on board the multiple narratives and entertaining characters of popular drama. The genre would have its heyday in the 1990s, but the medical environment had already provided some forerunners – following a hospital, in *Bolton Hospital* (BBC 1977), and a health centre, in *Best of Health* (Central/ITV

1982). Now, in 1987, the opening up of the schedules offered new opportunities for ITV. Producer Nick Gray describes below how he developed the long-running documentary series, *Jimmy's*, for the daytime slot. Promoted as 'the daily life of a hospital' it offered a detailed insight into the politics of an NHS in the late 1980s, as well as into the daily dramas of patients and staff.

Jimmy's: Flowing without interruption through our living room

Producer, director and deviser, Nick Gray, writes[4]

What is Jimmy's? It's the local nickname of a hospital in Leeds, actually called St. James's University Hospital. And *Jimmy's* is the name of the series we – Yorkshire Television – made there for ten years between 1987 and 1997. It had a modest beginning in the ITV Daytime schedule and grew to become a peak-time staple. At its most popular *Jimmy's* attracted audiences of ten million viewers. When in 2005, to celebrate its half-century, ITV invited viewers to vote for their Greatest Shows Ever, *Jimmy's* came in at number 36, up there between *Blind Date* and *Sunday Night at the London Palladium*. It was described as 'an emotional roller-coaster of a series'. *Jimmy's* did not have a Cilla or a Brucie. Our so-called stars were a lot of Yorkshire folk, although some of the administrators and doctors were from out of town.

The opening titles to each programme placed the hospital in an urban landscape surrounded by Victorian terraced housing and modern tower blocks. This is Harehills, a multi-cultural area of Leeds where at night the ambulances went about with a police escort. 'You don't want to go in there', a paramedic said to me one night when we were filming with them. We were outside a club where there had been a gang clash with multiple stabbings. The paramedic said: 'Upstairs, there's claret all over the walls.' Actually we made a story of it: following the surgeons and nurses as they treated the petty gangsters, with members of the opposing gangs meeting on the ward. But this is getting ahead in the story. We put a caption at the end of the titles which reads 'St. James's is the largest general hospital in Britain. What follows is what happens there...' And that's what we set out to do – cover what happened in the hospital.

---

[4] A version of this paper can be found on the research website at http://www. broadcastingnhsbook.co.uk/

The idea for the programme started in 1987, when ITV and BBC opened up daytime TV. Schools programmes were moved, and great slabs of airtime were available. Among other programmes, the BBC scheduled an Australian drama serial called *Neighbours* and ITV started *Jimmy's*. The BBC executive who bought *Neighbours* said to me recently: 'Hey, it cost £2,000 an episode and we could play it twice a day. It was a no-brainer.' *Jimmy's* cost a lot more than that and looks more like public-service broadcasting than the Australian serial. Today of course, ITV has given up on most of that. Back then, there were only four channels: and in ITV there was plenty of money about, some opportunities, some artistic freedom, but also a sense of public-service broadcasting. It was the era of *Brideshead Revisited* and that even higher achievement *Jewel In The Crown*. At Thames TV Jeremy Isaacs, responsible for the great documentary series *World At War*, scheduled an evening that included an hour about classic silent films, followed by the innovative drama series *Rock Follies*. ITV could not consider such a schedule today.

When ITV was planning the new daytime schedule, the Big Five companies – Thames, London Weekend, Granada, Central, and Yorkshire – pitched their programme ideas. Yorkshire Television, based in Leeds, had a strong documentary-making tradition and our Programme Controller offered an up-to-the-minute factual programme from an institution like a hospital which would reflect national events. He came back announcing that he had secured 26 half-hour slots over 13 weeks for this putative twice-weekly programme. I was given the task of producing and directing and we immediately set about making a different kind of programme.

We stuck with the hospital idea and selected St. James's, handily situated only a few miles away from our studios. It might have been the largest general hospital in Britain, but it wasn't the best known. It wasn't even the best known in Leeds. That was the Leeds General Infirmary where Jimmy Savile of *Jim'll Fix It* worked occasionally amid a blaze of publicity as a porter. We had several meetings with St. James's General Manager. We said that we were asking for an 'Access All Parts' agreement. No part of the hospital should be automatically out of bounds. After all, we argued, the hospital as part of the National Health Service belonged to the public: the public were entitled to see how its money was being spent. He replied that it was an argument with merit, but that his board was suspicious. At that time the main media story about the NHS was 'Health Service in Crisis'. But we both knew that for the series to work it would have to be a joint venture, and a long-term one. It was agreed that we should research, make two pilot programmes, and see how we went. We put in an Associate Producer, and two researchers (one of whom lived in the Nurse's Home for the duration of the first series) and started looking for people, stories, and issues. We were looking for good characters, representative of all strata of the hospital, and stories that would be followed over a period of time. At the beginning it was not just doctor-patient stories, but others that showed the workings of the hospital, taking the audience to places that normally they would not see. Thus we covered union matters, the privatisation of the cleaning services, as well as ethical issues about, for example, bed shortages and organ transplants. And there was plenty of material: on site each day there could be as many as 10,000 people.

We researched the project for twelve weeks before we shot the first frame of film, a prodigious amount of time which would probably not happen in TV today. What we agreed with the Hospital was a series that was going to be positive, that would 'demystify' the hospital experience for the public, that there should be instructive health messages, and that it should show some of the hospital what others in the hospital did. In the end the General Manager guaranteed full access, which meant that we could reflect all sides of a story. We had no formal agreement with the hospital (no money changed hands), and individuals could opt out (in the event, very few did). We agreed a 'Code of Conduct': we must ask everyone's consent, stop filming if anyone objected, show anyone what we filmed (we were on site every day), and screen each programme before transmission for the General Manager in case of factual error. Yorkshire Television retained editorial control.

Over the course of the next few weeks we developed our format, and what ITV Daytime got was the first evidence of a phenomenon that became known as the 'docusoap'. Because the form and structure of 'docusoaps' have now settled, it is difficult to appreciate how revolutionary *Jimmy's* was. The series was constructed like a drama serial (in the 1970s I had directed YTV's soap-opera *Emmerdale Farm*) and had four or five storylines running in each programme. It was based on 'pure' observational filming techniques. There was no reporter. There were no interviews. There was no commentary. Thus the audience had to pick up and run with the stories on the basis of character, dialogue and action, as in a drama. We knew we were inventing a new form – threading several narratives together in a single programme – and knew the risks. We filmed many differing stories and shot each programme on average over a period of three days. More recent documentary series have used a sneering narrator making fun of the contributors. No narration means not having to take an obvious attitude: but the themes are all there in the selection of stories and the editing. In house there was a lot of discussion about the form. One executive stated that without a commentary the audience would not know what was going on. We were resigned to the fact that if the audience did not catch on, the bosses would descend on us and insist on changes, or drop it. But the opposite happened. Nancy Banks-Smith wrote in *The Guardian*: '*Jimmy's* has no commentary... This was the life of St. James's Hospital, Leeds: the trivial, the terrible, and the cheerful, flowing without interruption through our living room. Very difficult to do and very beautifully done.'

As it was airing at 12 o'clock midday, *Jimmy's* didn't receive the same scrutiny from the bosses as peak-time programmes. From September 1987 it started transmitting twice a week, like the drama soap operas of the time – *Emmerdale Farm*, *EastEnders*, *Coronation Street* – but in the new ITV morning schedule. The serial started to be noticed – not just in the hospital, which was brought to a standstill for half-an-hour twice a week – but elsewhere. It was hailed as the most innovative programme on offer in the new daytime schedule. Even the Fleet Street critics reviewed it. Philip Purser in the *Daily Mail* noted that 'Reality is selected, not manipulated, to make art.'

The programme-makers for *Jimmy's* were recruited through Yorkshire Television's Documentary Department, led by John Willis. We were a unit that had worked together for at least five years, making programmes for ITV and Channel 4 including the flagship documentary series *First Tuesday*, a series whose dull title cleverly guaranteed YTV 12 slots a year (on the first Tuesday of each month!). On *First Tuesday* we were encouraged to give a voice to the under-privileged, taking the side of the victim, the oppressed (in the UK and around the world). We invariably used a human story as a narrative to examine issues. We were aware of our role in ITV's commitment to public-service broadcasting and of the opportunities offered for crusading journalism. And, with the way ITV was set up, we had many opportunities in an expanding department.

How did *Jimmy's* represent the staff and patients? How did we tell the stories? We showed the *process* of work. We followed the 'clinical continuum', of illness, diagnosis, treatment, operation, recovery, as well as the process of how the cleaners and caterers were privatised. The hospital was a microcosm of society. Watching *Jimmy's*, you learnt a little about medical matters but that wasn't the main subject of the serial; you found out a bit about how the hospital worked but that wasn't what the serial was about. The main subjects of the films were the human stories. Some of those stories did not turn out as we imagined: there were unpredictable twists and turns in the narrative. We were following a union representative when she became a patient in the hospital – she was diagnosed and treated for breast cancer. And a jolly porter we were featuring had circulatory problems in his leg. We filmed his leg amputation. He was a smoker, so we got a medical message in there. There were occasional disasters. One case we were following ended in tragedy when the patient suddenly died of an illness unrelated to his treatment. Actually, in the majority of cases, patients recovered. I believe they recovered more quickly because they were filmed. Not only did they receive better treatment from staff as the cameras were on them, but they also had the attention of the production crew and film unit who cheerily popped up all through the day, showing interest.

What does the viewer learn from this type of programme? Themes emerged: how people react in a crisis, how the hospital works. By showing how some people behave – doctors telling patients the news of their conditions or patients dealing with that news – it helps people who may face similar problems in their lives. In the best traditions of ethnographic observation filming, we became part of the hospital. We were there every day. We had our badges and our bleeps, and wore greens in operations. We had the same dedicated film crew throughout. When the programmes were shown, all medical activity stopped in all the wards so that the staff and patients could watch. And remember that after a programme was shown we needed their consent to continue filming. It was as much their programme as ours. St. James's was our hospital, Yorkshire Television was their TV station: part of the strong relationship that formed between the regional ITV companies and their viewers. We were serving the region, but also showing the region to the rest of the country.

The series *Jimmy's* recorded the mood of the workplace during a decade of change in the Health Service, including the privatisation of some of its services. It was always intended that the hospital would keep the tapes of all the programmes as a record of what happened. But during a reorganisation of the Health Service in 1999 when

Jimmy's became The Leeds Teaching Hospital, they were apparently thrown away. ITV keep the master tapes in a warehouse somewhere in Leeds. So now *Jimmy's* is a folk memory, as are other things that define the region, like Yorkshire Television, the Yorkshire Ripper, the coal industry, or the grocer's daughter from Grantham, Mrs. Thatcher.

Edwina's visit

It was November 1987. In June the Conservative government had been elected for its third term, and now St James's was visited by Edwina Currie, Junior Minister of Health. 'Her PR Department admitted that the motive of the visit was that she wanted to appear on our programme,' said Nick Gray. And the programme gave a revealing insight into Currie's own attitudes as well as the government's thinking. 'We caught her on the radio mike saying haughtily: "I can see six nurses over there, and four are overweight". And "I look at services like kitchens...we could do them cheaper".'

When she stepped outside the hospital she was met by a noisy demonstration. There were COHSE banners, Socialist Worker banners and nurses in uniform. 'We represent the people of Leeds and we want to keep our services.' (Memories of the miners' strike and the closure of the pits were raw in Yorkshire. Other viewers might well be reminded of the demonstration in *Casualty*.) The microphone captured her muttering, 'is there a back way in?' before she hurried away, surrounded by her dark-suited advisers. The press cameras went with the retreating Minister, but the *Jimmy's* cameras continued to film from the point of view of the patients and the hospital staff. 'Currie was an outsider entering the hospital, and we, and the audience, were on the inside.'

The radical political comment which so annoyed the Thatcher government had not been driven out of either the BBC or ITV by the need to develop popular formats in the second half of the 1980s. Both *Jimmy's* and *Casualty* demonstrated a commitment to a broad interpretation of public service in which entertainment had its place and where there was no rigid demarcation between 'quality' and the 'popular'. But, in 1987, the government would be elected for a third term, with an even greater commitment to monetarist economics. An increasing acceptance of privatisation and commercialisation would affect the NHS as well as broadcasting, and would characterise third-term politics. These changes to the two public services are the topics of our last two chapters.

11
The NHS and Third-Term Politics

I Third-term politics

The Big Bang and the return of inequality

'From the rock market to the stock market' proclaimed the advertisement. 'Virgin Music is going public. After the big bang how about a little pop!' And a traditional boss in a three-piece suit begins to rock and roll around his panelled office (1986).

It was autumn 1986. *Casualty* started its first series; the NHS was gearing up for an AIDS explosion; the sale of BP shares had been launched with spectacular fireworks, symphonic music and a call to 'be part of it', and October saw the 'big bang' in the city, when financial services were deregulated. The Stock Exchange was opened up to anyone who could obtain a licence, traders could make money on their own behalf, mergers and acquisitions were encouraged, banks and brokers became bigger, foreign banks bought into the City and salaries rose (Vinen 2010:182–185). As the closed, upper-class club of London's stock market was opened up, the class composition of the City began to change, making space for ambitious young men and women from grammar schools and polytechnics. It was 'the end of gentlemanly capitalism'. 'You, too can be part of it.'

But there were many who could not be 'part of it'. Over the winter of 1986–1987, both *Panorama* and *This Week* mounted two-part investigations into inequality and the NHS. Heavy industries, including coal, steel and shipbuilding had been running down over previous decades, but now the decline was rapid. 'The collapse of steel has laid waste entire communities, stricken by unexpected and devastating poverty,' ran the commentary on *This Week*'s 'Lessons from the dead' reporting from Sheffield (19 February 1987). The consequences for personal health were severe. On the Manor estate, one man in every three was on the dole; a family of four children all suffered from minor ailments. 'If you live in a poorer part of the city your life expectancy is at least five years lower than if you live in the richer suburbs. You are twice as likely to have a fatal heart attack and three times more at risk of dying from lung cancer.' Seventy primary-school children fell down 'dead' in front of the camera to make the point. Inequalities in health had widened since the Black Report (Hopkins 1991:233; Oppenheim and Lister 1996).

By 1987, with an election due, health and inequality were both high on the public agenda. 'Do you not see a nation divided by the Big Bang in the city?' Robin Day asked the Prime Minister in a pre-election *Panorama* (8 June 1987). 'Are you concerned about City salaries?' To which Margaret Margaret Thatcher replied with absolute confidence, 'The City is becoming the foremost international financial centre in the world. It *earns* for the nation.' From across the Atlantic, Gordon Gekko's celebrated catchphrase 'greed is good' entered popular mythology (*Wall Street*, 1987), but, in *Spitting Image*'s 'The Chancellor of the Exchequer talks frankly about the Big Bang': 'It's simply screwing people on a massive scale. That's certainly how they understand it in the City' (26 October 1986).

As election day approached, concerns over the NHS and the encouragement of private medicine contributed to 'Wobbly Thursday', when the Conservatives' popularity dipped dangerously (Letwin 1992:208). Mrs Thatcher had admitted that she herself used private medicine, and despite her insistence that 'no-one would accuse me of being thoughtless of other people', the image of an uncaring government was sticking. Small wonder Conservative ministers had been angry when the issues had been dramatised for a wider audience in *Casualty*.

In the event, the election brought Margaret Thatcher her third-term victory. But concern over the NHS did not go away. 'Opinion polls and the BBC assured everyone that the nation was thinking of nothing other than "the health issue",' wrote Shirley Letwin. 'Labour MPs talked of "murder" and the *Daily Mirror* described Mrs Thatcher as "cold-hearted". Prime Minister's question time was nearly monopolised by the health issue' (p. 215). Unlike the demonstrations earlier in the decade, protests were backed by doctors and other professionals. 'Trimming the fat from the NHS budget has bared the bones of NHS medicine…and launched a wave of professional anger,' wrote Steve Iliffe (1988:15). A petition signed by a 1,000 doctors and professors was handed in at Downing Street by five consultants (Marks 2008:166).

Despite the protests, the newly elected government hardened its position, and there was a more confident move towards market-based solutions. 'The "think-tank" industry and advocates of insurance systems, vouchers and health maintenance organisations' were no longer kept at arm's length (Iliffe 1988:19,44). John Moore, who shared Margaret Thatcher's approach, replaced Norman Fowler as Secretary of State. He made private health care partially tax deductible and the idea of switching to a universal health insurance scheme or introducing an internal market was publicly discussed. 'Lets make the 40th anniversary the end of the beginning' was the slogan (Iliffe 1988:19).

'Is a move towards privatisation inevitable?' David Dimbleby asked the Prime Minister. She responded, 'we are looking at all possibilities'. And, almost incidentally, she announced a government Review of the health service (*Panorama* 25 January 1988).

The year of hubris

Margaret Thatcher had 'returned from the 1987 campaign full of an almost maniacal zeal in which no sector of public life escaped her attention', wrote Andy McSmith (2011:281). The euphoria was reflected by the puppets of *Spitting Image* on election night. In a chilling parody of young Nazis in the film *Cabaret*, a fair-haired youth, filmed against a blue sky, began to sing 'Tomorrow Belongs to Me'. As the bystanders joined in the affirmation, the camera tilted to a bowler hat in one hand while, with the other, he raised his rolled umbrella in a pseudo-Nazi salute. 1988 became, in the words of Andrew Marr, the 'year of hubris', when 'the Thatcher revolution overreached itself' (Marr 2007:464). It would be the year of the Review of the NHS and the equally contentious White Paper on Broadcasting.

In factual programmes, considerable scepticism continued to be displayed about the marketisation of the public services. However, the *context* was changing. Across the broadcast output the aspirational culture was reflected in advertising, drama, consumer programmes and game shows. While programmes about the health service were documenting hospital closures and funding shortages, there was a tangible shifting of attitudes in the narratives, mannerisms and vocabulary of the surrounding material. Advertising breaks revelled in the colour-saturated multitextured and luxurious imagery inspired by the glamorous American soaps, *Dallas* and *Dynasty* (which were topping the audience figures at the time). Impeccably groomed women swished their fur coats, pursed their red lips and tossed their luxuriant hair; expensive cars gleamed and spun around impossible roads; banks and insurance companies offered enticing loans. In an ITV thriller 'a couple of city whizz kids' made *A Killing on the Exchange* (6 March–10 April 1987 LWT/ITV), while the BBC's popular drama *Howards' Way* (1985–1990) celebrated a yacht-owning, fashion-seeking lifestyle. 'It was Thatcherite Britain and we thought "let's go for it",' remembered actor Stephen Yardley, who played the flashy self-made entrepreneur who set out to make as much money as possible (*The Cult of Howards' Way* BBC4 25 February 2008). A reviewer pointed out that when terrible things happened to the characters in *Howards' Way*, this should not be interpreted as critique or retribution. It was just that cliffhangers were needed to keep the audience hooked, and hyperbole was intrinsic to the genre. In aspirational fantasy land, the worst of disasters could be followed by dramatic, if unrealistic, recuperation (Naughton 27 November 1986, *The Listener*). The series was quoted by the BBC as an antidote to what Norman Tebbit described as 'all these left-wing plays'. In *Howards' Way* 'they're all Thatcherite people doing well for themselves' (Horrie and Clarke 1994:131).

The visible lure of personal prosperity was contributing to the social realignment of the working class, which we have been tracing. This new image was more attractive than old-fashioned cloth-cap solidarity or trade-union activism. High incomes were aspired to rather than resented. As the inequality gap widened, the unemployed and those outside the new prosperity were becoming separated off, described as an 'underclass' (Field 1989; Murray 1990). By contrast, if you became part of the new aspirational world you could run your own business and claim a share in rising prosperity without changing your accent or your manners. You could, in the words of comedian Harry Enfield's track-suited builder, triumphantly shaking his wad of notes at his audience, earn 'loads o' money' and flaunt it (C4 *Friday Night Live* 1988).[1] For some it seemed as if the promises made in the 1979 Conservative election broadcast were coming true.

Meanwhile, current affairs programmes continued to document the bleaker side, investigating increasing inequality and the deep unease about changes to the NHS which ran across the class structure.

Current affairs: Salvage and entitlement – 'I thought the NHS was for everyone'

> Doctors make life and death decisions in ways that are becoming more and more arbitrary and unjust and depend more on whipping up public emotion to raise funds, than any serious assessment of how limited resources could best be used.
>
> (Professor Alan Maynard in *This Week* 'Who Lives, Who Dies?' (8 January1987))

---

[1] Clips can be accessed at BFI Screenonline through libraries, colleges and universities at http://www.screenonline.org.uk/media/stream.jsp?id=1367569.

While dramas and docusoaps, in their many different registers – from the playful avant-garde of *The Singing Detective*, through to the popular melodrama of *Casualty* and the lived reality of *Jimmy's* (which some viewers mistook for a drama) – were posing ways of *living through* social and political changes; the work of current affairs programmes was to offer ways of *thinking* through and analysing those same changes. 'Issues' may be incidental to a drama or a docusoap: viewers and listeners are left to observe and interpret in their own way. But current affairs addresses them head on. In a current affairs programme, a journalist faces the camera and engages directly with the audience. The points are explained; the arguments on both sides presented; witnesses and experts introduced; the facts laid out. Current affairs deals, above all, in political debate. Despite the strictures of John Birt (see Chapter 8), and the distinction between on-the-ground reporting and a more analytical approach (see Chapter 3), most journalists felt that it was everyday experiences, real-life examples, which got their points across. Consequently, the experience of patients – of ordinary people caught up in the system – remained the rhetorical focus of most of these programmes, generating emotional engagement while setting out to the underlying issues.

As the 40th anniversary of the service approached, the story of little Matthew Collier drew attention to the public service principles of universality and entitlement. Matthew became 'a symbol of the sickness afflicting the National Health Service' (*Panorama*). Matthew had died in January 1988 at the age of four, following a heart operation which had been postponed three times. The case had become a cause celebre, and allegedly was one of the factors which provoked the government's Review. His fate was used as a key example both in *This Week's* 'Right Wing Medicine' (20 January 1988) and *Panorama's* 'Can We Afford the Doctor?' (4 July 1988) which began with his grieving parents laying flowers on his grave. They had taken the NHS to court over the delay and the ruling had raised significant questions over entitlement to treatment. 'I thought the NHS was for everyone,' said Matthew's father, Barry. The ruling had suggested that this was not so. The court had accepted the urgency of the situation, but had refused to intervene, implying that the NHS could *not* guarantee an automatic right to treatment.

The issue of entitlement had been taken up by economist Professor Alan Maynard, interviewed in *This Week's* 'Who Lives, Who Dies?' (8 January 1987). Emotion should not influence decisions, he argued. At a time of limited resources, only a cost–benefit analysis could offer a rational measure of the quality of life. For example, expensive treatment to extend the life of terminally ill cancer patients should be given a low priority, and 'most people think being senile and a double amputee is worse than death'. A Centre for Policy Studies (CPS) pamphlet by Oliver Letwin and John Redwood, developed the approach. 'A system in which queues are the only method of rationing the amount of health care cannot eliminate waiting lists,' they argued. The solution was money. Only a 'charge for every service' would be effective. In a financially based system, entitlement could be purchased (1988:8). The inevitable questions about vulnerability and need were easily dealt with. Those who could not pay may rely on a safety net which would provide the minimum. And the myth of origin was challenged: 'In 1948 NHS patients were not meant to imagine that they (unlike those in the private sector) were entitled to receive luxury treatment. The spirit was that of wartime' (p. 6). The obvious conclusion, as reporter Jane Corbin made clear in 'Can We Afford the Doctor?', was that a two-tier health service was not only considered acceptable, but desirable. Universality, the CPS was arguing, should no longer be a basic principle.

Writing in 1988 from a left-wing perspective, Steve Iliffe also argued that the myth of origin could be misleading, and could lead to distorted priorities. It was indeed a myth, since some aspects of health provision, including dentistry, opticians and private beds in hospitals, had never been completely free. Nor had provision ever been equally available to all, since the NHS had inherited a patchwork of hospitals and services, which responded to the 'inverse care law': the best-resourced provision tended to be in the wealthier areas where it was least needed. Consequently, in the allocation of resources 'cure' had priority over 'care', and services were dominated by 'diagnosis' (by GPs) and 'salvage' (by high-tech hospitals). By the 1980s, emergency 'salvage' was available to almost everyone (in 'No Time to Lose' *This Week* had reported on hospitals specialising in trauma and the introduction of an air ambulance service, 15 October 1987) but long-term 'care' was not (Iliffe 1988:54–57).

The broadcast output shared a fascination with 'salvage'. The effects of poverty and disadvantage, evidence of the need for 'care', as documented in 'Lessons from the dead' (19 February 1987), were less prominent than more the more dramatic stories of rescue and cure. As Ewart Plimmer argued in the very first episode of *Casualty*, A&E felt it had the right to take equipment for other parts of the hospital, because 'we're on the frontline damn it!' A critique which focussed on the underfunding of such high-profile services, Iliffe argued, would not take into account the unequal distribution of resources. Because of their much higher profile, a successful campaign could mean more money going into the acute services which already took a disproportionate amount of NHS funds. The question of 'need' should be put into a broader context rather than being left to the economists and cost-efficiency experts. For him, one priority would be to control the 'medical-industrial complex' of private medicine (Iliffe 1988:49–60).

II Patients as commodities

Commercialisation and the politics of health provision

Wine is poured and glasses clink. Junior Health Minister Edwina Currie was addressing a reception given by the insurance company Private Pension Plan. 'We are determined to ensure that there are no unnecessary obstacles to your industry responding to consumer demand,' she told them (*Panorama* 'A terminal case' 1 February 1988).

It was a rare glimpse of lobbying by a company which stood to benefit from an increased involvement of commercial interests in the NHS. As we have seen, current affairs had largely focussed on the less contentious areas of patient experience and the intensity of the medical encounter. But some journalists were beginning to look more closely at the private health industry. 'The glossy commercials and brochures suggest you could be buying your way into a more comfortable, more efficient version of the NHS. But, the small print on the contracts often sets rules and limitations that come as a shock to patients brought up to expect the complete health service,' concluded Margaret Jay in *This Week*'s 'Private Health: Too High a Price?' (24 March 1988).

As the NHS marked its 40th anniversary, programmes reflected a growing nervousness about the government's Review and rumours of moves towards commercialisation. In *Panorama*, a BMA spokesperson complained that it was all 'behind closed doors. There are no terms of reference; no published papers.' Jane Corbin reported that the Review was, indeed, taking evidence from economists, private companies and key American health officials ('Can We Afford the Doctor?' 4 July 1988). American chains were already establishing hospitals in the UK and the American system of privately funded medicine had long been admired by free-market theorists. Speaking from the glittering prosperity of downtown New York, Jane Corbin declared: 'In America the consumer is king.'

While the brief of mainstream current affairs was to give equal space to spokespeople from both sides of an argument, Channel Four had licence to be more radical. A number of documentaries on the channel had looked at the American system and did not like what they saw. Joan Shenton's series *Who Cares* had compared, unfavourably, the treatment of lung disease in the UK and the USA (New York) (C4 7 May 1985). Now a three-part series set out to demonstrate without equivocation the disadvantages of the system: it amounted to *Kentucky Fried Medicine*.

Kentucky Fried Medicine

Kentucky Fried was transmitted in the *Eleventh Hour*, a late-night slot given over to experimental or challenging programmes (23, 26, 30 May 1988). But Channel Four, too, needed to be cautious about the power of commercial interests. Producers Yvette Vanson and Tony Wardle had been careful to give a right of reply to the companies they criticised, and their plan was that the final programme would feature a debate between advocates of the American system and opponents of it. Contributors included representatives of the four big American medical chains: Humana, American Medical International, Hospital Corporation of America and National Medical Enterprises, all of which were setting up hospitals in the UK. They were supported by representatives of the UK's right-wing think tanks, and their opponents included doctors, community workers and campaigners from both sides of the Atlantic. In the event, instead of concluding the three-part series, the debate was transmitted as the first programme. This may well have made less sense to viewers, since they had not seen the examples the participants discussed. However, they did see a clear exposition of the two sides of the argument, and the private health providers, who would be strongly criticised in the series, got the chance to put their case in advance.

The two subsequent programmes focussed on the experience of the less well-off members of the American population. Dr Mark Nelson, from Harlem Hospital, New York, described the situation in a publicly funded hospital: 'We are short staffed; there's a shortage of beds; nurses are overworked and underpaid; machines don't work.' Meanwhile, resources were lying idle in private hospitals, 'but they turn our poor black patients away'. He added that there's no preventative medicine in the USA. 'Half our kids haven't had basic immunisation. In Harlem there are 16 infant deaths per 1,000.'

In rural Kentucky, where there was only one hospital in a radius of 80 miles, its owners, Humana, would not allow patients to leave until their bills were paid. A shopkeeper who had signed a promissory note for his wife's caesarean could not raise the money and found that the company could now put his shop up for sale. Another patient was forced to file for bankruptcy, even though he was insured and thought his bills were paid. When a trailer park resident fell ill, his relatives called an ambulance and later found him left under a tree. Viewers were told that 250 thousand patients per year are picked up in this way then 'dumped'. The programme ended with a caption: 'Channel Four asked Humana and HCA to comment. Humana's Vice President responsible for Public Affairs replied: "Over 500,000 people are treated in our hospitals every year. No emergency treatment is ever denied for economic reasons...I co-operated in good faith and regret that the tone of the programme does not represent the true situation." '

The programme pointed out that American hospitals had huge departments for billing and administrative costs, which partly accounted for the high cost of health provision in the USA. (Administrative costs were 22% of the health budget in the USA, but only 5% in the UK.) Every charge had to be worked out and the insurance companies needed to check every item. They employed 'telephone gunners' and 'collection agencies' to reclaim unpaid bills. An insurer commented, 'If we had a service we didn't charge for we'd be moving towards a "socialist system".'

Arguments: Stigmatising the public?

The arguments for and against private medical care on the American model were woven throughout the programmes and marshalled in the debate transmitted as programme 1. They demonstrated a confluence of political ideology, economics and social behaviour, and are worth summarising here with a few selected quotes:

In favour of American-style private medicine:

Quality
'Quality is in the mind of the customer. The quality will improve when providers begin to see their users as customers'.
  Bob Graham Chief Executive BUPA

'Quality is driven by choice'.
  John Cassell Director of Marketing and Development at American
  Medical International Health Care Group

Consumer choice
'People have the right to choose how they will spend their [money]...and many will choose to spend it on health care.
  Margaret Thatcher (in a clip taken from a previous interview)

The government should 'extend to health care the same consumer choices which they enjoy elsewhere'.
  Quoted from the Conservative Political Centre

Financial incentives
'If we treat public servants the same way as we treat business executives, we will probably receive more humane and efficient health care'.
An American speaker

Cost effectiveness
'Private medicine runs a tighter operation'.
Representative of the Hospital Corporation of America

'We've helped the NHS save £100 million per year on domestic services alone. A private contractor gives better value for money'.
John Hall, Contract Cleaning and Maintenance Association

'We should not waste resources on people who can afford to go private'.
Eamonn Butler, Director of the Adam Smith Institute

'The NHS should be a safety net. When people can afford to pay for themselves they should'.
Bob Graham of BUPA

Against American-style private medicine:

'Need' rather than 'choice'
'We have to base our provision on needs not choices...I work with people who have made poor choices...'
Prof. Helen Deines, University of Louisville, Kentucky, USA

Inequality
'It just gives the better off the chance to jump the queue'.
Geoff Raynor, Health Policy and Advisory Unit

Relationship with patients
'People feel for the NHS. It's *theirs* – you expect a caring relationship. There's less waste, less duplication. Lets build on it'.

'The UK system is extraordinary value for money, driven by a sense of commitment to patients. It's an insult to say I'd work better for more money.'
Dr Paul Noone

Inefficiency
'It leads to underfunding and neglect in public hospitals'.
Dr Mark Nelson, Harlem Hospital

'The commercial sector doesn't have enough back-up: so it's unsafe – especially at night, when there may be only one doctor on duty'.
Dr Steve Iliffe, a London GP at the time

Preventative care
'Good medicine concentrates on prevention. Health is linked to housing and economic security'.
Maggie Kuhn, who founded the Grey Panthers in the USA

Patients become commodities: It stigmatises the 'public'
In an internal market 'We will be looking at people as individuals with a price on their heads rather than with a series of medical needs'.
Dr Steve Iliffe

'When you sell health care you have to look at patients as either profitable or not profitable. That's the theme in the USA'.
Dr Nelson, Harlem Hospital

'It would destroy universal access, it stigmatises the public'.
Shirley Goodwin, General Secretary, Health Visitors Association

Shirley Goodwin concluded, 'We should fight not just for the health service but for all public services, including water and housing'.

Professor Helen Deines of the University of Louisville, Kentucky, (home to the private health provider, Humana) and a long-standing campaigner on the issues of health, added: 'There's something I'd like to say to British people ... once you've done it, once you've dismantled the public sector you're not going to be able to rebuild it. That's what I'd like you to think about.'[2]

III Working for Patients?

White Paper on the NHS 1989

Partly as a response to concerns over the NHS in newspapers and the broadcast media, Margaret Thatcher separated health from social services and put Kenneth Clarke in charge of health. He supervised the White Paper which followed the health service Review. Its title *Working for Patients* (1989) echoed *Patients First* from a decade earlier, and it was greeted with equal scepticism. But the conditions were different. Not only had the rhetoric changed, but significant moves towards a greater involvement of commercial interests had already taken place. A White Paper precedes an Act of Parliament, and this one put forward measures

---

[2] In Louisville, Professor Deines went on to document how Humana diverted funds earmarked for indigent care for their own profit. Ultimately, the insurance company had to divest itself of its hospitals: http://www.churchofepiphany.com/news/2010/feb/McLaughlin (last accessed July 2012).

which would create an 'internal market'. It proposed self-governing hospital trusts which would be able to determine their own prices and negotiate individual pay settlements with their staff. Hospitals would sell their services to fund-holding GPs who could 'shop around' for the best (and most economical) deal for their patients. The NHS would be able to buy and sell services from the private sector (Letwin 1992:216). In anticipation, 500 National Health Service Trusts had already been formed. 'What we are trying to do is to introduce a competitive challenge into the NHS as a spur to efficiency, diversity and choice,' stated the NHS Chief Executive on *File on Four* ('Opting Out' BBC Radio 4 13 June 1989). The White Paper had nothing to say about the causes of poor health, nor the environmental issues to which numerous reports had drawn attention, nor to long-term conditions like asthma, diabetes or mental illness (see Chapter 5).

The proposals were formalised in the 1990 Act, which was followed by, 'a veritable explosion in the number and pay of NHS managers as every trust needed its separate accounts department, personnel department and so on. In the five years 1985–91 the cost of administering the NHS rose, after inflation had been taken into account, by 23%.' 'The number of nurses fell...and the best paid NHS managers were on six figure salaries' (McSmith 2011:290).

The GPs were vigorously opposed to the proposals. A commercial relationship would 'generate a culture of distrust' between doctor and patient, said one. 'If you could manage twenty families on your list for the same cost as a single chronically ill patient, it would be difficult to accept that patient, since they would be a financial burden on the entire practice' (*Panorama* 'NHS plc? What's in It for Patients?' 13 March 1989). This position was vocally supported at the GPs' annual conference (*This Week* 'Kill or Cure, Mr Clarke's Prescription' 27 April 1989). The BMA had spent millions on advertising and leafleting campaigns, opposing the measures, and, at the conference, angry doctors unanimously condemned the changes, arguing they would distract from their main commitment to do the best for their patients. They were particularly outraged by the requirement that they should be required to work for a minimum number of hours, should meet certain targets and that there would be a system of payment by results. 'The government have dealt with trade unions. Now they have a harder task,' was how Olivia O'Leary introduced the *This Week* programme. Secretary of State Kenneth Clarke insisted that this *is* a trade union (implying that this somehow detracted from the legitimacy of the arguments). In an interview, he repeatedly referred to GPs as 'he', and O'Leary gently reminded him that many GPs were, in fact, women, many of whom worked part-time because of childcare commitments. They would be disadvantaged by the new arrangements.

As always, commentary flowed across the broadcast genres, beyond the main news bulletins and into the local news and beyond. In a BBC arts programme about Ronnie Scott's London club, jazz devotee Clarke was placed awkwardly at a table with Labour's John Prescott. 'Closed any hospitals recently?' Prescott demanded[3]; and Channel Four gave over one of its open-ended late-night discussions *After Dark* to an edition on medical provision (1 July 1989).

Programmes in general offered very little support for the White Paper's proposals, and Yvette Vanson's polemic, *Stitching Up the NHS* (C4 28 August 1989) once more vigorously attacked the market principle. Contributors agreed that GPs' budgets and fundholding would lead to 'turning people away who might use up the budget'. Then there were hospital closures. 'I'm a Conservative but closing small hospitals is a bad thing to do,' declared Rae Festig, who was leading a campaign to keep a local hospital open in Rye. 'You can't think of people as tins of beans. They are people.' But an NHS regional manager declared: 'There are still savings to be made. In the last few years we've cut the fat off the edges of the beef, now there's the fat marbled within the meat itself. The question is, how can we get that fat out, without over-cooking the joint?' Vanson had approached Health Secretary Clarke for an interview, but, the commentary explained, 'he first demanded to see the other interviews; that his should come last; and that he should view the programme before transmission. We couldn't accept these proposals.'

Viewing the current affairs programmes of the last years of the 1980s, there is a curious sense of repetition as programme after programme detailed delayed operations, hospitals with boarded-up windows because they could not afford maintenance, surgeons unable to carry out necessary procedures, disgruntled and distressed relatives, managers closing wards and whole hospitals to save money. St Mary's Paddington would close for six weeks in the summer of 1990. When asked what the surgeons should be doing during this time, a hospital

---

[3] The clip appeared in a BBC *Omnibus* retrospective, *Ronnie Scott and All That Jazz* (30 October 2009).

manager replied, 'Anything but treating patients...they can go and play golf' (*This Week* 'What's Up Doc' 29 March 1990).

As the White Paper moved towards becoming an Act of Parliament, there was an extraordinary discrepancy in understanding between the desperate consultants –'we want to work: we don't want to play golf'– and the politicians who simply denied there was a problem. In the same programme, Kenneth Clarke asserted: 'I don't think there is a financial crisis. They treat more people than before. As we bring in our reforms, GPs will manage their own budgets, hospitals can compete. Private hospitals are looking forward to the Bill.' When the Prime Minister had appeared on *Panorama*, she declared, 'We are in an enviable position because of eight years' work, eight years' prudent finance, eight years' encouraging enterprise – so we can *increase* money for hospitals' (25 January 1988). In interviews like these, Margaret Thatcher's points were emphasised by the intensity of her visible presence. When, in response to her constant repetitions, David Dimbleby mildly suggested 'you must understand that I must move the interview on...', she responded with her most patronising smile, 'and *you* must understand that I must make the basic points'.

And finally

On BBC News, newsreader Nicholas Witchell introduced: 'A White Paper of 100 Pages. The most far-reaching proposals since 1948.' He continued: 'The idea of the White Paper is to improve services for patients. It's the concept of the internal market which should lead to improvements... waiting times should be cut... patients can choose their doctors.' In a mocking echo of that broadcast, comedian Steve Punt announced, 'The government's Health Service Review is absolutely wonderful. Some grumpy health workers disagree. Here's a report.' This was the audience-feedback series *Network*, with a commentary on television news from the neglected perspective of ancillary workers (20 March 1989).

And from 12 September 1989, once more strikers would be on the streets collecting signatures and donations, as a six-month ambulance workers' strike began. The strike 'received an amazing degree of popular backing, illustrated by the millions of pounds collected in buckets by ambulance crews. Rarely – if ever – have members of the public queued to donate money to workers involved in a dispute... At one stage, pollsters registered more than 80% backing for the ambulance staff, while five million people signed a petition in support.' 'Flashing blue lights and 999 sirens provided excellent TV pictures... The service has something of a glamorous image for outsiders,' wrote *Daily Telegraph* labour correspondent Kevin Maguire.[4]

From the early days of cinema, 'ambulance chasing' had been a documentary genre which could create excitement and suspense, while celebrating heroic rescuers. Every episode of *Casualty* began with the siren, the flashing light and the desperate rush to A&E, and these were echoed by factual programmes. 'Blue light' documentaries would become a staple of the more populist schedules of the 1990s (*Blues and Twos* (Carlton/ITV 1993–1998) innovated with the use of small, mobile cameras which could get very close to the scene of an accident). The focus was firmly on emergency and the drama of 'salvage'.

But when, in October 1989, *This Week* spent 48 hours in Sheffield, and followed both the routine of the strike and the paramedic crews as they responded to emergency calls, the crews made it clear that pay was not the only issue. Their concerns were wider. They were also questioning the direction of government policies ('A Call for Help' 5 October 1989).

Despite the strength of the opposition, in 1990, the White Paper became the National Health Service and Community Care Act. It confirmed an 'internal market', with self-managing trust hospitals (referred to as 'opted-out') and fundholding general practitioners (Leathard 2000:53). The NHS faced a major structural upheaval.

For Rudolph Klein, 'behind the stately façade, the workmen are beginning to gut the old building'. But for Shirley Letwin and the neo-liberal campaigners, the changes had fallen short of what might have been expected. David Green of the Institute of Economic Affairs accused the government of 'going native' (Klein and Green quoted by Letwin 1992:227, 225).

---

[4] From *COHSE Journal* May 1990. Kevin Maguire was writing in a personal capacity. To be found on the website at http://cohse-union.blogspot.co.uk/2008/06/ambulance-dispute-1989–1990.html (last accessed July 2012).

12

'Quality' and the Broadcasting White Paper

I Competition, choice and quality

Maximise consumer welfare? (Or 'you're going to be raped anyway')

'The entire edifice of micro-economic theory is based on the simple proposition that the goal of all economic activity is to maximise consumer welfare,' wrote the neo-liberal economist, Cento Veljanovski (1983:44), and this was the spirit in which the White Papers on Broadcasting and Health were presented to the public. *Working for Patients* promised to 'improve services to patients' while *Broadcasting in the '90s: competition, choice and quality*, stated firmly: 'The government places the viewer and listener at the centre of broadcasting policy' (Home Office 1988, para. 1.2). Viewers should be treated as 'consumers', but, as we have seen, there was more than one inflection to the meaning of 'consumer' (and even 'customer'[1]) in circulation. However:

> It is hard not to be struck by the remarkable gap between the agenda of modern consumerism – producer obligation, honest representation, quality and standards – and that of the economists whose abstract consumers are much less flesh and blood than the ones who really watch TV.
>   wrote Geoff Mulgan in a British Film Institute booklet (1990:11).

---

[1] In the *After Dark* discussion, Dr Ian McColl insisted that the only way to ensure that patients were treated with proper respect was to see them as 'customers' (C4 1 July 1989).

The demand for changes to the structure of broadcasting was not coming from viewers and listeners, but from entrepreneurs anxious to get into the market or to increase their stake. Consequently, the White Paper on Broadcasting echoed the radical tone of the Peacock Report. Similarly to that on Health, it stressed deregulation and lighter regulation. The aim to promote 'competition and efficiency' echoed through both documents (para. 10.6).

In parallel to the debate on health, an intense debate on broadcasting was conducted in the public arena: in the pages of newspapers, at public meetings and seminars, in campaigning books and pamphlets, as well as on television and radio. Once more, however, the commercial lobbying went on behind the scenes. Andrew Davidson has given a detailed account of the powerful interests who wanted access to the airwaves and their lobbying of the government, including personal contact with Margaret Thatcher (Davidson 1992:33). This time there was no equivalent to the informal alliances of producers, aspirant filmmakers and advocates of minority interests who had put their case to the Annan Committee in the 1970s. These 1980s entrepreneurs represented wealthy companies which wanted to extend their media interests. They included, for example, Carlton Communications, a company with a reputation for asset stripping, which owned video-editing firms, props hire companies and other electronic businesses but had no track record in programme production. Meanwhile, Rupert Murdoch, owner of five national newspapers, *The Times*, *The Sunday Times*, *The Sun*, *The News of the World* and *Today* was making no secret of his desire to control a television outlet, and his contempt for the very idea of public service (Murdoch 1989).

Just as *Working for Patients* aimed to restructure the very basis of the NHS, *Broadcasting in the 90s* laid down a challenge to the existing broadcasting ecology. Its aim was similar: a drive for a more competitive market, creating more spaces for commercial interests. To achieve that end it proposed that the regulator, the IBA, should be abolished and replaced with an Independent Television Commission (ITC) and a Radio Authority, both with greatly reduced regulatory powers. Aspirant commercial companies should make a financial bid for a licence to broadcast, and the franchises would automatically go to the highest bidder. Channel Four should sell its own advertising in competition, rather than collaboration, with ITV. (This, the White Paper claimed, would protect the channel from 'sterile elitism or precious self-indulgence' (para. 6.23).) And it paved the way for a fifth and possibly even a sixth commercial terrestrial television channel. Above all, the White Paper encouraged new technologies and new forms of delivery, especially satellite (Home Office 1988, Section V).

As for the BBC, the White Paper argued that, like the NHS, the Corporation should move towards forms of marketisation, because the licence fee 'insulates the BBC from its customers and from market disciplines' (paras. 3.12–3.13). Consequently, 'the government looks forward to the eventual replacement of the licence fee' (para. 3.10). The White Paper boasted about the 'double squeeze' the government had already put on the Corporation (granting a reduced licence fee and linking the fee to the retail price index (RPI)). It noted with satisfaction that this had already forced the Corporation 'to target its activities more effectively' and it praised the new management regime (para. 3.3). However, it insisted that the Corporation should go further. It should subcontract many of its activities; its transmission facilities should be privatised (para. 9.3); and its night hours should be sold off to a commercial company or used as a subscription service.

But progress from White Paper to the Broadcasting Act was not smooth. Tension continued between the Home Office and the Department of Industry, and in Parliament there was virtually unanimous opposition from both sides of the House and from both Chambers. Eight hundred amendments were put down. The areas of greatest concern included the loss of the regional nature of ITV and the danger of cross-media ownership, which would open the door to powerful proprietors, many of whom were not based in the UK. 'The Government has allowed a dangerous concentration of newspaper ownership in this country... the White Paper contains no adequate safeguards to prevent the domination of the networks by those with deep pockets and shallow concerns,' declared MP Robert Maclennan (Stevenson and Smedley 1989:15).

Meanwhile, the public consultation brought around 3,000 responses, both from insiders and ordinary viewers. The White Paper had given rise to a renewed assertion of public service principles, but these tended to be expressed as a defence of the status quo, rather than the dynamic forward projection which had characterised submissions to the Annan Committee. The British Film Institute (BFI) published a representative summary of the responses, described as 'a genuine reflection of the strength of critical opposition to the Paper'. The overwhelming view was that, far from putting the viewer at the centre, 'the viewer will be the loser' and 'choice will be reduced' (Stevenson and Smedley 1989:2, 24, 26).

Ironically, a less regulated media would become a more compliant media. 'Market disciplines' were likely to lead to 'more effectively targeted' programmes that were less troublesome to the government on all channels. Changes to the broadcasting ecology would mean changes to the conditions of possibility for programming. The more 'popular' programmes, which would result from an aim to maximise profits, would be less challenging than the uncomfortable, so-called 'public service' output, in particular, those awkward current affairs series which had been protected by the IBA. 'If ITV can become more commercial', predicted media journalist Brenda Maddox, 'it won't do programmes like *World in Action* and it will only be the BBC that can do investigative journalism.'[2] The aim was to make television more like the press, which is 'overwhelmingly controlled by supporters of the present government' declared Lord Bonham Carter in the House of Lords (13 December 1988, p.7).

Lord Annan, whose report had led to the establishment of Channel Four, summed up the attitude of the Department of Trade and Industry. 'The Secretary of State said to TV Britannia "you're going to be raped anyway, so why not lie back and enjoy it. You will have a wonderful choice of lovers"' (Stevenson and Smedley 1989:8).

A major cause for concern was a potential reduction in quality through commercialisation, and the issue of 'quality' became central to the debate.

II Mobilising 'quality'

Mobilising 'quality': A campaign and a political tool

> As viewers exercise greater choice there is no longer the same need for quality of service to be prescribed by legislation or regulatory fiat.
>
> (*Broadcasting in the 90s*, para. 6.9)

> The regulator in this case is the viewer. If they don't watch, a channel will have to close down.
>
> (Tony Currie, Controller of Programmes at the Cable Authority)[3]

'Each stage in the history of broadcasting in this country has been characterised by a debate about a word... [which has] stood in for a series of interwoven discussions held across the nation, which it has been impossible to untangle... [they are] cultural, political and social,'

---

[2] In a discussion about the banned programme *The Zircon Affair* (BBC 1988).

[3] In *The Television Village* (C4 15 May–19 June 1990).

wrote Anthony Smith (in Mulgan 1990:1). Now, as the 1980s drew to a close, within the public discourse, the broad and uncompromising concept of 'public service', whose fortunes we have been tracing, was being replaced by a more pliable point of reference. 'Quality' was a concept which could be bent to a number of different political and commercial ends. The White Paper had found no contradiction in linking 'quality' with 'competition' and 'choice' in its title. However, for a substantial proportion of the organisations, interest groups and citizens who responded to the Paper, 'quality' was precisely what would be lost in a no holds barred competitive regime 'geared primarily to maximising profits'. In particular, the projected franchise auction would inevitably 'lead to cuts in budgets' and 'a narrower, coarser ITV' (Stevenson and Smedley 1989:22–36).

The rhetoric of those advocating deregulation and commercialisation had not been overly concerned about 'quality'. Theirs was an appeal to 'freedom'. 'Roll on the government's plans to promote competition and freedom in TV' was how Rupert Murdoch's *Sun* greeted the White Paper (8 November 1988, O'Malley 1994:38). The Institute of Economic Affairs (IEA) responded with *Freedom in Broadcasting* (Veljanovski 1989). In broadcasting, just as in health, its writers argued, deregulation and a free market were exactly what the new legislation should be aiming for. The concept of 'quality' was no more than a sham, a front for regulation. In its evidence to the Peacock Committee, the Adam Smith Institute had declared:

> The 'quality' argument is elitist, as a small group decide what the majority should see. High ratings ought to be accepted as the yardstick of what people want, and should not be regarded as an object of disdain.
>
> (Peasey and Docherty 1986:30)

That judgement would be echoed by Rupert Murdoch in a speech to the 1989 Edinburgh Television Festival, which would become notorious. The battle would be political and cultural as well as commercial:

> Much of what is claimed to be quality television here is no more than the parading of the prejudices and interests of the like-minded people who currently control British television ... This public-service TV system has had in my view debilitating effects on British society, by producing a television output which is so often obsessed with class,

dominated by anti-commercial attitudes and with a tendency to hark back to the past.

(Murdoch 1989:39)

At the time, Murdoch had just sidestepped the UK regulatory regime by launching his Sky channels on a Luxembourg-based satellite (February 1989).

The White Paper gave a new impetus to a much older debate about the nature of the 'popular', a supposed opposition between 'quality' and 'popular', and the validity of cultural judgements. Since the 1970s, journals such as *Screen* had been arguing vigorously for a serious consideration of 'popular' forms, seeking to redefine 'quality' and rejecting precisely that elitism sneered at by Rupert Murdoch (Dyer 1985; McGuigan 1992). However, the debate had many facets. 'Quality' was a theoretical debating point, but it had long been a practical issue for programme makers (see Chapter 7), and now it became an important *political* tool. Following the Peacock Report, the concept was taken up by some campaigners as a last bulwark against destructive commercialisation, more easily defended than the highly contentious 'public service'. Establishing the importance of 'quality television' could combat the deregulation which could well lead to an impoverished output – a possibility echoed within the White Paper itself, which repeatedly insisted that wider choice must be achieved '*without detriment to standards and quality*' – apparently recognising the likelihood of that very outcome (para. 1.2, my italics; see also para. 4.1).

The Paper put forward its own version of 'quality' in its recommendation that ITV companies should make a financial bid for their licences. The ITC would be compelled to accept the highest bid, but only after the applicants had first passed a '*quality threshold*'. This included regional programming, 'high-quality' news and current affairs, and programmes to appeal to a variety of tastes and interests. It also included 'consumer protection', that is, offences against 'taste and decency', elsewhere in the Paper referred to as 'standards'. A minimum of 25% of programmes should be commissioned from independent producers and a 'proper proportion' should be of EC origin (paras. 6.10–6.11). 'Quality', a cultural judgement, became a 'qualification', a practical hurdle (Kerr in Mulgan 1990). Among the outraged reactions to the White Paper, the reduction of 'quality' to a mere 'threshold' was possibly seen as the most shocking. Once over the threshold, the highest bidder in the ITV auction would win out regardless. 'Why compel the ITC to accept the highest bid even if it knows, and the informed public also knows, that the highest bidder is either a crook or a shark who will do his best to evade every control and peddle trash,' demanded Lord Annan in the House of Lords (Stevenson and Smedley 1989:8).

There was intense campaigning to modify the White Paper's proposals, and the most politically effective was the Campaign for Quality Television (CQT). Originally set up by producers from Granada's *World in Action*, the Campaign placed an advertisement in the press headed 'Will Quality Television survive?' 'We will be able to make fewer high quality programmes', it stated; 'you are likely to get more junk television'. The Campaign published an open letter to the Prime Minister arguing that the proposals could lead to 'a serious reduction in the ability of British television to produce high quality drama, arts, documentaries, current affairs, religious and children's programmes...a narrowing of real choice for viewers'. 'What quality there is on ITV has stemmed from obligation rather than market forces,' they insisted (quoted by Stevenson and Smedley 1989:38). These were experienced television journalists with a great deal of political nous, and they increased their public profile by recruiting television personalities, including comic performers Rowan Atkinson, Terry Jones and Michael Palin. They lobbied David Mellor, the new Home Office Minister responsible for broadcasting, and, in the words of historian Andrew Davidson 'an extraordinary courtship between producers, performers and Minister underscored key changes in the legislation' (Davidson 1992:20).

The slipperiness of 'quality': quality and public service

> The richness and ambiguities [of the term 'quality'] should be seen as a virtue, not as a problem. A desirable broadcasting system will support a range of different and often contradictory qualities.
>
> (Mulgan 1990:7–8)

> Quality, for some good reasons, has become a bad word. The consequence of this is that only the most conservative ideas about quality are circulating.
>
> (Brunsdon 1990:67)

While the political and legislative possibilities of this key word in the conflict of ideas were being exploited, its ambivalence was debated by literary and media theorists. The Broadcasting Research Unit (BRU) and the British Film Institute both set out to explore the concept in the context of its highly charged political mobilisation. There was a considerable difference in their positions, which hinged on the legitimacy of making value judgements. This was, itself, considered suspect by those who pointed to the social and cultural context for such judgements. In *Screen*, Charlotte Brunsdon argued that it was important to take into account the 'historical and cultural privilege with which aesthetic judgement is encrusted' and to recognise that 'the value audience members... gain from particular programmes does not necessarily correlate with traditional ideas of quality' (p. 89). Perhaps in a fragmented, multifaceted society, ultimate judgements of 'quality' simply could not be made. For literary theorist Terry Eagelton, 'quality' is 'whatever is valued by certain people in specific situations according to particular criteria and in the light of given purposes' (quoted by Mulgan 1990:48). The work of French sociologist Pierre Bourdieu, who had drawn attention to the social aspects of hierarchies of taste, was increasingly influential (Garnham and Williams 1980).

By contrast, the Chair of the BRU, Richard Hoggart, whose powerful defence of public service had influenced the Pilkington Report nearly three decades earlier, stated uncompromisingly that

> though each programme will have to be judged in the first place by criteria peculiar to itself, these criteria are neither self-contained nor self-sufficient. Any kind of programme may be trivial, banal, patronising, tendentious, phoney, dishonest, evasive; such value judgements are not to be eroded by appeals to the demands of particular types of programmes and to the assumed tastes of the intended audience.
>
> (BRU 1989:1)

The Broadcasting Research Unit, which had produced its influential definition of public service broadcasting in the run-up to the Peacock Report (see Chapter 7), now compiled statements from eight prominent broadcasters, journalists and academics. Its pamphlet, *Quality in Television* (1989), considered three aspects: 'quality in broadcasting as a whole' (it 'should enhance rather than diminish the total life of the community in which broadcasting takes place' p. 4); 'quality in broadcasters' ('respectful broadcasters respect their subject matter and the content of a programme: they respect the participants in it and they respect its potential audience' p. 6) and 'quality in programme making', as well as in the programmes themselves. The grounds for judgements about specific programmes were made clear. 'In the trivialising programme the subject, whatever it is, seems to be quickly exhausted. The non-trivialising on the other hand seems to be bred of a limitless enthusiasm'

(p. 4). Contributors were not impressed by the emphasis on 'consumer sovereignty' in the White Paper, which implied nothing more than the ability to turn a programme off (p. 25). And the appeal to needs as opposed to wants was reasserted: it would be a pity if broadcasters followed 'what people think they want rather than what they will, in fact, enjoy'. 'Public-service broadcasting only has its sole raison d'etre in...that soberly stated and splendid purpose, the dissemination of education, information and entertainment; and then only if the institutional structure is truly enabling...public service broadcasting claims the support of authentic democracy' (p. 32).

The British Film Institute, a powerful force in the vigorous theoretical debates of the time, issued six booklets on 'The Broadcasting Debate', including its *Responses to the White Paper*. Geoff Mulgan, editor of No. 6 *The Question of Quality*, argued that the BRU had fallen back on 'old hierarchies of judgement', which should be questioned rather than simply accepted. He criticised the 'strongly paternal, moral, sometimes even moralistic tone [which] pervades the collection' (1990:5–6), and offered instead a broad outline of the *contexts* within which 'quality' could be assessed, ranging from producer professionalism, to the aesthetic of the medium itself, its role in ritual and communication, its place in the televisual ecology, its role in citizenship and its contribution to diversity. The real danger is 'when only one view crowds out the others' (pp. 7–8).

Meanwhile, just as the concept of 'public service' had been narrowed down in the public discourse, Paul Kerr noted that the concept of 'quality' could also become a narrower tool. It could become an attractive commodity offered to advertisers. He quoted the US trade press, 'Quality TV attracts Quality audiences'. Programmes like *Hill Street Blues* attracted an 'up-market demographic' and so were attractive to advertisers despite their relatively low audience figures (in Mulgan 1990:50). In the USA, 'quality television' had become a genre. (Kerr had been one of the authors of the BFI's monograph on the American company MTM and its self-description as 'quality television' (Feuer et al. 1984).) It seemed that relying on 'quality' as substitute for 'public service' could direct attention away from the *structures* of broadcasting.

Concluding the BFI booklet, John Ellis was pessimistic: 'Broadcasting has lost its sense of purpose,' he wrote, 'the doctrine of PSB has been discredited...Discredited a. by market arguments, b. by democratic values' (Mulgan 1990:33). He added: 'No-one has a clear idea of what should replace it.' He was wrong. The Institute of Economic Affairs, with its influence on the Peacock Committee and the government, had a very clear idea of what should replace it: it was *'choice in the multi-channel world'*. This was the subtitle of the Institute's contribution to the debate, the booklet *Freedom in Broadcasting*.

BSkyB, freedom and the age of plenty

The renewed attacks on concepts of 'the public' and 'public service' from a market perspective, to which the evocation of 'quality' had come as a response, were made as multichannel broadcasting was becoming a reality. The conditions for a 'true market' in broadcasting, envisaged by the Peacock Report, seemed just over the horizon. For neo-liberal campaigners, here was an unprecedented opportunity to throw off the old shackles and launch a new age. *Freedom in Broadcasting* was published in March 1989 and coincided with the launch of Sky Television with five channels. Sky was owned by News International, whose controlling shareholder was Rupert Murdoch.

Without extra funding to cover the costs, the BBC had withdrawn from its satellite agreement in 1986. The IBA had then awarded a contract to British Satellite Broadcasting (BSB) (a consortium of Granada, Anglia, Virgin, Amstrad and Pearson) to broadcast three channels from a new high-powered satellite. However, the huge engineering tasks involved meant that BSB was pipped to the post by Murdoch's Sky, which simply rented channel space on the Luxembourg-based medium-powered Astra satellite. Conveniently, this also meant that Sky was not subject to the cross-media ownership regulation, which would be part of the Broadcasting Act. A clause, widely referred to as the 'Murdoch loophole', exempted broadcasters not broadcasting from within the UK (Barnett 2011:115).

When BSB began transmission in April 1989, it soon became clear that it would not be able to compete with the already established Sky, especially as subscribers needed to purchase a special square aerial. 'It's smart to be square', said the ads, but the 'squarial' was incompatible with Sky's small round dish, which many viewers already had in place. In November, 'Murdoch engineered a merger with BSB on terms widely seen as a takeover' (O'Malley 1994:10). The story was that, despite existing regulations, Margaret Thatcher personally nodded it through (Goodwin 1998:50–51). BSkyB was created and the Third Age began in earnest.

The government was firmly harnessing changes in technology to changes in economic structure and changes in concepts of 'the public'. Breaking down a broad unified 'public' into individuals 'consuming' individual programmes was the desired consequence of these changes. A response to the White Paper from an advertising executive illustrated the point. 'We are trying to reach AB businessmen,' he stated. 'At the moment, even if I buy *News at 10*, I've got to buy a lot of women – a lot of housewives – and a lot of C2, D and E men. So there's a lot of wastage. Now, hopefully, with the fragmentation of the media, that wastage will reduce' (quoted by Hood and O'Leary 1990:196). Like the users of the NHS, in the new television landscape, viewers, too, would be more easily packaged as commodities.

Geoff Mulgan had written of the gap between the 'abstract consumers' evoked by economists, and the 'flesh and blood' consumers who really watch television (Mulgan 1990:11). In early 1990, Granada Television put together its contribution to the debate, involving some real, flesh-and-blood viewers. Commissioned by Channel Four, the current affairs department under Ray Fitzwalter set up an experiment to test reactions to the new age of television.

III   Waddington and the Broadcasting Act

The Television Village: Give them rubbish

Waddington, in rural Lancashire, had several times won the title of the county's 'best kept village'. Now it became 'the television village'. Satellite dishes were imported, a receiving centre established, homes were wired up, a local television channel was set up and licensed by the Cable Authority. Contacts were made across the globe, and the scope ran from the international to the very local, as volunteers got a glimpse of the future with an unprecedented 37 channels. 'They've been confronted with what the Broadcasting Bill calls "choice" and lots of it.'

Waddington was a largely middle-class haven. Conveniently, its local MP was David Waddington, who had recently taken over from Douglas Hurd as Home Secretary, and would be responsible for taking the Broadcasting Bill through Parliament. The participants were comfortably off, educated and articulate. Across the six programmes, they watched Sky Sports, CNN, Sky News, the Home Video Club (soft porn and horror), as well as Discovery and many other channels. They each kept a diary of their viewing and, as the experiment progressed, discussed their experience and their reactions. The vicar preached about television in the village church and, in the final programme, Home Secretary Waddington answered questions which covered the spectrum from children's programmes to the all-important issue of quality.

In programme 3 (29 May1990), participants were asked to assess the 'quality' of the material they were viewing. Sport was admired, the porn channel was received with some amazement ('why is it always the women who take their clothes off?'), but the villagers were mostly dismissive of their new fare. 'We've got 25 channels but the quality leaves a lot to be desired.' 'We had agreed that when we were married we'd take out a satellite subscription. But having seen this I don't think we should.' 'I was told by people who'd lived in USA and elsewhere that British television is the best in the world. I thought "no" – but having seen the cable I know what they mean.' On the whole there was approval for the BBC, and the points made were not dissimilar to those from the experts responding to the BRU; 'the BBC has an educational value: it has a variety of programmes; it's part of our lives'. 'You've got the BBC service the same as you've got the National Health Service. It's there for general use.' But when Village TV interviewed MPs from the Home Office Committee that had considered the Bill, Conservative Ken Hind reasserted that competition would bring pressure for greater quality. He was convinced that 'BBC audiences will shrink' when there were more channels.

In the most revealing episode, Home Secretary David Waddington himself faced a village hall meeting ('The shape of things to come' 19 June 1990). His attitude was largely sulky and unengaged; his only moments of animation when he expressed his distaste for the terrestrial channels. When a questioner posed the now familiar suggestion that 'quality will suffer because there will be a drop in income', and added 'the government should back the "quality" channels', his response was disdainful. 'Over the years the public have been given increasing choice. There was opposition to ITV when it was first introduced. The question assumes that the current licence holders are not in it to make money. They *are*.' And he displayed an ignorant contempt for the current system. When a questioner described the material on several of the new channels: 'these things we have seen: there's violence as well as porn', he responded, 'there's plenty of violence on BBC and ITV'. And his dislike of the BBC was thinly disguised. 'The licence fee is index linked – we've given the BBC "a bit of a squeeze": everything will change after Charter renewal in 1996.' For the questioner, 'seeing some of the junk that's been beamed down here, I think the licence fee is terrific value for money'. He got a hearty round of applause.

Throughout, the Home Secretary's manner bordered on the dismissive. It seemed that this was something he did not know much about and he was clearly not interested in taking part in a debate. To the question 'Why are we getting more channels?' he responded: 'If there's the technology and companies prepared to offer increased choice and make money out of it, we can't stop them.' And, he added, 'if people are prepared to pay for rubbish it's up to the people'. In a rare moment of engagement, he responded to a questioner worried that her son 'just gets up and turns on TV'. 'We already watch far too much. What's put out by BBC and ITV is extremely dangerous. Considering the appalling amount of rubbish they put out at the present time, they really could appreciate much more rubbish.'

The villagers shared their impressions over a cup of tea. 'It's a Conservative area round here, so I thought they'd agree with free enterprise, but they don't. The audience wanted a public service.' 'I got the impression he doesn't watch much television. He gave the impression that the British public wants rubbish so we'll give them rubbish.' And from David Waddington, balancing his teacup: 'Actually I don't have much time to watch television.'

1990 Broadcasting Act

In broadcasting as in the NHS, programmes demonstrated a striking gap between the perceptions of politicians and those of the users and creators of the services. Just as Kenneth Clarke had denied there was any problem with the NHS, so David Waddington simply swept aside concerns about broadcasting. His attitude to television echoed that of Margaret Thatcher herself: it was a corrupting medium, not respecting of 'taste and decency', biased against business and commerce, and 'the last bastion' of restrictive trade-union practices. Its cultural contribution to national life was simply irrelevant (Hood and O'Leary 1990:118–119).

However, when the Broadcasting Act was finally passed, a number of concessions had been made to its critics. Although Channel Four was to sell its own advertising, it would remain a public trust; the new Independent Television Commission would retain some positive regulatory clout and the ITV 'auction' would be more flexible (Goodwin 1998:109 et seq.). In addition, the Home Secretary announced that he would 'strengthen the quality threshold'. In 'exceptional circumstances' a higher-quality bid could override a higher monetary one. Although David Waddington told the villagers that the concessions had been considerable, in the view of many broadcasters 'this was generally seen as little more than a gesture, a form of words' (Hood and O'Leary 1990:171). And Margaret Thatcher was not pleased that the 'auction' had been watered down. She complained that the 'quality' provision

> muddies the transparency which I had hoped to achieve, and produced a compromise which turned out to be less than satisfactory

when the ITC bestowed franchises in the following year 'in the old-fashioned way'.

(quoted by O'Malley 1994:204)

And many of the fears expressed by those who responded to the White Paper proved justified. As predicted, in a climate of increased commercial competition, it became more important for channels to compete for audience numbers. Like patients in the NHS, viewers were chiefly seen as commodities to be sold to advertisers. Inevitably, this led to a more populist approach, which was condemned by many commentators as 'dumbing down'. Without support from the regulator, current affairs series on ITV all but disappeared. *This Week* came to an end when Thames Television lost out to Carlton in the 1990 'auction'. Granada's *World in Action* continued until 1998, but the climate in the company became increasingly unsympathetic. A new management brought asset stripping, mergers and severe cut-backs (Goddard et al. 2007; Fitzwalter 2008). Across the output there was less space for programming given over to debate and analysis. The conditions of possibility for critical programming had decisively changed.

> Where in the 60s and 70s discussion of broadcasting concerned itself with the ethos and responsibilities of a profession, with its modes of representation, its access and accountability, today's debate is primarily about business and competition and profitability.
>
> (Mulgan 1990:10)

Public service in broadcasting became one element, rather than the controlling principle in the broadcasting landscape.

Meanwhile, Stuart Hood, a former Controller of BBC Television, noted that 1989 was the 100th anniversary of the birth of John Reith:

> it is remarkable that (at time of writing) neither the Chair nor the DG of the BBC has created an opportunity... to speak out in defence of public service and the role it might have in a world so different from that in which Reith formulated the concept. One cannot imagine Reith remaining silent in similar circumstances.
>
> (Hood and O'Leary 1990:222)

Concluding Comments: Public Service or Kitemark?

The man in the pink suit

As Margaret Thatcher completed 10 years in power, Masden Pirie of the Adam Smith Institute celebrated her achievements:

> The last 10 years...have witnessed the end of the consensus under which...Britain had been governed since the end of World War 2...In one area after another, seemingly intractable problems have been tackled and decline has been replaced with success. The successes in the economy and other areas of national life have bred with them a culture of success, a spread of ideas that enterprise and initiative can bring results, that talent and work will be rewarded.
>
> (1989:4)

Television advertisements echoed that triumphalism. To celebrate the newly founded First Direct's telephone banking, a man in a pale pink suit sang as he danced ecstatically through the City of London, scorning its sober suits and glass towers (1990). For the *Daily Telegraph*, a working-class boy scanned the job ads and applied for 'Export Sales Director' (1990). For Norwich Union Health Care 'it's no longer a question of public health for all or private health for some...For as little as £9 per month we carry on caring no matter what!' (1993). This was the 'culture of success' which, the Adam Smith Institute claimed, had restructured the class system. The businessman's paper was now for everyone; there was easy access to the banks and their loans; ordinary people could buy better health care; top jobs were open to all. The dry language of efficiency and monetary economics was increasingly familiar in journalist-led programming, but it was in the mobilisation of narratives, imagery and emotion that the shift in attitudes and values became tangible. The whole population was invited to share the euphoria of the man in the pink suit.

Information, cultural creativity and conditions of possibility

In this book, we have been tracing the practice and the concept of public service across the Thatcherite 1980s by exploring the complex and shifting relationships between the political domain and the broadcast output. We have considered three aspects of that output: the flow of information – chiefly through current affairs and factual programmes; cultural creativity across the genres; and the institutional background which makes the programmes possible (see Introduction p. 15). Thus, we have observed how the output reflected, contested and mediated political debates, at the same time as legislation and political moves were changing their ability to do so. Moves towards deregulation, the destabilisation of the BBC and a mistrust of public service meant that spaces for investigation and contestation were increasingly challenged.

Against the background of policy developments in health and broadcasting across the decade, we have looked at a wide range of programmes and traced the interaction between the genres. Thus, we have been able to give a flavour of the shifts in language and mood, as the roles within the NHS were redefined in various ways. Chapters 4, 5 and 6 traced the changes in attitude towards those who worked in the service at every level – from ancillary workers and nurses, through to surgeons and managers – as well as the redefinition of patients as 'consumers'.

We have observed the ways in which neo-liberal arguments, which seemed extremist and fanciful at the beginning of the decade, moved into the mainstream, and the anti-elitist critiques of the 1970s, arguing for democratic participation and citizenship, were captured by the appeal to consumerism and consumer power. Despite contradictions, conflict and vocal opposition, by the time of Margaret Thatcher's resignation in 1990, the grounds of the debate had visibly shifted. The NHS and some aspects of broadcasting were still considered to be 'public services' but ideas about what that 'public' consisted of, and what constituted a 'service', had changed. The concept had been first discredited and then redefined.

And then?

Both the Broadcasting Act and the National Health Service and Community Care Act were modified in response to the extensive campaigns which followed the two radical White Papers. But, in both cases, the campaigns had been largely defensive. The need to focus on specific details, such as redefining the 'quality' threshold, meant that, unlike in the 1970s, the wider project of developing alternative models based on citizenship, participation and a commitment to a public domain, had little hope of success. The founding of Channel Four in 1982 had been the result of such a vision, and had offered new possibilities, despite the complexities and compromises which left it vulnerable to conflicting ideologies. But, by the late 1980s, many individuals and groups who had promoted alternative futures for both broadcasting and health, found themselves defending the very institutions they had sought to radicalise (Keane 1991:116–124; Iliffe 1988:8).

Many who were committed to the public-service ethos of the NHS and the BBC, had nevertheless argued that those institutions had become monolithic, arrogant and inflexible (see Chapters 2 and 3). The Thatcherite rhetoric of personal autonomy and consumer power had shared this critique and appeared to echo the concerns of those who felt disempowered by unresponsive professionals. When Norwich Union declared 'we carry on caring no matter what', it must have seemed like the answer. Arguments for a democratic engagement between the services and their users in their capacity as *citizens*, had been pre-empted by an appeal to users as *'consumers'*. And the humanist meaning of 'consumer' would all but disappear into its commercial meaning (see Chapter 5). 'Wants' had triumphed over 'needs' and few policymakers were prepared to question that crude dichotomy, or to pay attention to the subtle dialectic between them.

One consequence was that many who sought to defend and democratise the practice of public service found themselves repeating an older rhetoric, retelling the myths of origin. Opponents could then portray them as backward looking, out of date. Professionals and workers who sought to create a more open and participatory relationship with users of the service found themselves outflanked by an aggressive managerial culture and an appeal to monetary values. There was little opportunity to engage with the real history of the two services, building on their strengths while recognising the necessity of compromise and political contingency. The dynamic of creative change found no political ground on which to move forward. The legislation of the early 1980s had expanded public service when it brought Channel Four into being, but the legislation of 1990 expanded a predatory commercial sector. Its deregulatory measures meant that hitherto protected areas were exposed. A creative interaction between different types of funding and different approaches to 'the popular' was replaced by a contest between two apparently opposing positions – 'public service' versus the free market.

Public service or kitemark?

Following the 1990 Acts, both the NHS and the BBC were seriously destabilised. Both were deliberately underfunded, and both were 'marketised' – restructured around a division between 'purchaser' and 'provider'. This enabled the development of an 'internal market', in which competition could take place, both within the services themselves and between parts of the service and commercial providers. In both broadcasting and health, private provision became increasingly influential.

The 'internal market' was introduced in the NHS in 1991. 'The idea was that it would make NHS more cost effective by making hospitals respond to customer demand (exercised on behalf of patients by health authorities or fundholding GPs)', writes Colin Leys. Hospitals were forced to compete with the private sector and it became a 'tightly controlled shadow market' (2001:170–171). The Act also transferred responsibility for the long-term care of the elderly, chronically ill and mentally handicapped to local authorities. Although this was represented as removing patients out of 'faceless institutions' and 'into the community', Leys notes that local authorities were obliged to use 85% of the funding they received for private care homes. 'A multi-billion-pound long term care industry had been created using public funds; publicly-provided care had been drastically curtailed, and then public funding had been reduced as well' (2001:172, 174). The private institutions were often worse staffed and the staff were worse trained. A two-tier service was being created. By the late 1990s, the industry looked forward to 'a time when the NHS would simply be a kitemark attached to the institutions and activities of a system of purely private providers' (Leys 2011:1).

For broadcasting organisations, the 1990 Act ushered in a decade of turbulence. Within the ITV, the lifting of restrictions led to takeovers and mergers. This gradually destroyed the distinctive characteristics of the separate companies and the regional basis of the network. Producer Nick Gray describes how Yorkshire Television, producers of *Only When I Laugh, Jimmy's* and *First Tuesday* overbid in the 1990 'auction'. This led to cutbacks in the output, redundancies and the closure of the highly successful Documentary Department. Eventually, the company was sold to Granada (Gray 2010). At Granada itself, long-standing executives with a background in programme-making were ousted, and a new management team focussed on maximisation of profit, slimming down, asset-stripping and empire-building (Fitzwalter 2008). By 2004, instead of a network of regional companies there was a single ITV PLC.[1] As Channel Four prepared to sell its own advertising, it needed to reposition itself as a competitor to ITV. Even though its remit to innovate remained in place, its role as an outlet for experiment and dissent was diminished (Born 2003). At the BBC, John Birt became Director General, and established a policy of 'producer choice': an internal market in which service departments must compete with outside providers (O'Malley 1994:163–165; Born 2004). With the licence fee pegged to Retail Price Index, the Corporation was faced with cutting substantial areas. In a 1994 Channel Four programme, ex-*Analysis* journalist Mary Goldring provocatively proposed 'doing the unthinkable': cutting *EastEnders* (it's very expensive); Radio 3 (it has low listening figures); local radio (it takes up a sixth of the licence fee); selling off facilities including transmitters; outsourcing services; and building up commercial activities such as merchandising spin-offs (*The Goldring Audit on the BBC* 6 March 1994). The actual process was not as dramatic as she had envisaged, but gradually sections of BBC activity were, indeed, hived off or subcontracted to commercial companies. Meanwhile, BSkyB was, at first, propped up by subsidies from Rupert Murdoch's newspaper interests, then began building its audience through the purchase of football rights and Hollywood movies. In a 1993 interview, David Frost asked DG Birt, 'when do you think Sky will be your main competitor?' Birt replied, 'by the end of the decade' (*Breakfast with Frost* BBC1 7 November 1993).

The net effect of the profound changes in television is that many people are working harder for less satisfaction, good people in every age range are scarcely working at all, career-structure has gone out of

---

[1] Only Scottish Television, Grampian, Ulster Television and Channel TV remained independent.

the window, even entrepreneurial enthusiasts are waking up to a crisis in training and a clutch of quite ordinary people are seriously rich.

> wrote media commentator Peter Fiddick as the changes brought by the Broadcasting Act began to take effect (*Guardian* 20.6.1994).

Globalisation and the public domain

As restrictions on overseas ownership were lifted, increasingly ownership moved to powerful international corporations. Globalisation, together with commoditisation, 'mediated the basic shift in the balance of power between market forces and political forces that marked the new era', writes Colin Leys. Before the 1980s, it could be said that markets were to a significant degree politically controlled, but 'politics are no longer about managing the economy to satisfy the demands of voters, they are increasingly about getting voters to endorse policies that meet the demands of capital' (2001:63, 68). Services, like broadcasting and health were removed even further from the democratic participation of those who use them. In addition, the rejection of entitlement, of equal access as of right, would impoverish the whole of society. Something was lost that is essential to democracy.

David Marquand has pointed out that 'citizenship rights are by definition, equal. Market rewards are, by definition, unequal... Without a vibrant public domain, ring fenced from the market and private domains, social democratic politics cannot flourish' (2000:27).

But, in the late 1980s, the man in the pink suit threw caution to the winds. More than two decades later, we are dealing with the consequences of the changes he was celebrating with such abandon.

Programme References

Notes on sources

BFI

Most television programmes quoted in this book can be viewed through the British Film Institute's National Film and Television Archive: http://www.bfi.org.uk/about-bfi/help-faq/archive-collections

Some (e.g. the first night of Channel Four) can be viewed free of charge in one of the BFI's mediatheques: http://www.bfi.org.uk/archive-collections/duction-bfi-collections/bfi-mediatheques

The BFI's online resource *InView: British History Through the Lens* includes material on the theme of health, including the 1948 public information films on the launch of the NHS. Its collections include selections from *Panorama, Open Door, This Week/TVEye* and *After Dark*. Access to the collections is available to schools, further education and research institutions: http://www.bfi.org.uk/inview/

Some programmes and clips can be accessed at BFI Screenonline through libraries, colleges and universities: http://www.screenonline.org.uk/

BBC

The BBC is putting an increasing number of archive programmes online. Selections include editions of *Panorama, Analysis* and *The Reith Lectures*, and a selection of programmes on health and wellbeing. http://www.bbc.co.uk/archive/

BUFVC

The British Universities Film and Video Council provides a number of online television and radio resources for academic users, including programmes from the ILR station, LBC: http://bufvc.ac.uk/tvandradio

Also

Some of the programmes discussed, including *Casualty* and *Yes Minister* are available as commercial DVDs, and a number of those referred to in the book, including the advertisements described in the concluding comments, are quoted from off-air recordings made by Patricia Holland.

Programme references

Ad Men and Number 10 (BBC4 16 May 2008)

After Dark open-ended discussion programme, beginning at midnight (Open Media for C4 1987–1997), pp.89, 129, 197, 200 footnote, 220

'What's Up Doc?' an edition on medical provision (1 July 1989) A list of *After Dark* editions is available at http://en.wikipedia.org/wiki/List_of_After_Dark_editions, p.197

After Margaret season of programmes about Margaret Thatcher (BBC Autumn 1993), p.69 footnote

AIDS week 26 programmes about AIDS on all television and radio channels (27 February–5 March 1987), pp.159–161

AIDS public information advertisements on all television channels (December 1986), to be found on the website of the AIDS charity Avert at http://www.avert.org/AIDS-history87–92.htm, pp.153, 159

'AIDS: The Last Chance' *This Week* (Thames/ITV 23 and 30 October 1986), p.162

'AIDS: The Facts' an *Open Air Special* (BBC2 5 March 1987), p.163

AIDS: The Facts syndicated to all Independent Local Radio stations across the network (ILR/LBC 7 January 1987)

'AIDS: The Fight for Control' *Panorama* (BBC1 29 June 1987), p.162

'AIDS Is a Four Letter Word' *Diverse Reports* (C4 17 September 1986), pp.157, 163

AIDS, The Unheard Voices Meditel for *Dispatches* (C4 November 1987): http://www.virusmyth.com/aids/video/jsunheard.htm, p.164

'AIDS: The Victims' *TVEye* (Thames/ITV 28 February 1985), p.156

The AIDS Catch Meditel for *Dispatches* (C4 June 1990), p.165

Analysis current affairs series (BBC Radio 4 1970–), pp.32–5, 75, 220

Angels drama series (BBC1 1975–1983), pp.52–54, 72, 109, 177

The Archive Hour (BBC Radio 4 2003–), p.2

Ashes to Ashes police series in which the protagonist is transported back to the 1980s (BBC1 2008–2010), p.2

'Ashes to Ashes' *This Week* (Thames/ITV 11 September 1975), p.55

Auf Wiedersehen Pet drama series. Witzend for Central Television/ITV (1983–1984, 1986), p.122

'The Battle for Guy's' *The London Programme* (LWT/ITV 2 March 1990)

Bergerac drama series (BBC1 1981–1991), p.166

Best of Health documentary series in a health centre (Central/ITV 29 July–5 August 1982), pp.89, 115, 178

The Big Flame drama in *The Wednesday Play* strand (BBC1 19 February 1969), p.76

The Black Stuff drama in the *Play for Today* strand (BBC1 2 January 1980)

Blind Date game show (LWT/ITV 1985–2003), p.179

Blues and Twos documentary series about the emergency services (Carlton/ITV 1993–1998), p.199

The Body Show dance workout programme (C4 2 November 1982), p.95

Boys from the Blackstuff drama series (BBC1 1 January–7 November 1982), pp.77, 122

Brass comedy series (Granada/ITV original series 1983–1984), p.122

Breadline Britain series about poverty (LWT/ITV 21 August–1 September 1983)

Breakfast with Frost Sunday morning interview series (BBC1 1993–2005): Interview with Director General John Birt (7 November 1993), p.218

Sunday Night at the London Palladium variety show from the theatre (ATV/ITV Original series 1955–1967), p.179

Supersizers Eat... The Eighties Sue Perkins and Giles Coren consume 1980s-style food and drink (BBC2 15 June 2009), p.2

Surgical Spirit hospital-based comedy series (Granada/ITV 1989–1995)

TVEye current affairs series (Thames/ITV, replaced *This Week* 1978–1986), pp.56, 71, 74, 76, 86, 107, 138–9, 141, 156, 162, 220

'To Mrs Brown a Daughter' was the first *TVEye* (7 September 1978), p.56

Take the Mike 'access' series (CPU/BBC2 1981), p.58

'Talking Point: Hospitals for Women Run by Women – Are They Something to Fight for or an Anachronism?' *Woman's Hour* (BBC Radio 4 8 February 1983)

The Television Village series on the future of television (Granada for C4 15 May–19 June 1990), pp.210–2

Thatcher: The Downing Street Years series based on Margaret Thatcher's memoirs (Fine Art production for BBC2 6–27 October 1993), p.69

'The Thatcher Effect' four programmes *Analysis* (BBC Radio 4 18 March–8 April 1987)

The Thatcher Phenomenon six programmes (BBC Radio 4 5 May–9 June 1985), pp.136–7

This Morning chat show with Richard and Judy (ITV 1988–2001), p.54

Telford's Change drama serial (BBC2 7 January–11 March 1979), p.54

This Week current affairs series (Thames Television for ITV 1956–1978, 1986–1992), pp.54–6, 73, 112, 156, 161, 173, 177–8, 185, 189-90, 196, 198–9, 213, 220

Time Shift archive series on British cultural history (BBC4 2001–), p.2

Tishoo drama in the *Play for Today* strand (BBC1 9 March 1982), p.162

Through the Night drama in the *Play for Today* strand (BBC1 2 December 1975), pp.51–2, 98

The Thorn Birds American drama series (produced 1983, screened on BBC1 1984), p.132

Tory, Tory, Tory series about the Conservative Party through the eyes of Margaret Thatcher's supporters (Mentorn for BBC4 8–22 March 2006), pp.32, 120, 136

'The Toughest Job in Medicine' *This Week* (Thames/ITV 9 April 1987), p.156, 162

24 Hours in A&E documentary series following the team at King's College Hospital, London (The Garden Productions for C4 2011–), p.194

'Unmasking Medicine' *Reith Lectures 1980* by Ian Kennedy (BBC Radio 4 5 November-1 December 1980), pp.88-9, 99 *see* http://www.bbc.co.uk/search/?q=Ian%20Kennedy%20Reith%20Lectures%201980%20Unmasking%20medicine

A Very British Coup political drama serial (Skreba Films/Parallax Pictures for C4 19 June–3 July 1988), p.58

Video Diaries members of the public film their lives and concerns (CPU/BBC1 1990–1998), p.58

The Walden Interview (LWT/ITV 1988–1990) *and Walden* (1990), p.32

Wall Street American film about stock-market traders (American Entertainment US 1987), pp.39, 186

Walter first in the *Film on Four* strand (Central Independent Television for C4 2 November 1982), p.95

The Wednesday Play anthology strand of single dramas (BBC1 1964–1970), pp.51–2, 59, 175

Weekend World current affairs series ((LWT/ITV 1972-1988), pp.32, 75, 149
Margaret Thatcher's first major interview as Prime Minister on *Weekend World* (7 January 1979), p.75

Well Being series on healthy living in association with the Royal College of General Practitioners (Homes and Associated for C4 12 November 1982–11 February 1983), pp.95–6

'What Are We Here for, Brothers?' *Analysis* (BBC Radio 4 3 November 1978), p.75

'What's Up Doc?' *This Week* (Thames/ITV 29 March 1990), p.198

Who Cares series on comparative health care (Meditel for C4 1985), p.192

'Who Lives, Who Dies' *This Week* (Thames/ITV 11 December 1986 and 8 January 1987)

Woman's Hour reports, interviews and debates of interest to women (BBC Radio 4 1946–), p.140

World in Action current affairs series (Granada for ITV 1961–1998), pp.54, 74, 86, 203, 213

Yes Minister comedy series (BBC1 1980–1984) *Yes Prime Minister* sequel (BBC1 1986–1988), pp.40, 77, 121–2, 147, 220
special edition with Margaret Thatcher (20 January 1984), p.122

'You Can't Put Dedication in the Bank' *This Week* (Thames/ITV 9 May 1974), p.87

The Young Ones 'alternative' comedy series (BBC1 1982–1984), p.128

Your Life in Their Hands medical series featuring operations (BBC1 1958–1964, 1980, 1986), pp.102–6, 107, 115, 116

The Zircon Affair intended as part of the *Secret Society* series transmitted in 1987. The programme was banned at the time but transmitted with a discussion the following year (BBC Scotland/BBC2 1988), p.219 footnote

References

Adam Smith Institute (1984) *Omega Report: Communications Policy* London: Adam Smith Institute

Adam Smith Institute (1984) *Funding the BBC* London: Adam Smith Institute

Adam Smith Institute (1986) *Response to Peacock Report* London: Adam Smith Institute

Adams, J. (1989) *AIDS: The HIV Myth* London: Macmillan

Annan Committee (1977) *Report of the Committee on the Future of Broadcasting* London: HMSO Cmnd 6753

Baehr, H. and Dyer, G. (1987) *Boxed In: Women and Television* London: Pandora

Barnett, S. (2011) *The Rise and Fall of Television Journalism* London: Bloomsbury

Barnett, S. and Curry, A. (1994) *The Battle for the BBC: A British Broadcasting Conspiracy* London: Arum Press

Beckett, A. (2009) *When the Lights Went Out: Britain in the 70s* London: Faber

Beveridge Report (1942) *Report of the Committee on Social Insurance and Allied Services* Cmnd 6404

Beveridge Report (1951) *Report of the Committee on Broadcasting* London: HMSO Cmnd 8116

Black Report (1980) *Inequalities in Health: Report of a Research Working Group* London: Department of Health and Social Services Reprinted with revisions in 1992 Harmondsworth: Penguin

Blanchard, S. and Morley, D. (eds) (1982) *What's This Channel Fo(u)r? An Alternative Report* London: Comedia

Bonner, P. with Aston, L. (1998) *ITV in Britain Vol 5 The Old Relationship Changes 1981–92* London: Macmillan

Booker, C. (1980) *The Seventies* Harmondsworth: Penguin

Boon, T. (2008) *Films of Fact: A History of Science in Documentary Films and Television* London: Wallflower

Born, G. (2003) 'Strategy, positioning and projection in digital television: Channel 4 and the commercialisation of public broadcasting in the UK' *Media, Culture and Society* Vol. 25 773–799 London: Sage

Born, G. (2004) *Uncertain Vision: Birt, Dyke and the Reinvention of the BBC* London: Secker and Warburg

Boston Women's Health Book Collective (1971/2011) *Our Bodies Ourselves* New York: Simon and Schuster

Briggs, A. (1961) *The History of Broadcasting in the UK Vol I: The Birth of Broadcasting* Oxford: OUP

Briggs, A. (1965) *The History of Broadcasting in the UK Vol II: The Golden Age of Broadcasting* Oxford: Oxford University Press

British Medical Journal (BMJ) (1979) ' "Patients First": Government proposals for the NHS' 15 December

Broadcasting Research Unit (BRU) (1985) *The Public Service Idea in British Broadcasting: Main Principles* London: BRU

Broadcasting Research Unit (BRU) (1989) *Quality in Television: Programmes, Programme makers, Systems* London: John Libbey

Brunsdon, C. (1990) 'Problems with Quality' *Screen* 31(1) Spring

Brunsdon, C. (1987) 'Feminism and soap opera' in Kath Davies et al. (eds) *Out of Focus: Writings on Women and the Media* London: The Women's Press

Brown, M. (2007) *A Licence to Be Different: The Story of Channel 4* London: BFI

Burns, T. (1977) *The BBC: Public Institution and Private World* London: Macmillan

Buscombe, E. (1974) 'Television studies in schools and colleges' *Screen Education* 12 Autumn London: Society for Education in Film and Television

Calhoun, C. (ed) (1992) *Habermas and the Public Sphere* Cambridge Mass: MIT Press

Campbell, B. (1987) *The Iron Ladies: Why Do Women Vote Tory?* London: Virago

Chignell, H. (2004) *BBC Radio 4's Analysis, 1970–1983: A Selective History and Case Study of BBC Current Affairs Radio* PhD thesis: Bournemouth University

Chignell, H. (2011) *Public Issue Radio: Talks, News and Current Affairs in the Twentieth Century* Basingstoke: Palgrave Macmillan

Coase, R.H. (1950) *British Broadcasting: A Study in Monopoly* London: Longmans

Cockerell, M., Hennessy, P., Walker, D. (1984) *Sources Close to the Prime Minister: Inside the Hidden World of the News Manipulators* London: Macmillan

Cockerell, M. (1988) *Live from Number 10: The Inside Story of Prime Ministers and Television* London: Faber and Faber

Cockett, R. (1994) *Thinking the Unthinkable: Think-tanks and the Economic Counter-revolution 1931–1983* London: Harper Collins

Cohen, S. and Young, J. (eds) (1973) *The Manufacture of News: Deviance, Social Problems and the Media* London: Constable

Collins, P. (ed) (2002) *Culture or Anarchy: The Future of Public Service Broadcasting* London: Social Market Foundation

Conservative Party (1979) *General Election Manifesto* London: Conservative Party

Cook, J. (ed) (1982) *BFI Dossier 17: Television Sitcom* London: BFI

Cooke, L. (2003) *British Television Drama: A History* London: BFI

Coote, A. and Campbell, B. (1982) *Sweet Freedom* London: Picador

Corner, J. (ed) (1991) *Popular Television in Britain* London: BFI

Corner, J. (1995) *Television Form and Public Address* London: Edward Arnold

Corner, J. and Harvey, S. (eds) (1996) *Television Times: A Reader* London: Arnold

Corner, J. and Pels, D. (eds) (2003) *Media and the Restyling of Politics* London: Sage

Couldry, N. (2010) *Why Voice Matters: Culture and Politics after Neo-liberalism* London: Sage

Crawford Committee (1926) *Report of the Broadcasting Committee* London: HMSO Cmd 2599

Curran, J. (1993) 'Rethinking the media as a public sphere' in Peter Dahlgren and Colin Sparks (eds) *Communication and Citizenship* London: Routledge

Curran, J. and Seaton, J. (1981/2010) *Power Without Responsibility: The Press, Broadcasting and the Internet in Britain* Seventh Edition, London: Routledge

Curran, J., Gurevich, M. and Woolacott, J. (eds) (1977) *Mass Communication and Society* London: Edward Arnold

Curran, J., Smith, A. and Wingate, P. (eds) (1987) *Impacts and Influences: Essays on Media and Power in the Twentieth Century* London: Methuen

Dahlgren, P. and Sparks, C. (eds) (1991) *Communication and Citizenship: Journalism and the Public Sphere* London: Routledge

Darlow, M. (2004) *The Independents Struggle: The Programme Makers Who Took on the TV Establishment* London: Quartet

Davidson, A. (1992) *Under the Hammer: Greed and Glory Inside the Television Business* London: Mandarin

Davies, C. (1995) *Gender and the Professional Predicament in Nursing* Maidenhead: Open University Press

Dickinson, M. (ed) (1999) *Rogue Reels: Oppositional Film in Britain 1945–90* London: BFI

DHSS (1980) *Patients First: Consultative Paper* London: HMSO

Department of Health (1989) *Working for Patients* London: HMSO

Department of Trade and Industry (1982) *The Future of Telecommunications in Britain* London: HMSO Cmnd 8610

Doyal, L., Rowbotham, S. and Scott, A. (1973) 'Introduction' to Barbara Erenreich and Diedre English *Witches, Midwives and Nurses* London: Writers and Readers

Dunkley, C. (1985) *Television Today and Tomorrow: Wall-to-Wall Dallas?* Harmondsworth: Penguin

Dyer, R. (1985) 'Taking popular television seriously' in David Lusted and Philip Drummond *Television and Schooling* London: BFI

Edwards, B. (1993) *The National Health Service: A Manager's Tale 1946–92* London: Nuffield Provincial Hospitals Trust

Elliott, P. (1977) 'Media organisations and occupations an overview' in James Curran et al. (eds) *Mass Communication and Society* London: Edward Arnold

Ellis, J. (2000) *Seeing Things: Television in the Age of Uncertainty* London: I.B. Tauris

Elstein, D. (1979) 'Smoking and the media' *Media Culture and Society* Vol. 1 271–276

Erenreich, B. and English, D. (1979) *For her Own Good: 150 Years of Experts' Advice to Women* London: Pluto

Evans, H. (1984) *Good Times Bad Times* London: Hodder

Feuer, J., Kerr, P. and Vahimagi, T. (1984) *MTM: 'Quality Television'* London: BFI

Field, F. (1989) *Losing Out: The Emergence of Britain's Underclass* London: Blackwell

Fiske, J. and Hartley, J. (1978) *Reading Television* London: Methuen

Fitzwalter, R. (2008) *The Dream That Died: The Rise and Fall of ITV* Leicester: Matador

Forster, L. and Harper, S. (eds) (2010) *British Culture and Society in the 1970s: The Lost Decade* Newcastle-upon-Tyne: Cambridge Scholars

Franklin, B. (ed) (1999) *Social Policy, the Media and Misrepresentation* London: Routledge

Franklin, B. (ed) (2001) *British Television Policy: A Reader* London: Routledge

Fraser, D. (1973/1984) *The Evolution of the British Welfare State* Basingstoke: Macmillan

Free Communications Group (1969) *The Open Secret No 1* London: FCG

Freedman, D. (2001) 'What use is a public inquiry? Labour and the 1977 Annan Committee on the Future of Broadcasting' *Media, Culture and Society* Vol. 23 195–211

Freedman, D. (2003) *Television Policies of the Labour Party 1951–2001* London: Cass

Gaber, I. (2002) 'A history of the concept of public service broadcasting' in Collins, P. (ed) *Culture or Anarchy? The Future of Public Service Broadcasting* London: Social Market Foundation

Garnham, N. (1973) *Structures of Television* London: BFI, British Film Institute Television Monograph No. 1

Garnham, N. (1983) 'Public service versus the market' *Screen* (24)1:6–27

Garnham, N. (1986) 'Media and the public sphere' in Peter Golding et al. (eds) *Communicating Politics* Leicester: Leicester University Press

Garnham, N. (1992) 'The media and the public sphere' in Craig Calhoun (ed) *Habermas and the Public Sphere* Cambridge Mass: MIT Press

Garnham, N. and Williams, R. (1980) 'Pierre Bourdieu and the sociology of culture: an introduction' *Media, Culture and Society* 2:209–233

Geraghty, C. (1991) *Women and Soap Opera: A Study of Prime Time Soaps* Cambridge: Polity

Glasgow University Media Group (GUMG) (1976) *Bad News* London: Routledge and Kegan Paul

Glasgow University Media Group (1982) *Really Bad News* London: Writers and Readers

Glasgow Media Group (1998) *The Circuit of Mass Communication* London: Sage

Goffman, E. (1959/1971) *The Presentation of Self in Everyday Life* Harmondsworth: Pelican

Goffman, E. (1971) *Relations in Public* New York: Basic Books

Goddard, P., Corner, J. and Richardson, K. (2007) *Public Issue Television: World in Action 1963–98* Manchester: Manchester University Press

Golding, P. and Middleton, S. (1982) *Images of Welfare: Press and Public Attitudes to Poverty* Oxford: Martin Robertson

Goodwin, A. and Whannel, G. (eds) (1990) *Understanding Television* London: Routledge

Goodwin, P. (1998) *Television under the Tories: Broadcasting Policy 1979–1997* London: BFI

Gorsky, M. (2008) 'NHS at 60: Perspectives on health care systems' in *Social History of Medicine* 21(32)

Grade, M. (2012) *Michael Grade on the Box* BBC Radio 2 programme 5 of 6 (30 April)

Gray, N. (2010) 'Jimmy's: the rise of the docusoap and the fall of YTV' on the research website: http://www.broadcastingnhsbook.co.uk/

Gray, S. (2008) 'Sir Bill Cotton, BBC's king of light entertainment, dies at the age of 80' *The Independent* (12 August)

Griffith, B., Iliffe, S. and Rayner, G. (1987) *Banking on Sickness: Commercial Medicine in Britain and the USA* London: Lawrence and Wishart

Griffiths Report (1983) *NHS Management Inquiry: Report to the Secretary of State for Social Services* London: Department of Health and Social Security

Gripsrud, J. (1999) *Television and Common Knowledge* London: Routledge

Habermas, J. (1962 translated into English 1989) *The Structural Transformation of the Public Sphere: An Inquiry into a Category of Bourgeois Society* Cambridge: Polity

Hall, S. (1977) 'Culture, the media, and the "ideological effect"' in J. Curran, M. Gurevitch and J. Woollacott (eds) *Mass Communication and Society* London: Arnold

Hall, S. (1979) 'The great moving right show' *Marxism Today* (January)

Hall, S. (1980) 'Popular-democratic versus authoritarian populism: Two ways of taking democracy seriously' in Alan Hunt (ed) *Marxism and Democracy* London: Lawrence and Wishart

Hall, S. and Jacques, M. (eds) (1983) *The Politics of Thatcherism* London: Lawrence and Wishart

Hall, S. and Whannel, P. (1965) *The Popular Arts* London: Pantheon

Hallam, J. (2000) *Nursing the Image: Media, Culture and Professional Identity* London: Routledge

Ham, C. (1992) *Health Policy in Britain: The Politics and Organisation of the National Health Service* London: Macmillan

Harvey, S. (1994) 'Channel Four Television: from Annan to Grade' in Stuart Hood (ed) *Behind the Screens: the Structure of British Television in the Nineties* London: Lawrence and Wishart

Harvey, S. (2003). 'Channel Four and the redefining of public service broadcasting' in Michelle Hilmes (ed.) *The Television History Book* London: BFI

Hayek, F.A. (1945 reprinted 1999) *The Road to Serfdom* Condensed Version London: Institute of Economic Affairs

Heller, C. (1978) *Broadcasting and Accountability* London: BFI

Hendy, D. (2007) *Life on Air: A History of Radio Four* Oxford: Oxford University Press

Hobsbawm, E. and Ranger, T. (eds) (1983) *The Invention of Tradition* Cambridge: Canto

Hobson, D. (1982) *Crossroads: The Drama of a Soap Opera* London: Methuen

Hobson, D. (2008) *Channel Four the Early Years and the Jeremy Isaacs Legacy* London: I.B. Tauris

Holland, P. (1982) 'Public opinion, the popular press and the organisation of ideas' in *Falklands/Malvinas: Whose Crisis* London: Latin America Bureau

Holland, P. (1983) 'The Page Three Girl speaks to women, too' *Screen* 24(3) (May/June)

Holland, P. (2000) *The Television Handbook* Second Edition London: Routledge

Holland, P. (2006) *The Angry Buzz: 'This Week' and Current Affairs Television* London: I.B. Tauris

Home Office (1988) *Broadcasting in the '90s: Competition, Choice and Quality* London: HMSO Cmnd517

Hood, S. (1980) *On Television* London: Pluto

Hood, S. (ed) (1994) *Behind the Screens: The Structure of British Television in the Nineties* London: Lawrence and Wishart

Hood, S. and O'Leary, G. (1990) *Questions of Broadcasting* London: Methuen

Hopkins, E. (1991) *The Rise and Decline of the English Working Class 1918–1990: A Social History* London: Weidenfeld and Nicholson

Horrie, C. and Clarke, S. (1994) *Fuzzy Monsters: Fear and Loathing at the BBC* London: Heinemann

Hunt Report (1982) *Report of the Inquiry into Cable Expansion and Broadcasting Policy* London: HMSO Cmnd 8679

Husband, C. (ed) (1975) *White Media and Black Britain* London: Arrow

Iliffe, S. (1982) *Condition Critical: Private Medicine and the NHS* Communist Party Pamphlet

Iliffe, S. (1983) 'Dismantling the Health Service' in Stuart Hall and Martin Jacques *The Politics of Thatcherism* London: Lawrence and Wishart

Iliffe, S. (1985) 'The Politics of Health Care: The NHS Under Thatcher' in *Critical Social Policy* 15(13)

Iliffe, S. (1988) *Strong Medicine: Health Politics for the 21st Century* London: Lawrence and Wishart

Independent Filmmakers' Association (1980) 'Channel Four and innovation' *Screen* 21(4)

Illich, I. (1976) *Medical Nemesis: The Expropriation of Health* New York: Pantheon

Illich, I. (1977) *Disabling Professions* London: Marion Boyers

Inglis, B. and West, R. (1983) *The Alternative Health Guide* New York: Knopf

Isaacs, J. (1989) *Storm Over 4: A Personal Account* London: Weidenfeld and Nicholson

Jacobs, J. (2003) *Body Trauma TV: The New Hospital Dramas* London: BFI

Jessop, B. et al. (1988) *Thatcherism: A Tale of Two Nations* London: Polity

Johnston, C. (1973) 'Women's cinema as counter-cinema' reprinted in Sue Thornham (ed) (1999) *Feminist Film Theory: A Reader* Edinburgh: Edinburgh University Press

Johnson, C. and Turnock, R. (eds) (2005) *ITV Cultures: Independent Television over Fifty Years* Maidenhead: Open University Press

Karpf, A. (1988) *Doctoring the Media: The Reporting of Health and Medicine* London: Routledge

Kavanagh, D. and Seldon, A. (1989) *The Thatcher Effect* Oxford: Clarendon Press

Keane, J. (1991) *The Media and Democracy* London: Polity

Kesey, K. (1962) *One Flew Over the Cuckoo's Nest* New York: Viking

Klein, R. (1983/2010) *The New Politics of the NHS: From Creation to Reinvention* Sixth Edition, Abingdon: Radcliffe Publishing

Kingsley, H. (1993) *Casualty: The Inside Story* London: BBC Books

Kuhn, A. (1982) *Women's Pictures: Feminism and Cinema* London: RKP

Kumar, K. (1977) 'Holding the middle ground: the BBC, the public and the professional broadcaster' in James Curran et al. (eds) *Mass Communication and Society* London: Edward Arnold

Lamb, L. (1989) *Sunrise* London: Pan Macmillan

Lambert, S. (1982) *Channel Four: TV with a Difference* London: BFI

Langan, M. (1998) 'The restructuring of health care' in Gordon Hughes and Gail Lewis (eds) *Unsettling Welfare: The Reconstruction of Social Policy* London: Routledge

Leapman, M. (1986) *The Last Days of the Beeb* London: Allen and Unwin

Leathard, A. (2000) *Health Care Provision: Past, Present and into 21st Century* London: Nelson Thornes

Letwin, S.R. (1992) *An Anatomy of Thatcherism* London: Fontana

Letwin, O. and Redwood, J. (1988) *Britain's Biggest Enterprise: Ideas for Radical Reform of the NHS* London: Centre for Policy Studies

Lewis, P. and Booth, J. (1989) *The Invisible Medium: Public, Commercial and Community Radio* London: Macmillan

Leys, C. (2001) *Market-driven Politics: Neoliberal Democracy and the Public Interest* London: Verso

Leys, C. and Player, S. (2011) *The Plot Against the NHS* London: Merlin

Lindley, R. (2002) *Panorama: Fifty Years of Pride and Paranoia* London: Politicos

Livingstone, S. and Lunt, P. (1994) *Talk on Television: Audience Participation and Public Debate* London: Routledge

Mack, J. and Lansley, S. (1985) *Poor Britain* London: George Allen and Unwin

Marks, J. (2008) *The NHS: Beginning, Middle and End?* Milton Keynes: Radcliffe Publishing

Marquand, D. (2004) *Decline of the Public: The Hollowing Out of Citizenship* Cambridge: Polity

Marquand, D. (2008) 'How did we get here?' *New Statesman* (14 April)

Marquand, D. (2009) 'The Warrior Woman' *New Statesman* (26 February)

Marr, A. (2007) *A History of Modern Britain* London: Macmillan

Marr, A. (2007a) *Andrew Marr's History of Modern Britain* programme 4 BBC2 (12 June)

Marris, P. and Thornham, S. (1996) *Media Studies: A Reader* Edinburgh: Edinburgh University Press

Marshall, T.H. (1950) *Citizenship and Social Class* Cambridge: Cambridge University Press

McCabe, C. and Stewart, O. (eds) (1986) *The BBC and Public Service Broadcasting* Manchester: Manchester University Press

McDonnell, J. (1991) *Public Service Broadcasting: A Reader* Broadcasting Research Unit London: Routledge

McGuigan, J. (1992) *Cultural Populism* London: Routledge

McSmith, A. (2011) *There's No Such Thing as Society: A History of Britain in the 1980s* London: Constable

Merrison Report (1979) *Report of the Royal Commission on the National Health Service* London: HMSO Cmnd 7615

Milne, A. (1988) *DG: The Memoirs of a British Broadcaster* London: Hodder and Stoughton

Miller, D. (1993) 'Negotiating HIV/AIDS information' in John Eldridge (ed) *Getting the Message: News, Truth and Power* London: Routledge

Mitchell, J. (1984) *What Is To Be Done About Illness and Health* Harmondsworth: Penguin

Mort, F. and Bland, L. (1984) 'Look out for the good time girl' in *Formations of Nation and People* London: RKP

Mulvey, L. (1975) 'Visual pleasure and narrative cinema' *Screen* 16(3) Autumn, reprinted in

Mulvey, L. (1989) *Visual and Other Pleasures* London: Macmillan

Mulgan, G. (ed) (1990) *The Question of Quality* The Broadcasting Debate Number 6 London: BFI

Murdoch, R. (1989) 'Freedom in Broadcasting versus the Public Service Tradition' MacTaggart Memorial Lecture in Bob Franklin (ed) (2001) *British Television Policy: A Reader* London: Routledge

Murdock, G. (1999) 'Rights and representations, pubic discourse and cultural citizenship' in Jostein Gripsrud (ed) *Television and Common Knowledge* London: Routledge

Murray, C. (1990) *The Emerging British Underclass* Choice in Welfare Series Number 2 London: Institute of Economic Affairs

Naughton, J. (1986) 'The fall of the house of Howard' *The Listener* (27 November)

Negrine, R. (1985) *Cable Television and the Future of Broadcasting* London: Croom Helm

Nelson, R. (1997) *TV Drama in Transition: Forms, Values and Cultural Change* London: Macmillan

Newman, G.F. (1983) *The Nations' Health* London: Granada Publishing

Nigg, H. and Wade, G. (1980) *Community Media* Zurich: Regenbogen-Verlag

Nunn, H. (2002) *Thatcher, Politics and Fantasy* London: Lawrence and Wishart

Oakley, G. (1982) 'Yes Minister' in Jim Cook (ed) *BFI Dossier 17: Television Sitcom* London: BFI

Oakley, A. (1984) *The Captured Womb: A History of the Medical Care of Pregnant Women* Oxford: Basil Blackwell

O'Malley, T. (1994) *Closedown? The BBC and Government Broadcasting Policy 1979–92* London: Pluto

O'Malley, T. (2009) 'Planning and competition' in O'Malley, T. and Jones, J. (eds) *The Peacock Committee and UK Broadcasting Policy* London: Palgrave Macmillan

Oppenheim, C. and Lister, R. (1996) 'The politics of child poverty 1979–1995' in Jane Pilcher and Stephen Wagg (eds) *Thatcher's Children? Politics, Childhood and Society in the 1980s and 90s* London: Falmer

Palmer, J. (2008) *Sixty Years of the National Health Service* London: Department of Health

Peacock Committee (1986) *Report of the Committee on Financing the BBC* London: HMSO Cmnd 9824

Peasey, J. and Docherty, D. (1986) *Summary of Evidence to the Peacock Committee* Broadcasting Research Unit Working Paper

Petley, J. (1997) 'Ken Loach and questions of censorship' in George McKnight (ed) *Agent of Challenge and Defiance: The Films of Ken Loach* London: Flicks Books

Philo, G. and Henderson, L. (1999) 'Why go to casualty? Health fears and fictional television' in Greg Philo (ed) *Message Received: Glasgow Media Group Research 1993–1998* Harlow: Pearson Education

Phillips, W. (1995) 'The world of the news' *Television: The Journal of the Royal Television Society* 32(6)

Pilkington Committee (1962) *Report of the Broadcasting Committee* London: HMSO Cmnd 1753

Pirie, M. (1989) *A Decade of Revolution in the Thatcher Years* London: Adam Smith Institute

Potter, J. (1989) *Independent Television in Britain Vol 3 Politics and Control 1968–1980* London: Macmillan

Potter, J. (1990) *Independent Television in Britain Vol 4 Companies and Programmes 1968–80* London: Macmillan

Pratten, S. (1998) 'Needs and wants: the case of broadcasting policy' *Media Culture and Society* 20(3) 381–407

Richardson, K., Corner, J. and Parry, K. (2012) *Political Culture and Media Genre: Beyond the News* London: Palgrave Macmillan

Riddell, P. (1987) *The Thatcher Government* Oxford: Blackwell

Rivett, G. (1998) *From Cradle to Grave: Fifty years of the NHS* London: King's Fund

Rivett, G. (2009) *National Health Service History* http://www.nhshistory.net/

Salvage, J. (1985) *The Politics of Nursing* London: Heinemann

Salvage, J. (1987) 'We're no angels: images of nurses' in Julienne Dickey and Teresa Stratford *Out of Focus: Writings on Women and the Media* London: The Women's Press

Samuel, R. (1994) *Theatres of Memory* London: Verso

Scannell, P. (1989) 'Public service broadcasting and modern public life' in *Media Culture and Society* 11(2) April 135–166

Scannell, P. (1990) 'Public service broadcasting: The history of a concept' in Andrew Goodwin and Garry Whannel (eds) *Understanding Television* London: Routledge

Scannell, P. and Cardiff, D. (1991) *A Social History of British Broadcasting: 1922–1939 Serving the Nation* Oxford: Blackwell

Seaton, J. and McNicholas, A. (2009) 'It was the BBC wot won it' in Tom O'Malley and Janet Jones (eds) (2009) *The Peacock Committee and UK Broadcasting Policy* London: Palgrave Macmillan

Seldon, A. (ed) (1980) *The Litmus Papers. A National Health Dis-service* London: Centre for Policy Studies

Selley, P.J. (1980) 'Review of *Health Rights Handbook*' *Journal of the Royal College of General Practitioners* (September)

Sendall, B. (1983) *Independent Television in Britain Vol 2 Expansion and Change 1958–68* London: Macmillan

Sennett, R. (1975) *The Fall of Public Man* New York: Knopf

Sennett, R. (1998) *The Corrosion of Character: The Personal Consequences of Work in the New Capitalism* New York: Norton

Shaw, G.B. (1906/1987) *The Doctor's Dilemma* Harmondsworth: Penguin

Shenton, J. (1998) *Positively False: Exposing the Myths around HIV and AIDS* London: I.B. Tauris

Simon, B. (1965) *Education and the Labour Movement 1870–1920* London: Lawrence and Wishart

Smith, A. (1974) 'The National Television Foundation: A plan for the fourth channel' reprinted (1976) in *The Shadow in the Cave: The Broadcaster, the Audience and the State* London: Quartet

Smith, A. (1977) *The Politics of Information: Problems of Policy in Modern Media* London: Macmillan

Smith, A. (1986) 'Licence and liberty' in Colin McCabe and Olivia Stewart (eds) *The BBC and Public Service Broadcasting* Manchester: Manchester University Press

Sontag, S. (1979) *Illness as a Metaphor* London: Allen Lane

Stevenson, W. and Smedley, N. (eds) (1989) *Responses to the White Paper* London: BFI 'The Broadcasting Debate' No. 3

Stimson, G. and C. (1980) *Health Rights Handbook* Harmondsworth: Penguin

Stoessl, S. (1987) 'Women as TV audience: a marketing perspective' in Helen Baehr and Gillian Dyer *Boxed In: Women and Television* London: Pandora

Stoller, T. (2010) *Sounds of Your Life: The History of Independent Radio in the UK* John London: Libbey

Street, S. (2002) *A Concise History of British Radio 1922–2002* Tiverton: Kelly

Sutherland, H. (2007) *Where is the Public Service in Light Entertainment? An Historical Study of the Workings of the BBC Television Light Entertainment Group, 1975–87* PhD thesis: Westminster University

Sykes Committee (1923) *Broadcasting Committee Report* London: HMSO Cmnd 1951

Taylor, P. (1984) *Smoke Ring: The Politics of Tobacco* London: Bodley Head

Thane, P. (1982) *The Foundations of the Welfare State* London: Longman

Thatcher, M. (1987) 'Aids, education and the year 2000' interview with Douglas Keay *Woman's Own* (23 September)

Thatcher, M. (1993) *The Downing Street Years* London: HarperCollins

Townsend, P. and Davidson, N. (eds) (1988) *Inequalities in Health* For the Health Education Council, reprinted with revisions in 1992 Harmondsworth: Penguin

Tracey, M. (1983) *In the Culture of the Eye: 10 Years of Weekend World* London: Hutchinson

Tracey, M. and Morrison, D. (1979) *Whitehouse* London: Macmillan

Travis, A. (2012) *Guardian* (17 March)

Tunstall, J. (1993) *Television Producers* London: Routledge

TUC (1979) *A Cause for Concern: Media Coverage of Industrial Disputes January and February 1979* London: Trades Union Congress

Veljanovsky, C. (ed) (1989) *Freedom in Broadcasting* London: Institute of Economic Affairs

Veljanovski, C. and Bishop, W.D. (1983) *Choice by Cable* Hobart Paper 96 London: Institute of Economic Affairs

Vinen, R. (2010) *Thatcher's Britain: The Politics and Social Upheaval of the 1980s* London: Pocket Books

Watney, S. (1987) 'Spectacle of Aids' in *October* Vol. 43 71–86

Webster, C. (1998) *National Health Service Reorganisation: Learning from History* Office of Health Economics Annual Lecture

Webster, C. (2002) *The National Health Service: A Political History* Oxford: Oxford University Press

Weeks, J. (1981) *Sex, Politics and Society: The Regulation of Sexuality Since 1800* London: Longman

Wenham, B. (ed) (1982) *The Third Age of Broadcasting* London: Faber

Whitehouse, M. (1993) *Quite Contrary: An Autobiography* London: Sidgwick and Jackson

Whitney, J. (1986) *Evidence to the Peacock Committee from the Independent Broadcasting Authority* London: IBA

Wilkinson, R. (1976) 'Dear David Ennals' *New Society* (16 December)

Wilkinson, R. and Pickett, K. (2009) *The Spirit Level* Harmondsworth: Penguin

Williams, R. (1961) *Culture and Society 1780–1950* Harmondsworth: Penguin (first published by Chatto and Windus 1958)

Williams, R. (1965) *The Long Revolution* Harmondsworth: Penguin (first published by Chatto and Windus 1961)

Williams, R. (1974) *Television: Technology and Cultural Form* London: Fontana

Wilson, H. (1961) *Pressure Group* London: Secker and Warburg

Wilson, S. (2012) 'Dramatising health care in the age of Thatcher' *Critical Studies in Television* Vol. 7:1

Wober, J.M. (1983) *'The Nation's Health': Viewers' Personalities and Attitudes to the Series* London: IBA

Wray, E. (2010) 'British Commercial Radio in the 1980s: the relationship between regulation and programme content' on the research website: http://www.broadcastingnhsbook.co.uk/

Wyndham Goldie, G. (1977) *Facing the Nation: Television and Politics 1936–76* London: Bodley Head

Young, H. and Sloman, A. (1986) *The Thatcher Phenomenon* London: BBC

de Zengotita, T. (2005) *Mediated: How the Media Shape Your World* London: Bloomsbury

Index

Note: Letter 'n' followed by the locators refer to footnotes